GOOD

—a n d—

EVIL

GOOD

— a n d —

EVIL

Richard Taylor

 Prometheus Books

59 John Glenn Drive
Amherst, New York 14228-2197

Published 2000 by Prometheus Books

Inquiries should be addressed to
Prometheus Books, 59 John Glenn Drive, Amherst, New York
14228–2197.
VOICE: 716–691–0133, ext. 207.
FAX: 716–564–2711.
WWW.PROMETHEUSBOOKS.COM

04 03 02 01 00   5 4 3 2 1

Library of Congress Cataloging-in-Publication Data

Taylor, Richard, 1919–
    Good and evil / Richard Taylor.—Rev. ed.
        p.   cm.
    ISBN 1–57392–752–X (pbk. : alk. paper)
    1. Ethics. 2. Good and evil. I. Title.
BJ1012.T37   1999
171'.3—dc21   99–044712
                                                              CIP

Printed in the United States of America on acid-free paper

To my precious children,
Aristotle Eli and Xeno Alexander

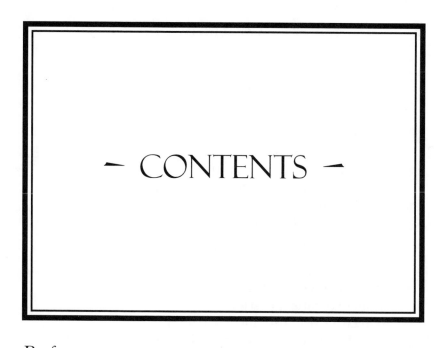

~ CONTENTS ~

PART 3: HUMAN GOODNESS

⌐ PREFACE ⌐

DURING THE CHRISTMAS break in 1969 I took leave from my university duties and flew to New Zealand. My first morning there I rented a typewriter and headed straight to the seashore, where I rented a simple cottage and spent the next ten weeks writing this book. I had taken a few notes with me, but visited no universities and undertook no research. The book was entirely the day-to-day product of my own thoughts. Plants were in bloom everywhere, and just across the bay the volcanic island of Rangitoto rose in glory. Each morning I got up at dawn and, to the accompaniment of the shorebirds, composed a few pages—sometimes very few, sometimes more—and then spent the rest of the day and evening enjoying that beautiful country and its people. I found a neighbor who was happy to earn a little extra composing the final typescript, which, having started from nothing, I was then able to mail to the publisher before my brief sojourn was over. All the ingredients of happiness fell into place in that brief time, and I cherish the memory.

My book came out as a trade book, but during the next twelve years it found widespread use in colleges. I had, almost as an afterthought, added a final chapter on "The Meaning of Life," a theme generally considered untouchable by academic philosophers, and this attracted more attention than anything I have ever written.

One large problem developed in those twelve years. The book had been written before gender-free prose had become the rule. "Man" meant human beings generally, "he" encompassed both male and female, and so on. My first task, therefore, in revising the book has been to clean this up, bringing the text into conformity with current usage. Besides this I have added some material and eliminated a considerable amount that I now see as boring and off the track.

I am, as usual, indebted to my one-time mentor, the late Roderick M. Chisholm, for my illustrations.

Richard Taylor

~ PART ONE ~

THE BACKGROUND: REASON AND WILL

- 1 -

ETHICS AND HUMAN NATURE

TRADITIONALLY, PHILOSOPHICAL ETHICS has tried to answer the question "What is good?" That is the question this book tries to answer.

The question is one about which everyone has an opinion. Indeed, virtually everyone, except the most thoughtful, assume that they *know* the answer, and that it is so obvious that they need not even give it thought. They may not formulate the answer in words, and of course if they do it will invariably turn out to be something silly, but most seem nevertheless to assume that no one could possibly have anything to say to them about ethics. If they read on this subject it is less with a view to learning than to appraising what they read in terms of what they imagine they already know. Their "knowledge," however, more often than not turns out to consist of nothing more than certain superficial attitudes having to do with the relations of husbands and wives, lovers and friends, rulers and ruled. Philosophical ethics is not so simple.

The question "What is good?" is a frightfully difficult one, and it cannot be answered without forming a certain general conception of human nature. The Socratic admonition "Know thyself" is especially pertinent, for how can you know what is your ultimate good if you do not know what you are? It is not enough to know that you are human, with arms and legs and so on, and that you have certain aspirations and ideals. You need to know what *kind* of being you are, what you share with the brutes and the angels, what makes you carry on as you do, and what is the source of your aspirations and ideals.

THE IMPORTANCE OF OUR QUESTION

The question "What is good?" is certainly the most important question you can ask. To say this is not mere rhetoric. There is simply nothing more important to which you can give your thought. For it comes to this: Each of us has one life to live, and that life can be, as it commonly is, wasted in the pursuit of specious goals, things that turn out worthless the moment they are possessed, or it can be made a deliberate and thoughtful art, wherein what was sought and, let us hope, in some measure gained, was something all the while worth striving for. Or we can put it this way: There will come a day for each of us to die, and on that day, if we have failed, we shall have failed irrevocably. This simple truth, so obvious, needs to be driven home. It is easy to make a mess of the whole thing, to end up with nothing, with no life that was really much worth living. Something that is so common must really be easy, and we have only to look about us to see how common it is. On the other hand it is not so difficult, really, to do better than this, to find our lives filled with sunlight and gold rather than darkness and dust, for many have managed to do it; it is, in fact, not so rare. But these beautiful lives that one sometimes sees are more often than not accidentally won; they are the outcome of steps casually and thoughtlessly taken, which in retrospect and in their combination turned out to be correct. It is probably for this reason that virtue is not the unique possession of the wise. Virtue, or the possession of what is really good, often exists in abundance in the most ordinary men and women. Without really trying, they have found—indeed, stumbled into—the whole thing. Now it is surely worth trying to discover whether virtue, which to such a large extent seems to be something distributed almost at random by accident or fate, may not to some extent be understood, so that you can have some inkling of what is and what is not worth having, without waiting passively to see what life may hold.

THREE TRADITIONAL ANSWERS

Traditionally, there have been three diverse and competing philosophical conceptions of what is good, namely, *virtue, pleasure*, and *happiness*, or what is better called well-being, the *eudaimonia* of the Greeks.

It is doubtful whether the first and third of these are answers to our question. If virtue is nothing but the possession of what is good, then clearly it is to no point to say that virtue is the greatest good. It is

simply an empty statement, and leaves one wondering what virtue is. Similarly, it is of no use to say
that human well-being is good, or even, that this is
happiness; for such an assertion, if it can even be
called an assertion, still leaves us wondering what
such happiness consists of, as Aristotle noted. What
we are seeking is not just more or less synonymous
expressions, but something we can actually recognize
as good, something real that we can set out to attain.

The second answer, on the other hand, that pleasure is the good, is without doubt an answer,
because feelings of pleasure are recognizably real
things. It appears, however, to be a wrong answer;
that is, the possession of pleasure, or even of a lifetime of it, is not the possession of virtue, not the
possession of what is really good. The consideration
of this must for now be postponed, however.

These three philosophical conceptions—virtue,
pleasure, and human well-being—will provide the
outline for the discussion that follows, for they more
or less supply a path from profound and serious
error toward something having at least some semblance of truth. And, as one best flourishes in love
and warmth only having tasted rejection, or best
appreciates light by emerging into it from darkness,
so also one can best see and recognize what is true
only after many false leads have been corrected and
errors overcome.

THE GREEKS AND THE IDEA OF
WHAT IS GOOD

Philosophical ethics, as distinguished from religious
and communal ethics, was the creation of Greek

thinkers at about the time of Socrates. Originally, the idea of anything's being good was no more than the idea of its being useful or efficient in the performance of its function, and this is still what is essentially meant. Thus, the Greeks observed that a good pilot is one who guides his ship well to the place it is intended to go; that a good sword is one that can be used effectively for the purpose for which swords are made; and that a good physician is one skilled in healing, thus performing the function of a physician. Goodness, therefore, was for the Greeks related to function. If one can say what the function of anything might be, then it is a simple matter to say what a good thing of that kind must be; namely, it is one that does actually perform that function well.

It is obvious that this is still the basic idea of goodness in all our practical life. We perpetually seek certain ends. Sometimes we attain them, sometimes we do not; but when we do, it is often with the help of something else, some instruments or tools or, as often as not, other people, and even various institutions. When things go well, when our ends are more or less satisfactorily achieved, then it is natural to express approval of those things that helped, us get there by calling them good. Thus, a good coat is one that is durable and warm; a good ruler or government is one under whose rule our interests are fulfilled; and a good bed is one that can be slept in soundly, and so on.

Suppose, then, that in such a context we ask, "What is a *good person*?" The answer comes forth at once: A good man is one who performs efficiently or well the function of a human being. And this at once invites the further question "What is the function of a human being?" Now this question, we note, does

not ask what is the function of this or that particular human being—this pilot, that physician, this or
that ruler, and so on. We know their functions, and
we thus know of what their goodness—as physicians, pilots, or whatever—consists. The question
asks instead what the function of a person, just as a
human being, might be.

It does not take much sophistication to see that
this is a strange question. Ordinarily, the idea of a
thing's having any function at all is one that is relative to human use; the function of a thing is ordinarily what it is used for, what it enables us to do.
Sometimes we do use other people to accomplish
our aims—we use physicians, pilots, and so on—so it
does make sense to speak of the respective functions
of those people; similarly, a content can be given to
the idea of a good pilot, good physician, good ruler,
and so on. But a person is not, just as a person, *used*
for anything; so in this sense, at least, people have
no function. Accordingly, in the context of this conception, a human being has no virtue; that is, there
is no such thing as a good person.

Yet this conclusion seems obviously wrong, and
the Greeks did not draw such a conclusion. There
are good human beings. But the Greeks could not
easily divest themselves of the idea that human
goodness must somehow be related to function, that
it must therefore be some sort of art or skill—that is,
the art or skill of performing one's function as a
human being. Many of the Socratic dialogues are
unintelligible if one lacks an appreciation of this
underlying conception. It became important to
Greek moralists, therefore, to discover what the
function or role of a human being, simply as a
human being, must be.

Human Goodness and Reason

The ancient moralists resolved this question in various ways, but in one way or another most of them settled on the idea that our function is the use of our rational powers. The question "What is the role or function of a person, simply considered as a person?" assumed in their minds the slightly different form: "What is *distinctive* of human beings? What differentiates us from the rest of nature?" It is not implausible to answer this by saying that humans, alone among other creatures, use reason, that we are *rational* animals. Our distinctive function or role is, therefore, the exercise of reason. A good person, accordingly, is in some sense or other a rational one, virtue is the exercise of reason, and vice the corruption of reason. Thus did Socrates identify virtue with wisdom, with the exercise of intelligence and thought. Plato, in keeping with the same idea, maintained that the best should rule, and had no doubt that these could be none other than genuine philosophers (philosopher kings) whose very mission would be to use reason and to govern in the light of it. Aristotle, similarly, after a lengthy consideration of all the "vulgar" or conventional virtues, concludes his discussion of ethics with a portrayal of the truly good person and the life of moral virtue. It is not surprising that this turns out to be the life of contemplation, or philosophy—that is, the life of thought and reason. The same basic thought underlies the Stoic philosophy, that natural virtue and the cultivation of one's rational faculty are inseparable. Of course not all the Greeks thought this way, but even those who challenged the idea, such as the Epicureans and other hedonists, could not dissociate themselves from it entirely. And this rationalistic conception of human goodness has, of course, been attacked by many philosophers since—by Hobbes, Hume, Schopenhauer, William James, and others. Still, it has persisted, and even today forms part of the ordinary notion of virtue in our culture. We can read Kant's pronouncement, that rational nature is alone possessed of dignity, and that rational beings are, by virtue of their rational element, to be treated as ends in themselves, without the least astonishment, so deeply embedded has this association of reason and goodness, first made by the Greeks, become in our minds. To describe someone as rational but without goodness, or as noble and good but bereft of reason, would seem paradoxical. It is, I think, worth reflecting on the more or less arbitrary philosophical origin of this idea.

RATIONALISM VS. VOLUNTARISM

Let us, in keeping with philosophical tradition, consider human nature as an amalgam of reason and appetite, or thought and will, or intelligence and desire, or cognition and conation—the contrast has been expressed in all these ways in philosophical literature. Now by this I am not suggesting that, as Plato sometimes put it, your "soul" is divided into diverse "parts," nor am I describing human psychology in terms of disjointed "faculties." I am only calling attention to the fact that we not only think and reason, but that we also will; that in addition to discovering, by thought, what *is* so, we also have certain desires, some abiding and profound and others fleeting and superficial, with respect to what in some sense *ought* to be so. In short, we have certain ideals and aspirations: we pursue ends, we *want* things, and we endeavor to get them; and this is all quite different from saying, which is also true, that we reason and think. This is a perfectly ordinary fact about us, and it is useful to express it more or less as Plato did, by artificially conceiving of human nature as an amalgam of faculties or parts. It calls attention to two rather dissimilar aspects of human nature.

We can thus, with extreme artifice but nonetheless usefully, represent *reason* and *will* by two separate circles, as follows:

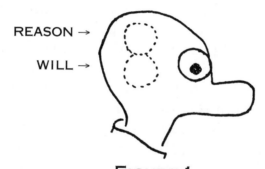

REASON →

WILL →

FIGURE 1.
THE AMALGAM OF REASON AND WILL

And we can now use this general picture to convey the broad ideas of what I shall call moral rationalism and moral voluntarism in this way:

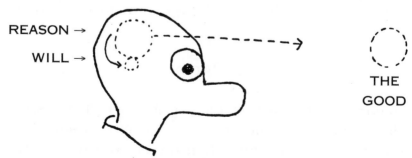

REASON →

WILL →

THE
GOOD

FIGURE 2. MORAL RATIONALISM

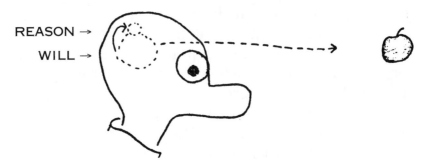

FIGURE 3. MORAL VOLUNTARISM

These two crude pictures represent very broadly two competing conceptions of human nature. According to both, a person is a combination of *reason*, on the one hand, and everything that falls under the head of desire, or what I shall call the *will*, on the other. This latter has sometimes been referred to as the *appetite* (as in Plato), as *conatus* or *conation* (by Spinoza and James), as *endeavor* (by Hobbes), as the *inclinations* (by Kant), and as the *passions* (by Hume); but the Schopenhauerian expression *the will* seems to be the best and least misleading expression. Figure 2, then, represents a person as a *rational being* and forms the basis of moral rationalism, whereas Figure 3 represents one as what I shall henceforth call a *conative being* and forms the basis of moral voluntarism. I shall now explain more fully what these two pictures mean.

MORAL RATIONALISM

According to the first conception, which is essentially a Platonic one, it is our reason that somehow sees what is good and then directs the will to the attainment of it. This is not a literal seeing, of course, so we represent it with an arrow composed of a dotted line. A thing is not seen to be good by the bodily eye; this was perfectly obvious to Plato, as it has been to all moral rationalists. We can, with our eyes, see things, but we cannot in that way see that they are good. So it must be by our reason that we somehow apprehend goodness, and Plato accordingly sometimes spoke of the "eye of the mind," this being that power by which we "see" purely rational things that are no part of physical nature. The good, which is among such rational objects, and is according to Plato the highest and noblest of them, is represented in our picture with a dotted line, to convey the idea that it is an abstract or ideal thing, not the sort of thing one could poke with a stick. The relative size of our circles is meant to suggest the relative importance or power of the things they stand for, reason and will. In the picture representing moral rationalism it is the reason that dominates the will, whereas in that representing moral voluntarism, it is the other way around. The curving dotted arrow in both pictures indicates which directs or governs which, reason governing the will in the one case, and will governing the reason in the other.

Figure 2, then, is meant to convey the idea that you are a kind of being who, endowed with reason, can discern good and evil. It is because of this, your possession of reason, that you are capable of being a moral agent. Having rationally discriminated good from evil, you can then direct your will toward the realization of what is thus seen to be good. This is the important part, the subordination of the will to the reason. A good or rational agent is one whose reason governs the will, and a life so ordered is both virtuous and rational. Vice, or the corruption of a person, consists of this order of things having become reversed, so that the appetite or will gains control over reason. The will, being provided with no inner eye like "the eye of the mind," is blind, and therefore wills whatever attracts it, which is more often than not something base. At the same time, reason, enslaved to this blind urge, is reduced to the degrading role of plotting the means by which the desires can achieve their arbitrary and irrational ends.

One cannot understand the Socratic and Platonic moral philosophies, or indeed most of the moral philosophy that has been fabricated since, without understanding this very general conception of human nature—which is not difficult, however, because it is approximately the idea most people, including those who are not scholars, have of themselves. Most, even now, would be offended at the thought that their conduct is not rational. Plato thought that we could not apprehend the good without willing it, that no one could voluntarily choose evil. Wickedness was for him, then, a kind of blindness or ignorance, and a state that no truly rational person need ever fear. The wicked tyrant who "has everything he wants" was thought of by Plato as an object of pity, his reason, which is the divine element in him, being enslaved to his will, which is base. Such a man only *seems* to have what he wants, and is in fact impoverished and helpless, for his rational element has become so eclipsed by his desires that he does not even know, cannot rationally apprehend, what he really wants, or in other words, what is truly good. In the Stoic philosophy, which drew its inspiration from Socrates, the will is so subordinated to reason that it almost disappears from the picture altogether. Apathy, or the desiring of nothing, became for the Stoics a primary virtue. The only life we should aspire to, according to these moralists, is a life "according to nature"— that is, according to our true nature or to reason. So long as we possess this we possess human virtue, they thought, however impoverished we may be with respect to everything else; and although we may be boundlessly rich in all other things, we still have nothing if we lack such rational virtue.

This idea is not an archaic one, for prevailing philosophical thought has always been Greek in its outlook even on the part of those thinkers who have been least aware of the Greeks. Even Kant never doubted that it is reason that counts, even in morals. So little did the will, or what he referred to as inclination, have to do with moral conduct that he was unwilling even to allow it to cooperate with the rational motivation of duty. Reason, for him, not only directs the will, but governs a recalcitrant will, much as in Plato. What human reason discerns, however, is not for Kant some abstract good, but rather an abstract "moral law" or formula of duty. This is not a significant difference between the Platonic and Kantian conceptions, but only a reflection of the influence of Christianity and its emphasis on dutiful conduct to other persons or to God. The fundamental conceptions of human nature are in all essential respects the same for both Plato and Kant; Figure 2 can represent the one as well as the other.

This conception of human nature, the conception graphically presented in Figure 2, still dominates moral philosophy. It is not that it is an idea that is defended; indeed, it is never even discussed. It is simply presupposed. There are countless philosophers and other intellectuals who simply assume that their behavior is rational, and who simply never doubt that a rational justification should be given, or at least be made available, for any mode of conduct or pattern of life that is claimed to be morally right. Indeed, to say that a mode of life has a moral justification simply *means* to the vast majority of contemporary philosophers that it can be *rationally* defended, and virtually all contemporary philosophical literature on this subject has to do, in one way or another, with the giving of reasons for this and for that, and with the intellectual problems that inevitably arise from the attempt to do this. It hardly occurs to anyone that there might be a kind of moral justification that has nothing whatsoever to do with reason, a kind of justification that rests more upon seeing than thinking, and involves wisdom rather than dialectic. That this is so is, nevertheless, the underlying theme of this whole book, and it marks a radical departure not only from contemporary thinking about ethics, but from the main stream of our philosophical tradition.

MORAL VOLUNTARISM

Let us next, then, consider Figure 3, which is intended to convey a much different conception of human nature than Figure 2. It is in fact almost the reverse of Figure 2. That it has some semblance of truth will, I think, be immediately obvious, but it is most assuredly not the picture of human nature that most philosophers have drawn.

According to this view, it is only because you have a will—that is, because you have desires, passions, wants, inclinations, or in short, because you pursue ends or objects of desire—that any distinctions of good and evil ever arise in the first place. The original goodness of something consists simply in its being desired, and the evil of any state of affairs consists simply in its frustration of desire. Were it not for this desiderative aspect of human nature, everything would be on a dead level, nothing would even matter. Things acquire the status of being good or evil only if someone—anyone—cares about them one way or the other. The question cannot even legitimately arise of whether what you will corresponds with what is rationally good. Reason, by itself, can make no distinction whatever between what is good and what is not. Reason can only, and within limits, see what is so, and can never declare whether it ought to be so. There is, therefore, a fundamental absurdity in the idea of reason *governing* the will, and the fact that this idea is very old and laden with great tradition makes it no less absurd. What is significant is that we will certain ends. From one sunrise to the next, this is what gives life meaning; indeed, it is the very expression of life itself. Human reason is employed almost exclusively in discerning the means whereby those ends, which are the product of the will, can be achieved. It is because of this that human reason and intelligence are rightly thought to confer upon us such an advantage over the rest of nature. What Plato and Kant thought of as the moral corruption of human nature is, therefore, human nature itself. Far from this conception being the enemy of morals, a kind of human nature that we are somehow called on to transcend, it is precisely because this is what we basically *are* that any problems of morals arise to begin with. Good and evil are not exactly the products of the will, but they are the reflection of it, for they would not even exist to a mind that was purely and exclusively rational. The will may be blind, in the artificial sense that no final rational justification can be given for the ultimate ends that you will, but it is not so morally blind as the reason, which by itself cannot even draw the distinction between good and evil.

In the pages that follow, then, I am going to develop a conception of moral voluntarism. To grasp this whole point of view is going to require a considerable readjustment of our philosophical thinking about morals. The justification of it will consist, in part, of the light it will throw on the errors of our predecessors, many of them great and illustrious, and the opening up of the blind alleys that they have created. The remainder of its justification will consist in the abolishment of mysteries, for many things will be found to make sense, to fall into place, when looked at in this light. This is probably the best kind of intellectual justification that can be given for any point of view, for a complete philosophy somewhat resembles a jigsaw puzzle. When everything fits, we know we have the thing right, and no further question of "proof" can be asked. When, on the other hand, something not only does not fit, but creates numberless new problems with every attempt to get it into the picture, we may suspect that it does not belong in the scheme at all. And this is surely what is true of many philosophical theories of morals. They more or less answer some immediate question that has been asked; but, as with many of the theories of Plato and Kant, they throw everything else out of kilter, giving birth to numberless new paradoxes that no imagination or wit can resolve, so that the general scheme becomes more disjointed than ever.

– 2 –

NATURE VS. CONVENTION

ONE CANNOT REFLECT on problems of good and evil without, consciously or otherwise, borrowing heavily from the ancients. People sometimes suppose, very naïvely, that they can turn their thought to such questions without preconceptions, thinking them all out for themselves *de novo*. They do not realize that many of the concepts in terms of which moral problems are framed are the legacy of a very old culture, and that their thinking is therefore quite thoroughly conditioned, sometimes by ideas whose authors are unknown to them. I propose, then, to take a fairly close, but not detailed, look at some of the more significant ethical ideas of the Greeks, particularly some of these whose validity is now widely taken for granted. This, I hope, will help us to shake ourselves free from the influence of some of them, for there is probably nothing so constraining to thought as an idea that is unconsciously and, hence, uncritically held.

TRUE MORALITY

I am going to use the expression *true morality* to cover that whole cluster of moral philosophies, ancient and modern, whose basic presupposition is that human conduct can be, in the philosophical sense, rational, and that only when it is such can it be virtuous or morally justifiable. I do not label these philosophies true morality because I think they are true. On the contrary, I consider them basically false, however venerable some of them have become. I so label them in order to express the idea of what is thought by many to be *genuine* moral philosophy, or simply moral philosophy that purports to have a rational basis. The expression *true morality* is apt, because there have always been many philosophers who have supposed that if morality is not discussed in the context of reason or of rational justification, then it is not really ethics that is being discussed—it is only anthropology or psychology or something of that sort. True morality, therefore, is simply rational ethics, as distinguished from all those nonphilosophical things with which ethics is sometimes confused. Or the matter can be put this way: There is a widespread presupposition that no treatise on human conduct can really be on the subject of morality if it does not somewhere contain certain claims, not merely about what we *do*, but about what we morally *ought* to do, and fortify these claims by some sort of rational justification. True morality is distinguished, then, not from what is false, but from what is considered specious, ungenuine, or unphilosophical.

WHAT IS AND WHAT OUGHT TO BE

It is, for example, a widespread assumption, and one having much philosophical authority to support it, that there is a real distinction between what is and what morally ought to be; or between fact, on the one hand, and value, on the other. Now this is not supposed to be merely the difference between what we have and what we would like, or between what we find and what we wish we would find, for those distinctions can be expressed without the use of any ethical notions at all. It is, rather, a distinction between two levels of being, two distinct realms of discourse. The realm of what *is*—of fact—is supposed to be the province of science and of observation generally. The realm of what *ought* to be is assumed to be the province of moral philosophy. It is supposed to be the role of philosophical ethics to discern what morally ought to be; that is, to state, and rationally defend, not what people, laws, institutions, and societies happen to be—because this might fall far short of the ideal—but what these morally *should* be. And it is assumed that there are truths concerning the latter as well as the former. They are not, to be sure, truths that can be proved by science, because empirical science is by its nature fettered to the world of what is. They are, accordingly, the province of philosophical ethics. It is assumed to be the task of moral philosophy to show, by reason, what ought to be; that is, what we ought to do, what our laws ought to be, and what our institutions ought to be. It is assumed, in short, that there are moral truths to be discovered by reason and enunciated by philosophy, just as there are truths about observable reality to be discovered by observation and enunciated by science. Any philosophy that rests on this assumption, whether it be wise or foolish, shallow or profound, true or false, I call a philosophy of true morality.

THE EMERGENCE OF ETHICS IN GREEK PHILOSOPHY

Classical Greek philosophy did not at first make this distinction. Indeed, the earliest philosophers said almost nothing about ethics at all. Philosophical ethics was first developed by Socrates and the Sophists of his period. Their predecessors had been concerned with nature or *phusis*, with what today is called physics, and, quite incidentally to this, with human nature. Some affirmed the existence of mind conceived as a force not significantly different from other forces in nature; others defended theories of atoms and considered people, like all other natural objects, to be composed entirely of these minute particles. Still others preferred theories of elements and qualities. The distinction, in any case, between what is and what ought to be was not at first significant, and the speculative interests of the Greeks were originally directed toward what *is*; that is, toward physical nature. The idea of moral goodness, so central to Socrates' thought, and derived by him from religion—that is, from the Pythagoreans and the Orphics—was for a long time quite foreign to philosophy. Human goodness was thought of essentially as art or skill (*areté*), and was therefore relative to the role or function of this man or that, as we have seen. Goodness, as so conceived, is not a moral concept at all.

The Sophists, however, became absorbed in another aspect of human experience, namely the laws, customs, and what can in a word be expressed as the *conventions* by which societies live—the rules and laws that in some sense govern human behavior. Thus arose the opposition that permeated Greek philosophy for so long, and still permeates philosophy under other names: the opposition between *nature (phusis)* and *convention (nomos)*. It is not at once apparent why these two ideas should have been thought to be opposed, but an acquaintance with some of the philosophical opinions of that age, together with a little reflection, will make it clearer. We shall also thus come to understand what was meant by the Cynic and Stoic maxim "Live according to nature"; how in one dialogue after another Plato was able to refute the moral relativisms of his day by assimilating morals to nature; how the concept of *natural* law gained a foothold on the legal and moral philosophy and the theological systems of Western culture; and, what is most important of all, how all those philosophies that I collect under the term *true morality* came to be born and to persist.

NATURE VS. CONVENTION

The basic problem of philosophical ethics eventually presented itself to the minds of the Greeks in the following way.

There is, they noted, a vast realm of truth that has nothing to do with human edict, fiat, or custom; that is in no sense fabricated or dependent on what anyone says or does; and that is, accordingly, constant from culture to culture and from age to age. This is nature, simply as we find it. That fire burns, that some human beings are male and others female, some light-skinned and others dark, that all are mortal, that the seasons succeed each other in a cyclic way, these are all truths of nature. They are not things that are so because someone has decreed that they should be so, or because people have become accustomed to so regarding them; they are so everywhere, no matter what anyone might think or do. They are not relative, then, to customs, laws, opinions, or conventions; they are things that are true, by nature.

There is, on the other hand, another realm of facts that is relative and variable, things that are so only because someone has in one way or another— that is, by edict, law, sheer custom, or otherwise— *made* them so. It is, for example, not by nature that some men are free and others slaves, that some are cultured and some barbarians, that some are ruled by tyrants and others by assemblies, that some are rich and some poor, or that one man is a physician and another a farmer. These may all be truths, to be sure, but they are truths of convention, things that are not given, but rather that are in one way or another made true. They are so, but they need not be so; having made them so, someone might have made them otherwise, with no violation of nature.

The terms *nature* and *convention* are very suitable for drawing this distinction, which is a very important one and not difficult to grasp. Once you have become aware of it, however, then some very disturbing questions suggest themselves. For example, with respect to those things that are true by convention, are any of them *also* true by nature? Raising this question implies, of course, that there are natural truths of morality and law, as well as conventional ones—or, in other words, that there is a natural or true morality, a natural or true justice that may or may not be embodied in existing practices and institutions. Given this assumption, then further and more disturbing questions arise. For example, what is natural justice? What is the actual content of true or natural morality? How is it discovered? And once it is known, might we not find that conventional laws and practices, although true by convention simply because they *are* conventional, are really false? Might not conventional justice be actual injustice, and conventional morality be immoral?

The laws and institutions of a society, for example, more or less express the conventional ideas of justice in that society. They are clearly man-made, could have been otherwise, and are in that sense arbitrary. Is there any reason, then, to suppose that they also express natural justice? If it should turn out that they do not, then do they merely fall short of natural justice, sharing the imperfections of all human contrivances, or might they, perhaps, be in absolute contradiction to it? The same sort of question can of course be asked concerning the extralegal customs and traditions that one assimilates from his culture—that is, the generally accepted morality. It is not enough that a set of moral attitudes and practices should be generally accepted and perhaps hallowed by long tradition; this only shows that they are conventionally true and, thus, in the last analysis, perhaps arbitrary. The question can still be asked whether they correspond with what is right and good by nature—with a true morality that is not man-made, variable, and arbitrary—whether they might be incompatible with what is naturally right, and even in complete opposition to it. If the latter should be true, then it would follow that the generally received morality is in truth *immoral*, a violation of natural or true morality.

It became very important to Greek thinkers to answer these questions, and it has been important ever since. Indeed, virtually all of moral philosophy is, in one way or another, the attempt to answer them. Even philosophers who have been only vaguely aware of the Greek distinction between nature and convention, and have hardly appreciated its significance, have been wholly dominated by it. So long as we suppose that there is such a thing as real justice or true morality, then we must determine what they are and answer the question of whether conventional justice and morality do or do not reflect them. The alternative, which few philosophers have been willing to consider seriously or to defend with consistency, is to suppose that all morality is *merely* a matter of convention, that there is no real truth to be discovered in this realm of what *ought* to be, and that justice and morality are in this sense purely arbitrary. What human beings have made, they could have made differently. Unless we suppose that there is a natural justice and a true morality we cannot say that any laws or conventional moralities are really any better than any others, nor can there be any rational basis on which to criticize or reject any laws or customs whatever. If there is no true morality, then there is left only convention, and this has no more foundation than that it was fabricated, willy-nilly, by human beings. It would seem to have, in other words, no foundation at all.

All of Socratic and Platonic ethical philosophy revolves around this distinction. Socrates' quest, in all the Socratic dialogues, is to find what genuine virtue is and what a really good person is—that is, one who is good according to what is good by nature, as contrasted with one who is merely deemed good by the conventions of his day. Plato's *Republic*, similarly, is a lengthy essay on justice, and its avowed aim is to portray both the just person and the just state, as nature or true morality would have them. These have so little to do with conventional justice that Plato did not for a minute assume that his just state exists anywhere, or even that it ever will. There can obviously be no merely conventional justice that nowhere exists, because conventional justice is identical with existing law and practice. The absorption of ethical philosophy into theology, resulting from the rise and spread of Christianity, did not represent a radical departure from the Greek development of ethics, for it involved only the substitution of what is considered to be according to God for the Greek idea of what is according to nature. Whether you defend a philosophical ethics that is deemed to be according to nature, or one that is claimed to be according to God, you are in either case defending what is claimed to be true—that is, a true morality—or claims concerning what truly ought to be, as contrasted to what, by custom or convention, exists.

THE PROBLEM OF MORALITY
IN SOPHISTIC PHILOSOPHY

The early Greek moralists made various uses of the distinction between natural and conventional virtue. Some, obsessed with the idea that conventional virtue is the corruption of natural goodness, advocated various philosophies of life according to which the conventional virtues were to be ignored or positively scorned as evils. Such were the programs of many of the characters who appear in Plato's Socratic dialogues, as well as of the Cynic and Stoic schools of philosophy that came later. Others, like Socrates, Plato, and Aristotle, declared conventional and natural justice to be compatible, identifying the latter with the rational ideals of philosophy and reserving the former for the ordinary non-philosophical citizens or the "vulgar." The fame of these three as moralists probably rests, in fact, upon their apparent reconciliation of the two ideas.

The opposition between nature and convention found one of its earliest expressions in the opinions of Hippias, about whom little is known. He is supposed, however, to have declared that there are certain unwritten laws that were instituted by the gods rather than by men, which accounts for their invariability and their authority over all societies everywhere. One such unwritten law is that all are fellow citizens, regardless of the state to which they owe conventional allegiance. Now this is a startling idea, when one considers it, for nothing would seem to be more conventional than citizenship. You are a citizen of this or that state purely by virtue of your place of birth or that of your ancestors, and this is hardly something that is invariable or according to nature. By convention, moreover, members of different states are *not* fellow citizens; to be a citizen of one is normally to exclude being a citizen of another. Yet Hippias declared that, in some sense, all members are fellow citizens, independently of their conventional citizenship. The only sense in which this can be so is that they have this common bond by nature. The implication is that if foreigners do not *treat* each other as fellow citizens, then, although they may be violating no man-made laws, they are nevertheless violating a *law*. Such a law can only be a law of nature or, what amounts to much the same thing in the context of Hippias' thought, a law of the gods.

THRASYMACHUS AND THE WILL OF THE STRONG

The conflict of these two ideas is beautifully expressed by some of the characters presented in Plato's dialogues. In his *Republic*, for example, he has Thrasymachus present and defend a conventional conception of justice, but one that has, according to Thrasymachus, a natural explanation. Justice, according to Thrasymachus, is "the interest of the stronger." This is easily misinterpreted, but it is clear enough what Thrasymachus means. By "the stronger" he means those who happen to hold power; they need not be strong in any natural sense. It is, he observed, those who hold power who make the laws and establish the standards of conduct for those who are ruled. Now these laws, although fabricated, are not arbitrary. They have a definite purpose, and that is to advance the interest of those who make them. That interest, however, does not coincide with the interests of the governed, who must obey them; it is, on the contrary, usually opposed to these. The relationship of rulers to ruled is essentially that of masters to servants, and whatever serves the interests of the former can hardly serve also the interests of the latter. Thrasymachus aptly compares the relationship of rulers to ruled to that of a shepherd and his sheep. A good shepherd tends his sheep, to be sure, and decides all things for them, sometimes in such a way as to suggest that he even places their welfare above his own. Thus, he protects them from predators and from storms, often at great trouble to himself. In fact, however, he does these things only to take advantage of them in the end, to slaughter them and thus promote his own interests. And so it is with people. Rulers promulgate the principles of justice and induce the herd of men to uphold them, but such principles are never in the ultimate interest of those upon whom they are foisted. Their only effect is to render it easier for the authors of these principles to exploit.

If we generalize this theory a bit, it is certainly not implausible. Laws and the conventional standards of conduct are obviously created by those who have the power to create them; that is, by those who, in a broad sense, govern, or comprise, in contemporary language, "the establishment." They are in this sense made by "the stronger." And it is not hard to suppose that the guiding principle of such laws and conventions is precisely the interest of those who establish them. You can find considerable confirmation of this in your own experience. But if this is so, and if the relationship between governors and governed is as Thrasymachus supposes, the implications are momentous. One such implication is that there is nothing about justice that is inherently good; on the contrary, the principles of justice can be nothing but evils to those who must submit to them. One really ought, therefore, to disregard such principles whenever he can get away with it, out of consideration for his own interest—unless, of course, he happens to be a ruler. If conventional justice is only the man-made expression of power, then a wise person, realizing this, will quite properly violate its principles whenever possible. The wise will, in other words, practice injustice. And, in fact, Thrasymachus thought, people do only shrink from injustice out of fear of punishment. Injustice is bad only in its consequences. Considered apart from these it is usually something good—that is, something serving one's own interest—and its opposite, justice, is an evil.

GLAUCON AND ADIEMANTUS

In the same dialogue, Glaucon and Adiemantus outline similar theories, but without advocating them. They are, in other words, theories that Glaucon and Adiemantus have heard and found persuasive, although they are themselves reluctant to accept them, and beg Socrates to exhibit what is wrong with them. The bulk of *The Republic* is, in fact, Plato's answer to these doubts, an answer that defends the view that true morality or natural justice is, in the individual, the governance of reason, and in the state, a rule by philosophers according to the principles of reason.

Glaucon observes that, by nature, the commission of injustice is good, whereas the suffering of it is evil. Anyone can see, in other words, that it is better, quicker, and easier to get ahead without regard to conventional restraints of justice than to try doing so within the confines of these, which makes the commission of injustice a natural good. Ideally, therefore, there should be no conventional rules of justice; we should all have exactly what we want, without restraint. But there is another side to this coin: If everyone were permitted such freedom, then each would be exposed to the risk of suffering at the hands of others. Everyone, therefore, arrives at a rule of compromise, to abstain from injury against each other, with a view to minimizing the risk of injury to themselves—and thus is born the whole complex of laws and customs expressive of conventional justice. Conventional or man-made justice, as opposed to natural justice, is simply that totality of rules that in various ways says: "Do not injure your fellows." And the reason for accepting such rules, onerous in themselves, is a purely practical one; namely, that by so doing you reduce the risk of something still worse, the suffering of injury from others.

Adiemantus reinforces this conception of conventional justice by noting, for instance, that justice is never praised as something good for its own sake, but only for its consequences, and thus are its principles conveyed to the young. No one pretends that adherence to any principle of justice is pleasant or agreeable in itself, but the rewards of such adherence generally outweigh their galling restrictions. If you act unjustly, for example, seeking only your own advantage without regard to others, then even though some things may thereby be made easier, you will nevertheless lose respect and honor from others, to say nothing of running the risk of severe punishment. If you restrain your natural inclinations by conventional principles, on the other hand, the opposite will be your return: honor and respect from others, a good reputation, and freedom from the pain of punishment. Still, the fact remains that vice and injustice, considered in themselves and independently of their consequences, are more pleasant and attractive by nature, and conventional justice is, from the standpoint of nature, burdensome.

This is obviously a rational and plausible theory. It is probably the first expression in philosophy of something resembling a social contract theory of a political society. It nevertheless, like the view of Thrasymachus, implies something profoundly odious to most philosophers, something that was in fact odious to Glaucon and Adiemantus: by nature there is nothing good about justice. Justice is by this theory a ball and chain, something we put up with, voluntarily, not as something good, but for the avoidance of evil. Were it not for the need to get along together safely, no one would respect any principles of justice. As it is, no one respects such principles for their own sake; we only grudgingly accept them. If in our philosophy we are to be true to the nature of things, then we should not sing the praises of conventional justice and forbearance, but the very opposite—we should recognize conventional injustice as what is by nature the true good. A few philosophers in the history of thought have actually extolled this idea—but only a few—and their ideas have always been reviled as warped and pernicious. Those many philosophers, on the other hand, such as Plato and Kant, who have defended the opposite idea, whether cogently or otherwise, have endeared their names to generations forever.

POLUS AND THE REWARDS OF INJUSTICE

Probably nowhere in literature is the contrast between natural, or true, morality and conventional,

or man-made, morality more clearly expressed than
in Plato's *Gorgias*. Here Socrates, having at length
gotten Gorgias and Polus to acknowledge that there
is such a thing as justice and that it is something
good, proceeds to develop a number of seemingly
paradoxical inferences from this acknowledgment—
inferences that are not, however, the least paradoxical if one once acknowledges this seemingly harmless point. Thus, Socrates maintains that a reasonable man, in case he has lapsed into injustice or
wickedness, will be his own accuser and, far from
trying to avoid punishment for his injustice, will
actually seek punishment. The basis of this is
simply that, justice being good, just punishment
must also be good, and a reasonable man will always
seek what is good in preference to what is evil—in
this case, in preference to the injustice and, hence,
evil that would result from anyone not receiving the
punishment he justly deserves. The worst thing that
can happen to you is to have a natural evil befall
you, and wickedness is a natural evil; hence, the
worst thing that can happen to you is to become
wicked or, in other words, to cease to be virtuous or
just. It follows from this, of course, that if there
were a wicked person upon whom we (rightly or
wrongly) wished to inflict evil, or who we wanted to
suffer because of his wickedness, then we should,
instead of seeking to have him punished, do the very
opposite! That is, we should protect him from punishment, abet his efforts to escape it, and all with
the view to maximizing the evil we wish to befall
him. Consequences such as these do surely follow
from the supposition that it can never be to any
man's interest to avoid what is good, that true justice is good, and hence that just punishment is good.

Polus finds such a point of view as implausible as any other unphilosophical person would. Surely it cannot be to any man's interest to suffer pain or loss, whether justly or not. On the contrary, experience abundantly teaches us that those who inflict harm on others, provided they escape punishment for this, are vastly better off than those who are thus harmed. Kingdoms have been built upon usurpation, murder, and intrigue, and it would seem laughable to point to the tyrants who have by such means engineered such power for themselves as miserable or unfortunate. They have everything they want, and are able to avoid what no one wants—namely, the fetters and confinements of justice. It is not the wicked who suffer, provided they can carry through their wickedness without incurring the punishment that is its normal return. It is, rather, the just who suffer, for it is in every case worse to suffer injustice than to commit it.

Polus nevertheless concedes to Socrates that it is in some sense *uglier* to commit injustice than to suffer it, and with this concession his whole position is soon undermined. For if acts of injustice are uglier than the suffering of injustice, they must also in some sense be more evil—and, hence, worse. We are thus brought back to Socrates' original position and all that it entails—that virtue or justice is a natural good, that a reasonable person will therefore prize nothing above integrity or virtue and just conduct, and will willingly choose these even when they involve suffering unjustly at the hands of others. These things do follow, and in particular it follows that a wise and reasonable person, given the choice between getting away with injustice and putting up with the hardships of justice, will voluntarily choose the latter. His choice will be governed by the simple and obvious principle that a reasonable person will always want to choose what is better in preference to what is worse, or what is by nature good rather than what is evil.

But is this fair? If acts of injustice are uglier and, hence, more evil than the suffering of injustice, in what sense are they uglier? The suspicion arises that Socrates is here exploiting different possible senses of "ugly" and "evil"; that injustice might, for example, be ugly only in terms of *conventional* morality, whereas Socrates has won his victory over Polus only by assuming, without actually affirming, that injustice is a natural evil.

Precisely this point is made by Callicles, who accuses Socrates of turning human life "completely upside down." He makes the point so well, and in a way that so beautifully expresses the contrast we are considering, that we can do no better than let him speak for himself:

> Now, Socrates, you know you really do divert the argument into such cheap and vulgar paths, saying that you're pursuing the truth, but really getting us into what is beautiful, not by nature but by convention. Yet these two are for the most part opposed to each other, nature and convention; so that if a man is timid and doesn't have the courage to speak his mind, he must necessarily contradict himself. So this is the clever trick you have devised to cheat in your arguments: if a man makes his assertions according to convention, in your questions you slyly substitute "according to nature," and if he speaks according to nature, you reply according to convention. So in the present

instance, when doing and suffering wrong were being examined, Polus spoke of what was uglier according to convention, but you followed it up as though it were a natural principle. By nature, in fact, everything that is worse is uglier, just as suffering wrong is; but to do wrong is uglier merely by convention.[1]

And with this observation, the opposition between natural and conventional good and evil is again before us. Socrates seems simply to have assumed that what is conventionally ugly and evil must also be so by nature, thus begging every question at issue.

---

1. Plato, *Gorgias*, trans. W. C. Helmbold (New York: Liberal Arts Press, 1952), p. 51.

– 3 –

THE ISSUE JOINED
TRUE VS. PRAGMATIC MORALITY

THE QUESTION IS still before us, then: What is really good? What is good, just, and noble, not by human opinion or contrivance, but in the very nature of things?

To this question Callicles has his own answer. It is an answer that is destined forever to be rejected by the majority of humankind, but it is nevertheless deserving of the most serious consideration, and one must understand what Callicles is doing. He is elaborating a philosophical position that is deemed by him to express a natural or true morality, and hence one that does not at all depend on prevailing opinions. Indeed, it will not find and does not need the endorsement of ordinary, decent, and well-mannered people, for in the very nature of the case their morality will be conventional. The morality of Callicles purports, however, to be a natural morality.

THE TRUE MORALITY ACCORDING TO CALLICLES

Callicles observes that people are by nature not equal, that they may be divided into the strong and the weak, the intelligent and stupid, those who lead and those who are led—in short, into superior and inferior. What he has in mind here is not certain distinctions of convention, such as distinctions of wealth and social position, but a natural one. Some are by nature superior to others. Philosophical or political claims of the human equality of all men are not only fabrications, but downright falsehoods. Some moralists and political leaders have urged that all should be *treated* as equals, and it has been fairly common to express this by saying that all are *in fact* equal, but as Callicles insists, they are in fact *not* equal. Some are by nature better men than others. Moreover, he observes, the superior are always and everywhere greatly outnumbered by their opposites. These who embody the ideal qualities of human nature are by the very nature of things few, whereas those who lack one or more of such qualities of body and mind as intelligence, courage, strength, and determination are very numerous.

It is, Callicles thinks, in the light of this fact that the origin and character of conventional morality, as well as its perniciousness, can be understood. For conventional morality, which among other things declares everyone to be equal, is nothing but the invention of the overwhelmingly numerous inferiors who, being by nature inferior, are quite content to declare themselves equal to all. The effect is to render the naturally superior equal to the inferior in the eyes of conventional morality. The underlying reason for such a dogma—or, rather, such a myth—

is not merely to enable the hoards of the inferior to feel that they are as good as others. It has a far more practical basis than this: the motive of self-protection. For, clearly, if some are superior to others, the latter are at the mercy of the former unless they take steps to protect themselves. Hence, conventional morality is invented by the multitude precisely to keep the strong from expressing their strength; to give everyone, whether deserving or not, an equal chance and an equal share of the goods and opportunities that the world offers. From these considerations it is very easy to see what the content of conventional morality or justice is going to be—namely, that not only are all people to be treated as though they were equal, but that everyone will have certain basic rights that it will be "wrong" to violate. Such qualities as humility, meekness, and cowardice—all the qualities of the weak and inferior—will be praised as the highest "virtues." They are precisely the qualities that the multitude, by nature, possesses.

Conventional morality is, therefore, according to Callicles, not only an artificial fabrication, it is a positively pernicious one, for it is an actual perversion of what is right and good by nature. Conventional justice is, in other words, what is in truth injustice, and in this conventional scheme of things what is really good becomes bad, what is right becomes wrong, and those very things that are by nature lawful and proper are declared to be wicked and criminal. According to the true morality, the superior should rule the inferior in their own interest, and the relationship of ruler to ruled should be that of master to servant, taking into account those who have worth and those who do not. "Nature herself," Callicles declares, "reveals it to be only just and proper that the better man should lord it over his inferior . . . men are acting in accordance with natural justice when they perform such acts, and, by heaven, it is in accordance with law, too, the law of nature."[1]

Now the temptation here is to say that these ideas of Callicles are plainly out of accord with the accepted concepts of morality, and even with the very meanings of our basic moral terms. This, however, would be entirely to miss the point. Callicles admits this, but he adds that the generally accepted notions of morality—that is, conventional morality —are in fact a perversion of morality, or the expression of what is in fact *immoral*. Socrates, accordingly, is not found to criticize Callicles' ideas on this ground. Socrates shares with him the conviction that there is a natural or true morality; he only insists that Callicles has failed to set forth its contents correctly. It is significant to note, however, that Socrates is able to "refute" Callicles only by first leading him into the declaration of *another* doctrine—namely, the doctrine of hedonism, which was no part of Callicles' original thesis. That original thesis was evidently not refuted by Socrates, and has probably never been refuted by anyone else— although it has been rejected by virtually every moralist who has considered it. Such is the weight of convention, even on the minds of those who are learned.

---

1. Plato, *Gorgias*, trans. W. C. Helmbold (New York: Liberal Arts Press, 1952), pp. 51–52.

PROTAGORAS AND THE
DOCTRINE OF PRAGMATISM

When you are confronted with such a doctrine as this, and see that it is a fairly obvious consequence of the presupposition that there exists a true or natural morality as contrasted with what is merely conventional, then you are apt to question that presupposition. Perhaps all morality is conventional; perhaps there is no true or false in this realm, but only a distinction between what is and what is not done. Perhaps, in other words, all moral distinctions are in the last analysis of human origin, such that nothing is in truth really right or wrong, just or unjust, but is only such within the framework of this or that artificial set of conventions.

This was the conclusion arrived at by Protagoras, one of Socrates' contemporaries and undoubtedly the possessor of one of the finest minds ever to adorn the human race. But Protagoras went further than this, maintaining that the distinction between objective truth and falsity is inapplicable not only to morals, but to anything whatsoever. He summarized this view of things in the famous and generally scorned epigram "Man is the measure of all things," to which he added, "of things that are, that they are, and of things that are not, that they are not."

The Protagorean theory of morals can thus be expressed in the following way: There is no natural morality, justice, or law. Laws and practices vary from one time and place to another, and none is objectively true or false. It is this latter claim that is significant. It has always been known that morality varies with climate and time, but faced with such diversity, most thinkers have wanted to ask: Which set of practices is the correct one? Given that different societies behave and think differently, which behave and think as they should? Which thoughts and practices come closest to what is in the nature of things *true*?

Protagoras dismissed all such questions as intellectually empty. Man, he said, is the measure of *all* things, and by this he meant, first, that the opinions and attitudes of every individual person are ultimate or final, that each is the final judge of things, and that there is accordingly no further standard by which the views of men can be judged as true or false; and secondly, that this holds, not only with respect to our opinions and attitudes concerning morality and justice, but with respect to everything whatsoever. Faced with the philosophical distinction between what is objectively true (by nature) and what is merely believed (by convention), most thinkers had assumed that in every domain of inquiry, including morals, something must be in fact true, in addition to, and (as with Callicles) perhaps even in opposition to, what is merely accepted. But Protagoras took the very opposite view. Faced with the same philosophical distinction between nature and convention, and driven to the conclusion that all morality is purely conventional, he went one step further and claimed that in every domain of inquiry, including, for example, physics and mathematics, all distinctions of true and false are purely conventional. Nature is the measure or standard of nothing; the thoughts, feelings, and opinions of human beings are the measure of everything.

Hence, if someone should, for example, declare it to be a warm day, and another should declare it to be quite chilly, there would be nothing here, according to Protagoras, for them to argue about. Each is expressing how things seem, and each is right—which amounts to saying that neither is right and neither is wrong. Similarly, if someone should declare that today is Monday, and another that today is Tuesday, then Protagoras would point out that nothing is more purely conventional than the names given to days. If someone were to decide to refer to a given day as Sunday and the day following as Tuesday, that would be no intellectual error. It would be confusing to others, no doubt, but there is no sense in which it would be false except within the framework of convention. It would only be speaking differently. Again, if someone declared a square to have four sides, and another said, on the contrary, that a square has six sides, then Protagoras would insist that neither can be said to be right or wrong, except with reference to certain conventional definitions of mathematics. But those are human conventions; they were not given by nature. And if someone says that grass is green, and another that it is blue, then we can only say, with reference to each of these, "So it seems to him." If we then go on to inquire which sees things as they are, then we have begun a vain and futile pursuit of "the truth." The most we could say is which sees things as most people do. There *is* no truth in these or any other matters over and above how things seem. Man— each individual man—is the measure of all things. That many agree on certain things does not make them more right than those who do not agree; it only gives a stronger voice to their views.

Protagoras did not stop with this purely negative view, however. Although he repudiated any real or natural distinction between true and false—and hence between just and unjust, right and wrong—he nevertheless insisted that some opinions, attitudes, and practices are *better* than others; that is to say, better *in terms of their consequences* to whoever holds to such opinions, attitudes, and practices. It cannot, for example, really matter so far as truth is concerned whether one insists on calling a given day Monday or Tuesday, but if everyone else refers to that day as Tuesday, then I had better go along with them—my affairs will go more smoothly and well if I do, and surely will be confused and go badly if I do not, particularly where appointments, meetings, and public events are concerned. Similarly, it cannot really matter in terms of the truth or nature what conventions of mathematics one adopts, but if certain conventions already prevail and are agreed to, then those should be my conventions too. Otherwise I shall not be understood, and things are apt to go very badly for me whenever I apply my mathematics to any of the affairs of life. And if the grass that seems green to most people seems blue to me, then even though there is no point in their maintaining that I am wrong, I can nevertheless conclude that there is something wrong with my eyesight, which means only that my eyesight is not normal, or like that of most men. I should, therefore, have it corrected if I can, for it is better and less confusing for me to see things as most people do.

PROTAGOREAN ETHICS

The application of this philosophy to morals is fairly obvious. We should abandon the search for any moral laws that are objective or natural, or for any distinction in nature between right and wrong or justice and injustice. All such distinctions are quite obviously conventional and relative. They differ from various times and places to others, and none are truer or more in accordance with nature than any others. What is moral or just is simply what is thought to be so by this group or that. No one can say who is right and who is wrong with respect to his concept of justice, for everyone is right—which amounts again to saying that no one is right and no one is wrong.

Still, Protagoras insisted, it is perfectly obvious that some practices, all equally conventional, are nevertheless *better* than others, in terms of their consequences to those who adhere to them. A society, for example, whose conventions forbade any carnal contact between the sexes would not be wrong, but it would be a society that would be destined to perish. Similarly, a society that entirely forbad the taking of life—human, animal, or vegetable—might stir a certain sentimental approbation in the hearts of some, but this would nevertheless be a very bad morality. Its adherents would die of starvation—and this is absolutely all Protagoras would mean by regarding it as a bad morality. It would work out badly in terms of its consequences. The good or the true is what works out well, enabling us to reach the goals we are seeking; the bad or false is what works out badly, frustrating men's endeavors. Beyond this there is no good or bad, true or false.

Furthermore, it is fairly obvious that different sets of conventions, wholly opposed to each other in their contents, might work equally well under different circumstances, from which it would follow, according to Protagoras' view, that they would be equally true—and Protagoras did not hesitate to draw this conclusion. Thus, the Athenians valued intellectual culture and individual liberty, elevating the pursuit of these above the military virtues and the rewards of discipline and authoritarian rule, and the Spartans reversed this scheme of values. On any doctrine of true morality, it would follow that not both systems of law, justice, and morality can be correct, because each seems to deny what the other affirms. But, according to the pragmatic view of Protagoras, each might be equally true, for the circumstances of each society might be such that its particular set of conventions worked best in enabling that society to survive and achieve its goals. There is, accordingly, no point in any philosopher attempting to appraise these moral systems in any abstract or intellectual way, or trying to determine which more closely approximates true justice. Philosophers, after all, are human, and can only measure things according to how things seem to them; and how things seem to this person or that must largely depend on the conventions—moral, social, religious, and whatever—that they have imbibed. The only thing to consider here is whether the various conventional moralities do in fact seem to work in getting us to where we want to go; and this is not, in the usual sense, a philosophical inquiry. It is a purely sociological question.

THE SOCRATIC QUESTIONS

With this seemingly simple but in fact fairly profound view of morals, Protagoras had little difficulty dealing with the problems that philosophers like

Socrates wrestled with so interminably and with so little result. Socrates, for example, was obsessed with the questions: What is the true good? What is the true definition of justice? What is a genuinely moral person? How is virtue learned—is it a gift of nature, a product of philosophy, an accident, or what?

With respect to the first question "What is the true good?" Protagoras simply held that there is no true good, in Socrates' sense. *Every* good is equally true to whoever holds it, provided it works—that is, provided its fruits are those that happen to be sought. It is no wonder, then, that Socrates and other moralists should labor so vainly to find the right candidate for this concept—the concept of a true good is only an abstract concept, and there is nothing in the world that fits it. This holds also for the true definition of justice. However one might define justice, it is never difficult to find another definition, quite different in its content, that is, nevertheless, just as good a definition for some society in some circumstances. Justice, like goodness, is simply that set of practices that this or that group has hit on to enable them to get on together as a group. Of course there is no single formula for this, or any single set of practices that does it better than certain others. For some cultures, a harmonious social life is accomplished through democratic institutions, for others it is through religion, for still others through authoritarian rule. All might, therefore, be equally just, which amounts to saying that there is no exclusive definition of justice.

The Protagorean answer to the third question "What is a genuinely moral person?" is interesting and at first surprising. You might expect him to say that there is no such thing as a moral person; that morality is not to be taken seriously; that anyone might do as he pleases without censure from a Protagorean relativist. But Protagoras did not say this at all. A genuinely moral person, according to Protagoras, is simply one who upholds and abides by the conventions of his culture, assuming that these conventions are well established and tested by time. There could be only two motives for rejecting or trying to overturn the conventional values of one's culture: (1) the belief that they are wrong, or (2) the belief that, although neither right nor wrong, other conventional values would work better. It was the first motive that led the Cynics and, to a lesser degree, the Stoics to reject conventional Athenian morality. They thought, following Socrates, that there is a true and higher justice or virtue than that embodied in conventional morality. The second motive is more or less typical of the practical revolutionary. But Protagoras did not believe that either of these two reasons is likely to be valid; certainly never the first, and seldom the second. There is no point in repudiating, and certainly nothing but folly, in trying to overthrow the conventions inherited from tradition, in the name of a truer or higher justice. There is no truer or higher justice than the conventions one happens to have inherited. As for attempting to replace conventions with others that it is alleged will work better in terms of the fulfillment of human interests, such an attempt must necessarily involve certain dislocations and confusions in a society and may sometimes even involve revolution, or the virtual destruction of a society and its attempted replacement by another. It is quite possible that this might sometimes be justified—in case, for example, conventional morality, quite suitable for an earlier age and other circumstances, ceases to work at all in newer circumstances and instead becomes a burdensome hindrance to stable and well-ordered social life. But the cost of such meddling and tampering with established institutions must necessarily be high, and it is not often that it will be justified in terms of the ends thus attained.

The practical consequences of Protagoras' philosophy are therefore extremely conservative. The revolutionary can draw no inspiration from his teaching, but only a dampening discouragement, for a revolutionary must above all be a believer in a true morality and in the injustice of the existing order. The effect of this teaching on all other believers in a true justice or true morality must be much the same, whether they be Stoics, Platonists, Kantians, Christians, or whatever. There is no point in criticizing existing morality in terms of any philosophical or religious principle of morals, because no such principle is true, and it is rare indeed that any such principle would work better in fostering social life than the precepts and practices we already have.

Finally, how is virtue taught? This is a question Socrates raised again and again, but he never answered it very convincingly; nor did he ever find anyone else who could. Protagoras gave his own answer in the Platonic dialogue bearing his name. It is an answer that deeply puzzled Socrates, mainly because he did not consider it an answer to the question he had asked.

To learn virtue or moral excellence, according to Protagoras, is simply to absorb the conventions of one's society. There is no other moral excellence. But it is fairly obvious how these are learned, that is, absorbed. Children begin to learn what is and what is not acceptable behavior as soon as they can understand a precept and appreciate the significance of praise and censure from their parents and nursemaids. The child who does the "wrong" thing learns in the most direct manner possible that he has done the wrong thing—he receives a reproach or a blow. Growing up under this kind of training, the child bit by bit learns what can and cannot be done—which means learning virtue or absorbing the conventional morality of the culture. When a boy learns to read, he is given legends and tales loaded with accounts of the deeds of great heroes—that is, men who have contributed greatly to the strength and security of the culture to which he happens to belong. Even music has the same effect, for as soon as a child learns to sing, the poems are again filled with the ideals and aspirations of the culture, so one is still learning virtue. There is no need to ponder long over the Socratic question "Where are the teachers of virtue?" They are, according to Protagoras, everywhere, for anyone who has any hand in passing on to the young the conventional values and practices of a society is a teacher of virtue. Even the conventional practices themselves serve to teach. One might as well, Protagoras thought, ask where the teachers of Greek are and, failing to find them, wonder how children ever manage to learn their native Greek. If Greek is the only language one ever hears, and if it is spoken constantly by all those around one, then obviously every such speaker is in effect a teacher of Greek. And so it is with morals. And, it might be added, just as the "best" Greek is that used by those who know and adhere to the traditions of the language, so also the "best" morality is that which is practiced by those who know and adhere to the traditions of a given culture.

THE SIGNIFICANCE OF PROTAGORAS

Protagoras' seemingly simple philosophy deserves pondering. You can see that it is by no means as superficial as it may initially appear. It is apt at first to seem overly simple just because we approach it with certain preconceptions of morality. It does not seem to provide the answers we are seeking. But you thus fail to see that it is those very preconceptions that Protagoras repudiates. It is for just this reason that Socrates at first failed to understand Protagoras and was so deeply puzzled by his discourse. Socrates raised certain questions of morality that, according to his presuppositions, ought to have answers. Protagoras answered those questions in terms of his own very different presuppositions, so that to Socrates they quite rightly did not appear at all to be answers to the questions he had asked. Because our own presuppositions concerning truth and justice are like those of Socrates, it is exceedingly easy for us, too, to fail to see the depth and originality of Protagoras' philosophy. We are apt to view it as not only superficial, but entirely negative and destructive. It is doubtful in fact whether any apothegm of morality has been held up to more scorn than the one coined by Protagoras: "Man is the measure of all things." And Protagoras is himself still presented as the *sophist*, par excellence, with all the pejorative connotations of that appellative. If, however, you are willing to question your most basic preconceptions of morality and justice, you will see that Protagoras' ideas not only go to the heart of certain philosophical problems, but that they are very far from being purely negative, skeptical, and destructive. Protagoras had an exceedingly valuable and highly original way of looking at things, and it was not for many centuries, until William James applied his great mind to philosophy, that anything quite like this was to be heard again.

– 4 –

SOCRATIC ETHICS

B Y SOCRATIC ETHICS I mean the moral ideas expressed by Socrates in certain of Plato's *Dialogues*, particularly the *Protagoras* and the *Gorgias*, but others as well. It does not matter whether the historical Socrates held these views, or whether they are merely Plato's ideas put into Socrates' mouth. However, I have no doubt that the historical Socrates is faithfully portrayed there. Indeed, it does not matter for this discussion whether there even was a historical Socrates. That is not a question of ethics, nor even a question of philosophy. I am concerned only with certain philosophical ideas, and because Plato has attributed these ideas to Socrates, I refer to them as Socratic ethics. It is the ideas that we are concerned with, and not the question of who really held them.

THE CHARACTER OF SOCRATES' THOUGHT

Two things invariably strike the reader of the Socratic dialogues. One is that they are usually inconclusive, even though ever so many positions are examined and refuted. The other is that Socrates always wins. You get the impression that the whole discussion is contrived, that Socrates is enabled to refute all his opponents only because Plato arranges for them to say just what is needed for this, that each such opponent sooner or later puts his foot in his mouth just because the whole discussion is, after all, in Plato's hands, and the outcome of every argument is a foregone conclusion.

These impressions are superficial. The inconclusive character of these dialogues is readily understood in terms of Socrates' conception of instruction and learning. It was his view that nothing of significance, and certainly nothing philosophical, is learned by being imparted by others, that you learn only by discovering truth within yourself. It does little good to be told, for example, that an unexamined life is not worth living. If that is how it is learned, it is hardly more than a precept and has no personal meaning. The only way you can learn that an unexamined life is not worth living, or anything else of a philosophical character, is to discover it within your own thought and experience. It must be the product of your own pursuit of philosophy. Plato's ethical dialogues, therefore, are enormously skillful attempts to induce you to think for yourself. The frequently paradoxical turns of thought expressed in them are perfectly calculated to achieve this, as is also their dialogue form. You more or less identify with one of Socrates' opponents, and thus find yourself vicariously refuted. The most natural response to this situation is to think harder—precisely what the dialogues are so artfully designed to achieve.

The impression that the arguments are contrived is also superficial and essentially wrong. Socrates always speaks from a deep conviction of certain ethical ideas that his opponents partially accepted or to which they were at least willing to pay lip service. He invariably leads his opponents to render these ideas explicit—to acknowledge them openly—and then draws the conclusions, usually entirely negative, that inevitably flow from them. It is for this reason that Socrates' opponents present the appearance of being led to refute themselves, for the points they concede to Socrates always contain implications that are inconsistent with what they have been maintaining. We have already seen a fairly characteristic example of this in Polus' concession that it is ugly to commit an act of injustice, which Socrates has little difficulty in showing to be inconsistent with Polus' earlier thesis that injustice is somehow better than justice.

I have said that Socrates always spoke from a deep conviction in certain ethical ideas, more or less inchoately shared by his contemporaries. He nowhere in the early dialogues expresses these ideas as a complete ethical philosophy. They are instead brought forth piecemeal, as the discussion requires. Only enough is enunciated to provide a lever for the refutation of whatever doctrine is under discussion. These ethical ideas do, nevertheless, constitute a complete and rational theory of ethics, and they provide the framework for all of Socrates' remarks.

It is my purpose now to render a part of that ethical philosophy explicit, and more important, to bring out the presuppositions upon which it rests. I believe that it is a profound philosophy, but I also believe that its presuppositions are profoundly and dangerously wrong. This is not to question the merit of Socrates as a philosopher, or the brilliance of his mind, or his genuineness as a man. Probably no philosopher has ever had a greater impact upon civilization, and this influence is certainly justified in terms of stature. The brilliance and profundity of a philosopher's thought can sometimes be measured by the brilliance and profundity of its errors, however, and my belief that Socrates' errors were profound indeed in no way modifies my estimate of him as one of the deepest and wisest persons who ever lived.

The examination of Socrates' moral philosophy is important, not just because it was possessed by a towering philosopher, but rather because his presuppositions are shared by almost everyone today, just as they were shared by his contemporaries. The framework of presuppositions within which we today think about moral problems is essentially the same as that of Socrates, and it is these that I mainly want to question. As long as we are willing to concede that there is a true or natural good, a real good and evil independent of human needs and feelings, and hence independent of human convention and contrivance—and most people seem to feel ashamed *not* to say at least this much—then the Socratic gadfly will always be around to bedevil us. We cannot have it both ways. We cannot uphold the basis on which Socrates reasoned, or even pay lip service to it, and at the same time pursue moral ideals that sooner or later clash with that basis.

SOME SOCRATIC QUESTIONS

Socrates' inquiries usually centered around the following questions, all of which are quite obviously variants of one and the same large question: (1) What is virtue or true goodness? (2) What is a genuinely just or virtuous person? (3) How is such virtue acquired? (4) Can one know justice? (5) If not, why not? (6) If so, why are there no teachers of such knowledge? And so on.

It is clear enough that all such questions presuppose that there is such a thing as goodness and, more than that, that the distinction between good and evil is by nature and not merely fabrication. Socrates never doubted this, even though at the same time he never defended it, other than by leading his interlocutors in one way or another to admit it. That is, it is always assumed that, just as fire is hot and ice cold, just as men sire children and women bear them, so also some things are good and some bad. Moreover, good things are assumed to be good because of the goodness that is in them, and goodness is thus thought to be a property that something might either have or lack. It is on the basis of this assumption, for example, that pleasure is proved not to be the same thing as goodness—for cowards and fools and other people lacking in goodness can nevertheless possess pleasure. By similar arguments goodness is shown to be different from strength, power, or any skill. Men possessed of strength or power, such as the various tyrants alluded to in the discussions, can nevertheless be lacking in goodness. Skills, on the other hand, can always be used for good or bad ends; they are "arts of opposites," such that anyone possessing any skill whatever, such as the skill of a physician or of a ruler, can apply it to the achievement of a noble end, or of a base one. The best healer, as Socrates observed, is also the most skilled poisoner. An art is good or bad depending on whether it is used for a morally good or bad end, which is enough to show that goodness is something independent of the art or skill itself.

Because, then, there is (it is assumed) such a thing as moral goodness, and because it cannot be identified with any of the numerous things that we are accustomed to calling good, the problem for Socrates is to discover its nature, which usually means, for Socrates, to define it, and thus be enabled to recognize it, or to know it. This seems to be a perfectly reasonable problem, and an exceedingly important one, perhaps even the most basic question of moral philosophy. I have myself suggested that the question "What is good?" is the most important one anyone can ask. But this presented itself to Socrates as primarily an intellectual inquiry, a question for philosophy to answer, and so it has remained ever since. That is, there is a built-in presupposition that there exists something called moral goodness. Because it is obvious that it is most difficult to define, and equally obvious that people are far from agreeing about what things embody it, it is assumed that it is something quite *elusive*. We cannot tell the difference between good and bad just by examining things, the way we can tell the difference between square and round, wet and dry, and such similar common properties. So moral goodness must be something hidden, rare, and difficult to discover. It can be discovered only through the exercise of reason; that is, through philosophy or, as Socrates sometimes expressed it, through the *mind's* eye. At other times he suggests that it can be discovered only through a process of "reminiscence," the knowledge of it being thought to be deeply buried within oneself. At any rate, moral goodness is assumed to be highly elusive of discovery, and yet the intellectual discovery of it is thought, quite naturally, to be the foremost task of philosophy. Such assumptions provide a very fertile field for philosophy, and it is no exaggeration to say that they not only kept Socrates busy at thought for most of his life, but have provided ample scope for the labors of most of the moral philosophers since.

VULGAR VS. PHILOSOPHICAL VIRTUE

Genuine moral goodness being something obscure, it is not surprising that the masses of humankind have no knowledge of it. What they have, at best, are certain opinions of it that might be correct but are, nevertheless, opinions only. This is the virtue of the vulgar, that is, of common, decent but unphilosophical people. It is also obvious that such vulgar virtue is one and the same as conventional virtue, or the established and accepted moral practices of one's social milieu. What Socrates was seeking, therefore, was not merely what was deemed good by his culture, not what this or that person found to be morally good, but another kind of goodness; namely, what is good *by nature*. He sought a kind of goodness that can be *known*, just as anything in nature can in principle be known. He simply assumed that there is such a natural goodness. His problem was that of discovering it, so that it could be imparted by instruction, so there could be teachers of it, so that differences of opinion in this realm could be resolved rationally, and so the conventional virtues could be measured against it—and, above all, so that there could be genuinely good persons. For it was another presupposition of Socrates that a knowledge of moral goodness would unfailingly produce genuine moral goodness in the possessor of such knowledge.

Natural moral goodness and conventional moral goodness being assumed to be two quite different things, it is of course possible that the two should quite fail to resemble each other, either in certain details or in their entirety. Because conventional morality is a matter of opinion only, it is perfectly possible that it should be false, that you might be quite wrong in believing that something is good, even though everyone might speak with the same voice on the matter. That an opinion is widely or even universally held is no guarantee of its truth. It is, therefore, quite possible that what everyone calls moral virtue is in fact moral vice, that conventional morality might in truth be an accepted system of immorality, that what everyone thinks of as justice might in fact be injustice—possibilities that Protagoras, as we have seen, considered scandalous and not even to be entertained. In fact, Socrates did not think this was so. He was exceedingly deferential to convention, and sometimes appealed to the laws and customs of his state as though they were fixed and natural moral principles, absolutely binding on himself. He was not, in other words, a revolutionary, bent on overthrowing convention in favor of a true morality, in spite of the fact that he appeared as a corrupter of conventional morals to his contemporaries. But Socrates did consider the ordinary person's conventional opinions on ethics to be inferior, just because they were mere opinions—not because he thought they were all false. He was only seeking something better; namely, a philosophical *knowledge* of virtue or justice, even though the path to which it directed its possessor might turn out to be much the same as the path of convention. Opinion can be wrong, but knowledge cannot. Knowledge, moreover, is abiding, whereas opinions are like the statues of Daedalus that moved about; they tend to slip away precisely when they are needed. This, again, suggested to Socrates' mind that once you possess the knowledge of moral goodness, you cannot be divested of it; you cannot substitute a groundless and possibly false opinion—and, hence, a merely conventional virtue—for what you once know to be true, and for what you know to be good.

THE INVOLUNTARY CHARACTER OF WICKEDNESS

This kind of thinking led Socrates to one of his most characteristic and startling doctrines, and one he never tired of reiterating; namely, that if you know the good, then you cannot choose evil. The implication of this is, of course, enormous. The knowledge of goodness being sufficient to guarantee a noble and virtuous life, an effective means to such a life is precisely that knowledge. And because such knowledge is gained through philosophy and nowhere else, it follows that the path of philosophy is at the same time the path toward goodness—not merely the path to the knowledge of goodness, but to the possession of true goodness itself. For genuine goodness in the conduct of one's life follows automatically from a knowledge of what true goodness is. You might have a true opinion concerning moral goodness, and lose it when it is needed for making a choice, but you cannot have knowledge of goodness and nevertheless choose what is evil, or even what falls short of true goodness. An incidental consequence of all this is that only a philosopher can display the highest goodness and justice that anyone is capable of achieving—a consequence that reverberated in Plato's philosophy, in his view that only philosophers are fit to be kings, and in Aristotle's conception of intellectual virtue, which he deemed to be akin to the blessedness of the gods and available only to the philosopher. This conception persists even today. The notion of a corrupt or vicious philosopher has at least an incongruous ring, for example.

Socrates went further than this, however, maintaining that you cannot even act contrary to your *opinion* of what is good, even though that opinion might in fact be false. Expressed more aptly, it was his view that no one ever voluntarily chooses evil. Such a view seems enormously paradoxical, but given Socrates' presuppositions it can be defended quite plausibly. Thus, whenever you are acting voluntarily or from choice, you are acting in the pursuit of some near or remote end, whether it be trivial or momentous. A chosen course of behavior, in other words, has some point to it, something it is aimed at achieving. Now obviously, it would seem, that which is aimed at must at least appear as something good to anyone who seeks it—for otherwise, why would you seek it? Could you with sincerity ever say of something that it appears to you ugly, painful, evil, or otherwise *bad*, and that therefore you have a keen desire to bring it about? Does not anyone, in describing anything in such terms, thereby declare his or her aversion to it? How can anyone want something, unless it appears to be something good in some sense? Why else would one want it?

Now to be sure, people sometimes pursue ends that they will admit are bad or wrong or in some sense evil, but in such cases they either see some good in it for themselves, or they are conceding only that it is evil in some conventional sense that they are rejecting, or else they are only expressing in words what they do not in fact believe. You might, for example, flee from danger in a cowardly way, admitting that this is wrong; but its wrongness would be outweighed by the goodness you would attach to your own safety. You would not be acting in such a way in order to achieve the evil, but rather, in order to achieve the good, in spite of the evil— such would be Socrates' interpretation. Or someone might, as Callicles advocated, seek to oppress and exploit inferior people, conceding that this is unjust according to conventional morality, but not really unjust according to nature. He would in that case be seeking what seemed good to himself. Or someone might speak an untruth—in order, for example, to save an innocent person's life—conceding that it is an untruth and in that sense wrong, but not really wrong under the circumstances; and so on. All such seemingly voluntary wrongdoing, Socrates thought, can be analyzed in some way similar to these. It can never be what it might at first appear to be.

VIRTUE AS KNOWLEDGE

Wrongdoing, then, or any sort of lapse from virtue, is always involuntary in this sense. No one can ever from choice seek what seems bad. The fact nevertheless remains that many do pursue evil and injustice. If it were not so, there would be no practical problems of ethics. Powerful kings are not always good kings, soldiers are not always courageous, judges are sometimes corrupt, and the most ordinary citizens time after time bring about perfectly miserable ends, apparently knowing quite well what they are doing. How can this be explained? How can one reconcile Socrates' seemingly unassailable theory with such commonplace facts of daily experience?

Socrates' answer is implied by his theory. That answer is *ignorance*. Those who bring about bad ends are acting from ignorance; they quite literally do not know any better. A very simple analogy may help to see this. Suppose a man is thirsty, and comes upon a well from which he is perfectly free to drink. He will want, then, to drink from that well, for this will certainly appear to him as good. But all this is consistent with the supposition that the well is in fact, and unbeknown to him, poisoned. If, then, he does drink from it, he will be doing what he wants to do (drink from that well), thereby seeking to realize a certain good; but from the perspective of a fuller knowledge of what he is doing, he is not doing what he wants to do at all. What he wants is to drink, not to drink poison. He drinks from the well out of ignorance, not really knowing what he is doing.

Socrates thought that all injustice, and all voluntary behavior whose consequences are on the whole bad, is to be interpreted in such terms. Injustice, whether in high places or low, whether on the part of those who are generally deemed knowledgeable and powerful or those who are simple and weak, is always the product of ignorance. No man who fully knew what he was doing—that is, knew what the consequences of his actions would be and that they would be bad—could possibly choose those actions. If he did, he would be deliberately choosing what he saw to be bad, which is an absurdity. He must see them as somehow leading to some good in order to choose them. But if they in fact lead to evil, then he has obviously misunderstood, has acted from ignorance, and did not really know what he was doing.

WHAT POWER IS

Consider the tyrant who "has everything he wants." His power is absolute, he is subject to no one's will but his own, and he need not answer to anyone for anything he does. He can abolish his opponents by the utterance of a command and seize as he pleases the possessions of anyone under his sway. Suppose, furthermore, that he uses his unlimited power for his own aggrandizement, impoverishing and reducing to misery those under him while he, at their expense, walks in a blaze of glory. Socrates said of such men, who were familiar figures in his day as they are in ours, that, contrary to what might first appear, they have *no* power; they really have nothing that they want and that they are in fact less happy than those whom they plunder. The philosophical basis for this seemingly paradoxical appraisal is fairly obvious. One has only to concede that the behavior of such a man is unjust, which it most obviously is, and that injustice is an evil, which none will deny, to be led to just that seemingly paradoxical view. For no man can knowingly and willingly choose what is bad. If, therefore, this tyrant chooses what in fact turns out to be evil—namely injustice—then he must be acting from ignorance. This is, of course, consistent with supposing that, from a more limited view, he gets what he wants—namely, self-aggrandizement—and that this appears to him as good. But from a larger perspective he surely gets what he does not want and what no one can want—namely, a state of affairs that is loaded with evil.

For what, after all, is power? It is not simply the lack of fetters and restraints, for a stone or a corpse might be unfettered and unrestrained, yet neither would possess power. To have power is to possess the unfettered and unrestrained opportunity to obtain what you want. The element of wanting something is essential. But if you then bungle this opportunity and get what you do not really want and what no one could want, then you are lacking in power. No one, however, can want evil, and this is precisely what the wicked tyrant in fact gets—namely, the evil of injustice—and he is, then, after all lacking in power. He has only the semblance of it, a specious and ungenuine power.

VIRTUE AND HAPPINESS

It is by a similar analysis that Socrates deems the wicked tyrant—and, by generalization, any wicked person—to be less happy than others, less happy even than his own suffering victims. For again, happiness surely consists in the possession of a true good, not something that merely seems good from some limited view, but is in fact evil. A man who is wicked, however, by necessity loses the greatest good anyone can possess, namely, the goodness that is inherent in justice. What he has are many possessions and the fear and envy of others, but these are sham goods in comparison to the greatest good of all, which he has forfeited. His condition is like that of an alcoholic who has free rein to satisfy his cravings, and fancies himself happy in the unbridled satisfaction of them, but who is by that very indulgence injuring himself further.

Given the choice, then, between committing injustice and suffering injustice at the hands of another, Socrates had no difficulty in inferring that the wise will choose the latter. He did not imagine that it is good to suffer injustice, but it is at least less bad than committing it. This of course accords with conventional morality, but it was not out of deference to convention that Socrates held this. He thought it was the inevitable conclusion of reason and philosophy. The production of injustice is *by nature* bad, because justice is by nature good. Someone who suffers injustice does not thereby produce it. No one, accordingly, would commit injustice except unwittingly—that is, out of ignorance of what is good. A wise person, who knows what is good, would therefore not commit injustice at all.

These ideas seem at first to go against common sense. We can sympathize with Callicles, who accused Socrates of turning everything upside down. Everyone wants to avoid being the victim of injustice at all costs. Thus, being undeservedly injured in one's body or possessions, for no other purpose than to advance the wicked ends of one's oppressor, seems to be an evil that everyone would want to avoid, no matter what. But Socrates maintains that there is a greater evil: namely, to be such an oppressor. And this is a greater evil, not just in the sense that it is condemned by conventional morality, but in the sense that anyone who fully understood what it is to be unjustly oppressed and what it is to be an unjust oppressor would voluntarily choose to be the former rather than the latter, provided one could not choose to be neither. And the seemingly unassailable argument for this is as before: There *is* such a thing as justice, it is a good transcending every other good, and no one, knowing or even believing that something is good, can voluntarily choose anything less good in preference to it.

From the same considerations it follows that if you lapse into injustice you will not only willingly submit to just punishment, but will eagerly seek it, and will in fact be your own first accuser—provided, of course, that you know what you are doing. Of course this is not how people do ordinarily behave. Thieves and murderers do not voluntarily present themselves in courts of justice seeking punishment, nor do cruel despots seek out just people in order to be condemned by them. But according to Socrates, this is only because they are ignorant. Such wrongdoers, suddenly vouchsafed the light of wisdom, would do precisely that. And the reasoning behind this seemingly paradoxical opinion is again quite impeccable: Someone who knows what is good and what is bad must thereby know that injustice is bad and that justice is by nature good, since this is manifestly true. Furthermore, he will know that just punishment, being an expression of justice, must therefore be good. And because it is good, he cannot fail to seek it, supposing that he recognizes its goodness. A wise man who has lapsed into injustice can therefore be compared with a sensible man who is beset with some curable malady of the body. Such a man, knowing that disease is bad and health good, will voluntarily seek a physician, not because he sees the medicine as good in itself, of course, but because he sees health as good and the bitter medicine as the means to it.

JUSTICE AS A STATE OF THE SOUL

This analogy is quite Socratic, for Socrates was impressed by what seemed to him an analogy between the just and the sick. Health he conceived, in keeping with the medicine of his day, as a certain harmony of the bodily parts and functions. Justice, accordingly, was thought of as a certain harmony of the soul's functions—a proper balance and integration of reason, desire, and the like. As the physician heals the body, so the philosopher heals the soul; that is, imparts justice by cultivating reason and subordinating the appetites to it. This is a somewhat more specialized conception of justice than the one that is at work in most of Socrates' discussions, but it is worth noting that in some ways it leads to the same conclusions. Thus, if justice is a certain state of a man's soul, then a wise man will cultivate that state and prize it above any earthly good; for just as no man would voluntarily relinquish his bodily health for something of ephemeral value, such as pleasure, so also no man would voluntarily corrupt his own soul for anything whatever. Socrates even sometimes described philosophy as the tendance of the soul, thinking again of its analogy with medicine, which is the tendance of the body. If, then, we think again of a someone who is given the choice between suffering injustice and committing it, and who knows the exact nature of the choice, we are led again to the conclusion that a wise person would choose to suffer rather than to commit injustice. You suffer if you suffer injustice, to be sure, but you suffer only with respect to externals, that is, possessions and the like. You are not thereby corrupted or made morally worse. Committing acts of injustice does corrupt, however, or make you morally worse; indeed, it is the very expression of such inner corruption. And because such corruption is, in the light of the conception of justice now under consideration, the corruption or ruin of your very soul—indeed, of your inner being—then it is the ruination of that which is to everyone the most precious of possessions. It is the dissolution of your very person.

When the matter is put in these terms, it is indeed easy to conclude with Socrates that no one would knowingly and voluntarily choose injustice in preference to justice, even though the former might, from a limited viewpoint, be highly profitable and the latter painful.

— 5 —

IS JUSTICE GOOD
FOR ITS OWN SAKE?

THE ENTIRE SOCRATIC system rests on a pre-supposition, never really proved, that there is such a thing as natural justice or virtue, and that it is something good, not merely as a means to good things, but for its own sake. This claim is loaded with significance, and whether you accept or reject it will probably determine, more than anything else, your whole outlook on morality.

THE TEST

What is basically at issue here can be aptly illus-trated with an experiment in the imagination sug-gested by, and in fact in its essentials the same as, one propounded by Socrates in Plato's *Republic*. The experiment is as follows.

Imagine two men, Mr. Adam and Mr. Brown—or,

for short, A and B. Now, in your imagination, endow A with every virtue, and B with every vice. We suppose, for example, that A is honest and considerate of others, truthful in his dealings with them, that he is kind, modest, courageous when courage is called for, temperate in his indulgence of pleasures, and so on. We suppose, in short, that this man, A, is the paragon of moral excellence, in whatever we consider moral excellence to consist. Next, endow B with all the opposite qualities. B, we thus suppose, is dishonest and disregardful of others, mendacious in his dealings with his fellows whenever this appears to him advantageous, cruel, vain, cowardly, and insatiable in his cravings of pleasures and possessions. We suppose, in short, that B is a model of moral corruption, a thief and murderer bound by no restraints whatever.

Let us suppose next, however, that each of these men is universally believed to be the opposite of what he in fact is. That is, A, even though he is the model of moral goodness, is erroneously believed by everyone to be totally corrupt—to possess, that is, the very qualities that are in fact possessed by B; and B, in turn, even though he is the arch criminal and the exemplar of moral corruption, is erroneously believed by all to be the model of virtue—to possess, that is, the very qualities that are in fact possessed by A. Everyone has, in short, a total misconception of the character of each of these men.

What we are here imagining is not, it should be noted, entirely absurd, although it is admittedly not easy to see how such total misconceptions could ever really prevail for very long. If you admit, as you must, that people are not always what they appear to be, then you must admit that it is at least possible that the contrast between what a man really is and what others think he is might be as complete as we are now imagining in the cases of A and B. Indeed, we know that good people have sometimes been put to death by others who erroneously thought they were wicked (Jesus is perhaps an example), and the wicked have gone to their graves with everyone singing their praises, never suspecting the baseness of their inner characters. In the examples we have imagined we are only supposing that this contrast between the appearance and the reality is total and complete, and that the misconceptions are never discovered.

Continuing our imaginative experiment, then, we next suppose that each of these men, A and B, receives from his society the desert appropriate to what he is thought by that society to be. Thus, A, the good man, languishes in a jail, with roaches and rats for his companions, and water and bread for his food. He dwells in dirt, and is spat on by his fellows, until eventually he is mercifully hanged. Why? Just because, as they suppose, he is wicked and evil, a thief and murderer, deserving of nothing else. He knows, of course, that he is none of these things, and is in fact the opposite, but his own witness to his character is not of much avail to him in these baneful circumstances.

The real thief and murderer, B, on the other hand (who has always managed to cover his tracks and conceal his true nature), walks through the world bathed in glory and leaving in his wake the admiration and praise of everyone. Medals are struck in his honor, public places inscribed with his name, and the highest offices thrust upon him—all of which tributes he exploits, of course, to further his own greedy ends, conveying always the false impression that his deepest interest is service to the public good. Parents point him out to their children as an object of emulation, and all vie for his approval. When he finally dies, full of years and loaded with honors, he receives a state funeral and the tribute of all who have heard his name. And why does he receive this enviable treatment at the hands of all? Simply because, as it seems to them, he clearly deserves it, considering his greatness, his goodness, and his devotion to the well-being of all. He of course knew otherwise, but nothing required him to correct the universally held misconception of himself that he had so skillfully created and he had, of course, every inducement to perpetuate it.

Now, with these two pictures before us, let us ask: Which of these two men is better off? One can find, in his answer to that straightforward question, the clearest indication of whether or not he really embraces the Socratic ethics. Our first man, A, possesses genuine moral goodness and the true beauty of a harmonious and well-governed inner life. He lacks only the usual consequences and rewards of such goodness. Our other man, B, possesses all the usual rewards of goodness and greatness, although he is really devoid of both, and his inner life is entirely base and corrupt. Which man, then, has what is truly worth having? Which has made his life really worthwhile? And if you were given the choice between these two lives, with no third alternative offered, which, in the light of wisdom, should you choose?

It will not do at this point to say that the situation just portrayed in imagination would not be likely ever to exist in fact. It will not do to say that our man B, for example, would surely be found out sooner or later and his rewards replaced with their opposites, nor will it do to insist that A's true nature, and the misconceptions that all have entertained concerning him, must surely be discovered before he is hanged and the injustices to him corrected and compensated. This would simply be cheating and refusing to face the challenge that the examples contain. It is not presupposed that situations like these often arise in the world, or even, that they ever arise. It is only claimed that it is possible, that things could happen this way, whether they ever do or not. And then our question is a fair one: suppose there were these two men, A and B, whose inner and outer lives were precisely as we have described them, which is the better life? Which has the most, or is lacking least, of what an intelligent person, knowing the true worth of things, would want?

The first man A, it is obvious, has nothing of any worth except real justice—provided, of course, that there is such a thing as justice. One could point to nothing else in his life as a thing of value. The dirt, the bugs, the obloquy, and the final pain of the gallows, cannot possibly be represented as things to be sought by anyone. Still, he *is* in fact, if not in appearance, a good and just man, provided such goodness and justice are something real and not just words that stand for nothing existing in nature. Man B, on the other hand, possesses everything that we seek—except, of course, justice or goodness. The honor, reward, praise, and esteem that he enjoys, his power, and his wealth can hardly be represented as things that we shun as evils. Still, he does utterly lack, in fact if not in appearance, justice and goodness, provided there really are such things as justice and goodness, and that these are not just philosophical abstractions.

Now if one supposes, with Socrates, that justice is something real, something that exists by nature and not just a conventional thing invented for the attainment of certain practical advantages, and that such justice is worth possessing for its own sake and not just for its consequences or rewards, then you cannot avoid saying that A is *better off* than B. For A, no matter what else he may lack—and he of course lacks everything else—does possess this, and this, according to Socrates, is worth possessing at *all* cost and sacrifice. If you further identify such justice with a certain kind of harmonious inner life, an inner life wherein your desires are under the governance of reason and intelligence, then you will affirm the same answer. For A does possess that inner life, he knows that there exist no real grounds for reproaching him, and nothing that is done to him or to the externals of his life can divest him of that justice.

If, on the other hand, you suppose that justice is only a conventional thing, a set of practices and precepts invented for the achievement of certain desired results, then you can hardly avoid saying that B is better off. Indeed, his position is enviable beyond comparison, for he has all the rewards of justice without having to pay any of the price of a just life. He has all of the rewards of crime and none of the cost of it. He is, to be sure, bereft of justice, but in case there is no such thing as genuine justice, in case this is merely a concept of convention and not one of nature, then it follows that, by lacking this, he lacks nothing real. And if, furthermore, the rational pursuit of what is by nature good, and the subordination of passion and desire to this rational end, is not something good for its own sake—in case, for example, there is no such natural good—then B, lacking this, again lacks nothing real. His reason and intelligence are subordinated to his desires, and as a result his desires are abundantly fulfilled. If, in view of all this, you conclude that B is better off, or even that his life is in the slightest to be preferred to A's life, then you can no longer pretend to give any credit to the ethics of Socrates. You cannot have it both ways. You cannot in sincerity nod approval of Socrates' high-sounding theme, and at the same time give the slightest preference to the life and fate of Mr. B. And on the other hand, if you find anything to be said in favor of A's life and fate, then you will find it very difficult to avoid the conclusions to which Socrates wants to lead you. For there is only one thing of any worth that A can possibly be said to possess, and that is justice. And because it is a justice that bears no fruit at all, and is insufficient to deflect any pain and misery to its possessor, it must be a natural justice, a kind of justice that contains its whole worth within itself, and not the kind of justice that is merely a tool for the attainment of certain desired ends.

It is doubtful whether many philosophers have faced this basic problem of ethics in terms of the contrast just illustrated. Most people seem to prefer to extol the idea of a true or natural justice, as opposed to a merely man-made justice, without considering what they are really committed to by such an idea. Plato faced the question quite clearly. Indeed, the imaginative experiment just elicited was probably his own invention, although he represents Socrates as its author in the *Republic*. In any case, justice was represented by Plato as a quality that could, at least imperfectly, be exemplified in societies, institutions, and laws, as well as in persons.

What Plato never seems to have doubted is that there is such a thing as true justice, that it is something that is not a human fabrication, but something that can be discovered by a rational person. At his hands it became detached from the physical world, which was reduced in his philosophy to a kind of shadow existence. Pure justice came to be thought of as something accessible only to the highest reaches of philosophical penetration, and he thought that the knowledge of it was the highest aspiration any one could set for himself. This thought has persisted, at least as a sentiment, for people still speak of justice and of moral goodness generally with a certain awe and reverence. It is, moreover, thought to be somewhat degrading to this noble idea to suggest that it might be a mere human contrivance, something that is quite variable from one time and place to another, and something fabricated for nothing more pretentious than the furtherance of certain utterly practical aims of social life.

IS THERE A TRUE OR NATURAL JUSTICE?

Let us, then, face the question: Is there any such thing as justice, as it is typically represented in Socratic ethics? We can grant at once that there is such a thing as mental health, that those who possess it are in one clear sense good and those who lack it—who are, in contemporary terms, "mixed up"— are lacking in something of great value. But this is not what we are asking. This is, in my opinion, the most valuable contribution to ethics that Socrates made; that is, his identification of moral goodness with certain perfectly natural characteristics and relations of one's inner life. But it is not the one that has endured. Most philosophers and moralists regard these as purely psychological observations, and rather archaic ones at that, having really nothing to do with philosophical ethics. I profoundly disagree with this appraisal, but because the Socratic reduction of morals to psychology is not the part of Socratic ethics that has endured in philosophical literature, it is not the aspect of Socratic ethics on which I shall dwell.

I want to consider only whether there is such a thing as justice, *by nature*; that is, whether the distinction between good and evil is, as Socrates always presupposed, a natural distinction rather than a human creation relative to ordinary human feelings, needs, and desires. Socrates thought that there is such a thing, and that it exists by nature and not by human contrivance or invention. By this he did not mean that justice is something automatically *produced* by nature—there is nothing automatic about a just person or a just government, for example—but that the justice or moral goodness of anything possessing it is an objective property of it whose nature can be discerned by reason, that is, by philosophy. If there is a genuine justice or a genuine moral good independent of human invention, then all the seemingly paradoxical conclusions that Socrates drew do follow quite inevitably. He was, moreover, quite right in maintaining that philosophy is the most important endeavor you can undertake, that philosophers ought to be honored above everyone else, even though they might sometimes, as Socrates often did, make all those about them feel like wretched fools. For if there is such a thing as pure justice or pure moral goodness, and if philosophy is the only road to the discovery of it, then surely everything else is of subordinate importance. And if, moreover, no one ever pursues an unjust or immoral end except through ignorance, then it is of the greatest possible importance to each individual to know what the true good is, or in other words, to pursue the philosophical life. You can neglect it only at your own peril.

But suppose we consider an alternative approach. Consider, first, that human nature is—as Socrates himself maintained—a combination of reason, or intelligence, and desire, or what I would prefer to call the will. That is to say, we not only discover, by reason and intelligence, that certain things are so; we also will that certain things should be other than they are. This is but another way of saying that human beings *pursue ends*, that they try to bring about certain states through their efforts. Thus, to take a humble example, you might be exceedingly poor. By your intelligence you can understand that this is so. It is the fact that is given. But you are not apt to like the fact; we can suppose that you want to be rich, or at least delivered from poverty. There is your end or goal, something that is *not* simply given to your intelligence, because it is a state of affairs that does not even exist and may never exist. It is an end or goal that is projected by your will; it is what you will should be so, although in fact it is not so.

This model of human nature, then, as an amalgam of intelligence and will, yields an elementary distinction between what *is* and what *ought to be*. By our reason and intelligence, drawing from the testimony of our senses, we discover what is, but what ought to be is the declaration of the will. This is to say that what *ought* to be is a desideratum, the object of desire, or simply what is wanted by this or that person, by some group, or perhaps by all. Thus, one can form in his mind a more or less accurate conception of things as they are. This is simply understanding, or the apprehension of truth, which is sometimes accurate and clear and at other times vague and inaccurate and infected with error. Along with such a conception of things as they are, you can form another conception of things as they should be. This simply means things as you would have them, things as you would want them to be. At this level, this quite clearly has nothing to do with understanding or the apprehension of truth. It has rather to do with the will. You find that the world, or some large or small part of it, is such and such; you will that it should be otherwise; and this latter finds expression by your declaring that something, which does not exist, ought to exist. Or you perhaps find that the world, or some large or small part of it, is such and such, and you will that it should be pre-cisely so. That is, you find that the world or some part of it, as it is, is precisely such as to promise ful-fillment of your aims and aspirations. In that case you declare that what is—the world as you find it—is what ought to be. In either case, it is clear that your declaration of what ought to be is the expres-sion not of your reason or intelligence, but of your will—that is, of your desires, aims, and aspirations, whatever these might be.

You can from this same point of view see how the distinction between good and evil arises. You do not look out at the world and at human practices and institutions and simply find that, among other things, some are good, some bad, and some a mixture of both. This is simply superficial. Nor does a person of great intellect and rational penetration manage to make these distinctions any better. Good and evil are not, as Socrates sometimes thought, elusive or deeply hidden properties of things that only a philosopher can hope to discern. The reason they are so hard to discern, even by a philosopher, is apparently that they are not qualities of things at all, just considered by themselves and independent of human needs and feelings. People pronounce things good to the extent that those things appear to promise satisfaction of their needs or the fulfillment of their aims and goals, whatever these might be. They pronounce things bad to the extent that they appear threatening, either as obstacles to what they happen to want, or as sources of just what they do not want. The distinction between good and evil is therefore relative to goals, ends, and wants—in a word, to the will—and has no meaning except in relation to this. To convince yourself of this, you need only to consider how such a distinction could ever even arise for a race of beings entirely devoid of will, whatever might be their endowments of reason and intelligence. Such a race of beings would have no ends and goals, no aspirations, would want nothing, and would shun nothing. How, then, could they pronounce some things good and others bad? How, indeed, could they even form an understanding of such a distinction? Everything, it would seem, would be on a dead level for such beings, nothing would offer any promise, and nothing any threat, for they would have no aims for which promise of fulfillment or threat of frustration would have any bearing.

Looking at things in this light, you can at once see both the truth and the error in Socrates' contention that no one voluntarily pursues evil or does injustice. Socrates evidently regarded this as a significant and somewhat surprising philosophical insight, filled with implications for ethics, and many since him have struggled to reconcile what appears so paradoxical in it with what at the same time appears quite impeccably true. Socrates, as we have seen, inferred from this thesis that all wrongdoing must be the product of ignorance, and forthwith concluded that the kind of ignorance involved must be ignorance of what is really good. This is in a sense true, but not in the sense that the good of which the wrongdoer is ignorant is some good existing by nature and independently of any wants and needs. Thus, if we consider again the thirsty traveler who comes to a well and wants to drink from it, not knowing that it is poisoned, we can indeed say that his undertaking *that* immediate end is a product of ignorance. He does not know that the well is poisoned, and that drinking from it would therefore be something bad. But this quite clearly presupposes that he wants to live, that he therefore does not want to be poisoned. The poisonous character of the well is not bad, considered by itself; it is bad only in relation to the fact that this man's desire to live greatly outweighs his desire to drink, however thirsty he might be. Good and evil, in this simple example, are quite clearly relative to needs—that is, to aims and purposes—and in isolation from these have no significance at all.

So when Socrates said that no one can voluntarily pursue an end that is evil, knowing that it is evil, he was quite right, but not in the sense that these words first suggest. The claim must not be understood to mean that anyone, knowing what is good, must seek it, or that the wise cannot fail to be just, and so on, for that is plainly contrary to what everyone knows to be true. All that the claim means, really, is that we do pursue goals, that we want to attain certain goals by our actions; in short, that we want to achieve those ends that we do in fact want. But this is a trivial truth, a mere tautology. For if the good, for this or that person, is simply the object of that person's desire or will, then we are told nothing on being told that people seek the good—or in other words, that they desire what they desire, and that they can fail to desire the good only from ignorance. Such ignorance is not ignorance of whether something is or is not in fact good, for good and evil are not, by themselves, facts to begin with. The kind of ignorance in question can be only an ignorance of certain real features of a situation that, if known, would affect one's desires with respect to it.

The philosophical theory underlying the foregoing remarks is, of course, very superficial as presented, and it would not take much acumen to riddle it with difficulties. No attempt will be made at this point to develop it, however, for my purpose has only been to suggest that there are alternatives to the Socratic conception of ethics and, in particular, to the idea that good and evil must be natural and not merely conventional things or, as some would now express it, that good and evil must be "objective." What is true by nature, I shall maintain as we get more deeply into the subject, is that we do have needs and desires, that we are desiderative or goal-seeking creatures. I have found it convenient to express this conception of human nature by saying that we are *conative* beings. Such a conception does not by itself make anything good or evil by nature, but it nevertheless provides the natural foundation for the distinction between good and evil and, indeed, for every moral distinction.

– 6 –

HEDONISM, THE DOCTRINE OF PLEASURE

SOCRATES WAS A lover of dialectic and argument and seems never to have doubted that through philosophical argumentation a rational person can arrive at the truth of things. There is, to be sure, more to it than this, for he thought that everyone, even the untutored slave,[1] is already possessed of the truth, which is buried deeply in the soul and obscured by all the solicitations of the senses and appetites. Nevertheless, it is through philosophical argument that the truth is brought forth. Socrates thought of the philosophical teacher, such as himself, as a spiritual midwife who assists in the birth, not of real children, but of spiritual children—that is, of philosophical ideas. He could not impart such ideas to others, but he could, through his dialectical probing and refutations, enable others

---

1. See Plato's *Meno*, 82a–85d.

to deliver forth their own ideas, and thereby discover the truth that was already hidden within them.

This method of philosophy, shorn of its Socratic psychology and epistemology, persists today. There are, and perhaps always will be, ever so many philosophers who would feel they had said nothing of philosophical significance unless they enunciated their opinions within the context of philosophical argument—that is, of rational proof. This approach to philosophy can, somewhat loosely, be called rationalism.

MORAL EMPIRICISM

Along with this rationalistic approach, however, there has always persisted another, which we may with equal looseness refer to as empiricism. It is the presupposition of empiricism, as it was not at all the presupposition of Socrates, that the truth of things is learned through perception or experience. The world is what our experience reveals it to be; there is no higher test of what is true. And if the world, as we experience it, appears to be other than what seems to be required by reason, then we should adjust our reason to our experience, and not vice versa. Thus, for example, if the physical world we experience, the world of matter in motion, appears to involve the existence of a vacuum—the reality, that is, of nothingness—then we should affirm that such nothingness or "the void" is real even if this appears plainly self-contradictory. We have already seen one outstanding example of empiricism in the philosophy of Protagoras, for this thinker affirmed that all experiences are true. If the world appears differently to different people, then we should say that their diverse and mutually inconsistent reports are nevertheless all true. It would be difficult to imagine a more extreme rejection of reason than this.

EMPIRICISM AND THE DOCTRINE OF PLEASURE

Of all the things that have ever been proposed as the unique and greatest good, perhaps none has won more adherents than *pleasure*. Feelings of pleasure, it would seem, are always good, and their opposite, feelings of pain, are always bad. One need not be a philosopher to arrive at this opinion, and it is perhaps for this reason that the everyday philosophy of vast numbers of people is the philosophy of hedonism, even though most of them may never have heard this word and perhaps never have read a philosophical book.

The reason for this is not too difficult to fathom. Most people are empiricists by nature. They go through the world assuming, without giving the matter further thought, that the world is pretty much what it seems, in their experience, to be. Hence, they believe material things to be real, and in fact the only realities, whether they actually profess such an opinion or not. Generally, it is just taken for granted. And they deem pleasure to be good, and pain bad, without bestowing much thought on the question. Things like this just seem fairly obvious, and not in need of much discussion or proof.

Probably the first thinkers to develop this point of view into a complete philosophy of life were Epicurus and his followers, and their philosophy still shines forth as a model of clarity and consistency. There have been hedonistic philosophies since, and we shall shortly give some attention to one of them, but no one has ever improved on the hedonism of Epicurus. By this I do not mean that his philosophy is true, for I think it contains a fatal though instructive flaw. It is nevertheless pure, golden, and consistent throughout.

Epicurus offered his instruction in a public garden in Athens, and his teaching was so persuasive that it was transmitted without basic changes from pupil to pupil for generations, long after the death of its founder and the decline of Greek culture. The basic principles of his teaching were very simple and, as it seemed to so many of his audience, very obvious, but their implications for a way of life were rather far-reaching.

EPICUREAN EMPIRICISM

Epicurus assumed from the start that the world is what it appears to our senses to be, and not what the shrewd dialectic of a Socrates or a Plato would declare it to be out of deference to the requirements of reason. Hence, matter is real, and it is the only thing that is real, because it is the only reality we ever experience. He conceived of matter as composed of atoms, or tiny hard particles, so small as to be invisible, in order to account for the coming into being and passing away of things, which is such a manifest aspect of our experience. Individual atoms are never created, are never destroyed, and never suffer any change at all within themselves. Nevertheless, the world changes; indeed, everything in the world is changing perpetually, and nothing, it seems, lasts forever. Such change can only be the coming together and the separation of the atoms of which all things are composed. Thus, when a man, for example, comes into existence, this only means that certain atoms that have existed from all eternity have been brought together by natural processes to constitute a human being. His growth consists of the gradual accretion of more atoms over a period of time. And his death is simply the separation and dispersal of the atoms of his body. In such processes of change, growth, and decay nothing is really reduced to nothingness, for all that is real is matter, and matter is composed of minute and imperishable atoms, each atom being eternal and indestructible.

Death, accordingly, is just what it appears to be, the decay and dissolution of the body, its reduction to dust. The philosopher should, therefore, not think of life as Socrates did—as a preparation for death and the liberation of the immortal soul from the body. There is no such immortal spirit or soul. The soul or mind of a man is, like everything that is real, composed of invisible atoms, that is, of matter, and all processes of sensation and thought are material processes. That is, they are changes in the relations and interactions of the atoms of which the soul is composed. In death, the soul, like the rest of the body, is simply diffused. There is, in our experience, no basis for affirming the existence of any spirit or any other nonmaterial reality, and it is on our experience that we must base our beliefs concerning what does and does not exist.

Because experience is our basis for affirming what does and does not exist, so also, Epicurus thought, it must be our basis for affirming what is good and what is bad. Experience consists of both sensations and feelings. By our sensations we learn what is real, and by our feelings we learn what is good. If our feelings provide no distinction between good and evil, then no such distinction exists. But of course our feelings do provide such a distinction, and in the clearest manner imaginable, for we feel both pleasure and pain. Moreover—and this is what is crucial—we always feel pleasure as good and pain as bad. It follows, then, that pleasure is in fact always good, and pain always bad—there is no other test of good and evil than this. What is felt to be good *is* good, whatever might be the arguments of philosophers, and whatever is felt to be bad is in fact bad. Upon this ultimate test every opinion of what is good and evil must finally rest.

One further point is to be made and we shall then have laid the foundation for the Epicurean way of life. That point, crucial to what follows, is that pleasure is the *only* ultimate good, and pain the only ultimate evil. Other things are good and bad only in relation to these. Nothing else is ever felt to be good, or to be bad, and if we hear others say that justice, for example, or honor, or courage are good, we must understand what is meant. If it is suggested that justice, for example, is the highest good, or is an ultimate good, then this cannot be so, for it is never felt to be such. On the contrary, the practice of justice is sometimes more or less painful. We can actually feel pleasure, and we always feel it to be good, but we do not in any similar way feel justice. If, therefore, we declare justice, or honor, or courage, or any of the other things that have found favor among the philosophers, to be good, it can only be in some derivative sense that this is so. One can only mean that the practice of justice, for example, is more often than not conducive to feelings of pleasure in the person who is just. This is doubtless true, but it still remains that pleasure, even in such cases as this, is still our guide to what is good. Divest justice and the other commonly accepted virtues of their pleasurable fruits, and they retain nothing whatever of their goodness.

PLEASURE AS THE NATURAL GOOD

That is the foundation for the Epicurean ethics, but two things should be noted at this point.

The first is that Epicurus, like Socrates and Plato and most of his predecessors, did not doubt that there is a natural good. That is, he assumed that something is good by nature, as distinct from those things that are merely deemed good by human convention. His problem was not to determine whether this claim is true, but simply to discover what that natural good is. Pleasure was declared by him to be good by nature, and not good merely because it was deemed good by people. Nor did he think of pleasure as something that is good merely in relation to what our human feelings, needs, and wants happen to be. Our feelings only inform us *that* pleasure is always and invariably good, just as our sensations inform us, for example, that fire is hot and water is wet. Our feelings no more *make* pleasure good than our sensations make fire hot or water wet. The philosophy of the Epicureans is therefore a philosophy of true morality, as it is defined here, because it affirms that the distinction between good and evil is a distinction existing in nature. It denies that things are good or bad only in relation to human feelings, needs, and desires. Epicurus has, nevertheless, advanced far beyond most of his predecessors (Protagoras being a notable exception) in relating good and evil to human needs. Our feelings, rather than abstract reasoning, are at least his criterion of what is true with respect to good and evil. He never supposed that, because we cannot tell good from evil just by looking at things, they must therefore be highly elusive, and that we can therefore hope to discover them only through the most abstract and subtle reasoning about things; and he would surely have laughed at the suggestion, sometimes made by Socrates, that the knowledge of the good is so deeply hidden that we can recover it only through a difficult process of reminiscence from a prenatal existence during which it was divinely implanted in us. That is good which our feelings immediately declare to be good, and that is the end of the matter for Epicurus. I do not know what he might have said had he been invited to imagine someone who found feelings of pain to be good and feelings of pleasure bad.

The second thing to be noted is that the Epicurean philosophy is not a philosophy of duty or of right and wrong. It is, rather, a philosophy of good and evil. His question was not at all, "What should I do in order to do what is right and avoid doing what is wrong?" Nor did he ask, "What is my duty?" His question was, rather, "What should I do, in order to live a good life?" And this, as I have indicated before, is quite obviously a question of the greatest importance, and an urgent one for anyone, particularly in view of the fact that each of us has only one life to live. We can, then, either make that one life a good one, or we can entirely waste the one chance we have at it. It can hardly be a matter of indifference to anyone which way to go. The Epicureans took for granted that a good life is, quite obviously, one that is most filled with goodness. The principle is, therefore, to find what goodness is, and then fill one's life with it to the utmost that is possible.

THE PROBLEM OF ETHICS

How this is to be done is quite plainly implied, in the most general way, in the philosophical foundations already outlined. If a good life is a life filled with whatever is good, and if pleasure is the only thing in nature that is good, then clearly a good life is a life filled with pleasure. The problem of ethics, however, is not simply to discover this general truth. It is, rather, how to accomplish this end. And that is in fact what most of the Epicurean philosophy was devoted to: to the discovery of those precepts and principles whereby you can embody in your life the greatest total pleasure and the least pain. Epicurean moral philosophy is therefore similar to an elaborate recipe, the aim of which is to concoct, not a good dish for the moment, but a good and secure path for the journey of a lifetime.

To deliberately contrive and plan a life of pleasure seeking, and one that will, to the highest degree possible, be successful in achieving it, is not so easy as it may seem. Pleasure getting is an art, requiring a good deal of thought and planning, as the Epicureans quickly discovered. Some pleasures are intense, whereas others are weak and feeble; some are lasting, and others are ephemeral; and some can be attained only by considerable effort or even pain, whereas others are easy and relatively cheap. The task, then, is to discover and combine those sources of pleasure that will yield in one's life the greatest and most durable total amount of pleasure with the least admixture of pain, to find just the right formula for this and reject all those that will divert the seeker from the correct path.

THE CYRENAIC PHILOSOPHY

The Cyrenaics,[2] a school of hedonists who had preceded the Epicureans, had, it seemed clear to Epicurus, rather abysmally failed in all this. The Cyrenaics had noted, quite correctly, that the so-called bodily pleasures—the pleasures of food, wine, sexual gratification, and bodily stimuli generally—are the most intense pleasures one can experience. They much exceed in their intensity the pleasures of the mind, such as those derived from philosophy, literature, friendship, and so on. So the Cyrenaics concluded that such bodily pleasures should in every case be sought in preference to the weaker pleasures of the mind. Again, the Cyrenaics had observed, also quite correctly, that the only pleasures that are real are those that are felt, and the only ones that can be felt are those felt at the present moment. The pleasures of yesterday can only be remembered, and those of tomorrow, anticipated. Therefore, they concluded, you should live for the pleasures of the moment, giving no heed to the past or the future. And finally, they observed that the only pleasures that you can feel are your own, not those of others.

---

2. The name is derived from the birthplace of its founder, Aristippus of Cyrene.

Their ethical formula, therefore, amounted essentially to this: Get, and increase to the highest intensity, the greatest amount of bodily pleasure for yourself in the present moment. Much the same idea has sometimes been expressed in the injunction: Eat, drink, and be merry. The Cyrenaic life was, in obedience to this principle, one of unabashed, unrestrained indulgence in bodily pleasure.

That is the conception of hedonism that has persisted in the popular mind, but it is very remote indeed from the hedonism of the Epicureans. The Epicureans accepted the basic Cyrenaic axiom, of course, that pleasure is the only thing in nature good for its own sake, and they further agreed that bodily pleasures are more intense than those of the mind, but this entirely leaves out of account innumerable important considerations. Although the bodily pleasures are more intense, for example, they are invariably of shorter duration. Thus, it is pleasant to be scratched when you itch—more pleasant, perhaps, than discoursing on philosophical themes in the company of warm friends—but as soon as the itching is banished, which is apt to be quite soon, the pleasure of being scratched is replaced with positive annoyance. Similarly, the pleasure of sexual intercourse can be great, but it cannot be prolonged beyond a certain point. Bodily pleasures, moreover, are usually purchased at a certain price in terms of pain. Thus, it is pleasant to drink or eat only if you are thirsty or hungry, and thirst and hunger are both painful. Immoderate indulgence in the pleasures of food and drink and other bodily stimulants is also usually followed by nausea, sickness, and pain, so that you invariably pay dearly for them. And finally, of course, life is itself shortened by unrestricted indulgence in pleasures of this kind, so that you forfeit forever the opportunity of adding more pleasures to it.

The Cyrenaic life can, somewhat crudely, be graphically represented: the horizontal line represents the boundary between pleasure and pain over a course of time, T_1–T_2; the degree of pleasure is represented by the departure of the line above it; and the degree of pain by the extent to which the curving line falls below the horizontal. Thus:

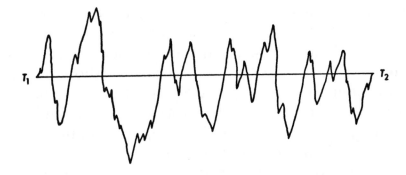

It can be seen from this drawing that the pleasures enjoyed over the period of time from T_1 to T_2 were both numerous and intense, their intensity being indicated by the heights of the curves above the horizontal. So far, then, so good. But now note that these pleasures, although great, were mostly of short duration, this being usually true of bodily pleasures of the kind represented. More significantly, they are generally preceded and followed by pains, these being represented by the depths of the curves below the horizontal. And worst of all, some of these pains considerably exceed in their intensity and duration the pleasures that preceded them, indicating that the individual pleasures were rather dearly purchased. Let us suppose, for example, that pleasure Number 2 in the drawing, which is clearly the greatest and most lasting of those represented, was derived from an evening of boundless imbibing of spirits, followed by gluttonous gorging with fine foods and delicacies into the early hours of the morning, topped off by a sexual orgy. Such a night would, no doubt, be memorable in terms of the sheer quantity of bodily pleasure thus achieved. But now note the curve that immediately follows it. This curve represents the nausea induced by the drinking, the gas pains and illness resulting from the gluttony, and the remorse and feeling of self-reproach produced by the orgy. This curve is larger, both vertically and horizontally, than the one that precedes it. Clearly, the pleasure was dearly purchased, and one can only conclude, on purely hedonistic principles, that it was not worth the cost.

THE EPICUREAN MODIFICATIONS

Taking such considerations as this into account, the Epicureans substituted the more refined pleasures of the mind for those of the body, not because they are stronger (for they are in fact feebler), but because they are of longer duration and are neither preceded nor followed by pain. Thus, you can discourse with friends for hours on philosophical, artistic, or literary themes without first feeling any pain or want akin to hunger or thirst as a precondition of such pleasure, and without suffering any disagreeable consequences. Such discourse might appropriately take place in some lovely garden, perhaps, and be augmented by fine wines, in moderate amounts, and perhaps by soft music, and whatever other adornments to the occasion promise to enhance and refine the pleasure of it, and never to threaten it. Such pleasures as this may reach no great heights, to be sure, but they can be lasting and, best of all, freed from antecedent or consequent pain, whether bodily or mental. After such an occasion, you can awaken the next day with a clear head and a vigorous body for the pursuit of still further pleasures of the same sort—delicate, refined, and best of all, lasting. You can, moreover, relive them in memory, as well as anticipate them before they are experienced, and such memories and anticipations are themselves quiet pleasures that may be indulged at will.

On the same scheme as before, then, one might graph the pleasure and pain over a period of time T_1–T_2 in the life of an Epicurean in the following way:

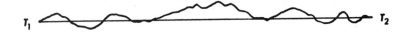

It will of course be noted that these pleasures do not compare in their intensity with those captured by the Cyrenaic; they are indeed wan and feeble by comparison. But note at the same time how little appears below the line separating pleasure from pain. We can suppose, for example, that pleasure Number 3 in this picture was that produced by an occasion such as that just described. We envisage the Epicurean lounging in his garden, surrounded by cultivated friends, a goblet in hand, his brow wreathed with a garland, just the appropriate quantity of good wine, sipped with moderation, and soft music in the air, appropriate to enhancing and refining the pleasure without distracting from the pleasures of the philosophical conversation in which all are engaged. Such conversation, we must suppose, never rises to argument, is free of any contention, and is seasoned, in just the right amount, with flashes of humor and wit, producing merriment without detracting from the serious level of the conversation, and never rising to raucous guffaws that would be abrasive. The picture can, of course, be filled out as you please, adhering always to the principle of moderation, gentleness, and refinement. Concerning such a pleasure as this we can surely say that, although it approaches no ecstasy, it is relatively lasting and unaccompanied by pain either before or after its enjoyment, and it is one that can be relived in the mind as long as the memory of it can be nourished. Clearly, if we measure this pleasure against that of the Cyrenaic, and judge it solely by the criterion accepted by both—namely, by the criterion of the total amount of pleasure and nothing else—the Epicurean comes out well ahead. The Cyrenaic was forced to conclude that the pleasure, although great, was not worth the cost. The Epicurean could declare that it was abundantly worth it. It cost little or nothing in terms of any pain, and rather than be unfit for further pleasures, he goes forth fortified and renewed for the enjoyment of still more of them.

The Epicurean, therefore, took it as his program not simply to achieve the greatest pleasures, but to enjoy the pleasantest life possible, taking his lifetime as a whole. To accomplish this program of life, you must frequently eschew many opportunities for pleasure that present themselves. Indeed, the best single formula for the attainment of pleasure was thought to be a purely negative one; namely, to avoid pain. If you can but get through life with the minimum of pain, whether it be the physical pain of sickness or wounds, or the mental pain of anxiety and remorse, then you will come as close as possible to the ideal, which is a life filled with goodness—that is to say, with pleasure. Such a life might be quite uneventful, but it will nevertheless far exceed, in the pleasure it embodies, the turbulent life of the less reflective seeker of pleasures.

THE MODERATION OF DESIRES

The Epicureans did not therefore advocate the indulgence of desire. On the contrary, they taught that desires should at all times be firmly controlled and, where feasible, entirely eliminated, for desire is always a state of want, and all want is painful. There are, in fact, different kinds of desire, and a wise person will deal with desires according to their kind. Some, such as the desire for food, are both natural and necessary. These are natural, in the sense that they are shared by all and are not artificially created by one's culture, and they are necessary, in the sense that their fulfillment is essential to life itself. Such desires, accordingly, ought not to be eliminated, because it would be impossible to do so and painful to try. At the same time, they should be indulged only in moderation, to avoid risking the pain that invariably accompanies overindulgence. Thus, food, for example, should be simple, healthful, and moderate—as much, but no more, than is necessary to live well and pleasantly, with occasional departures in one way or another as special circumstances suggest. The same principle will apply, of course, to the satisfaction of all other desires that are both natural and necessary, such as the desire for warmth, shelter, and so on. Another class of desires are those that, although natural, are not necessary—the clearest example of these being sexual desire. Such desires cannot be entirely eliminated, simply because they are natural, and any attempt to eliminate them would bring unavoidable pain. They should, however, be indulged no more than is necessary for the avoidance of pain, and must never be indulged in the pursuit of pleasure itself. And a third class of desires comprises, of course, all those that are neither natural nor necessary, such as the desire for wealth, honor, power, fame, and so on. Such desires are not natural, because they are entirely the product of social conditioning, and they vary from time to time and culture to culture. Nor, obviously, are they in any way necessary to life, or even to a life that is pleasant. The wise, accordingly, will wholly eliminate these desires, and with whatever strength necessary refuse to be seduced by their blandishments.

THE SOURCES OF GOODNESS

With these philosophical foundations secure, there remains only to consider the sources of pleasure and the means to the avoidance of pain. These are of course discovered by experience, and are not derived from philosophy. Perhaps the best one can do is take advantage of the example and counsel of others who have reached the goal, which is always the same: a life that is insofar as possible pleasant and free from pain. Certain things are of course obvious: For example, a healthy body, able to withstand the threat of disease, which is always painful; a cultivated mind, sensitive to the most exquisite and durable pleasures; and such externals as are needed for peace and comfort. But perhaps the greatest source of all, Epicurus taught—and one that can be quite easily overlooked by an inattentive mind—is friendship. It is impossible to live pleasantly if you are isolated and friendless, and quite impossible to live otherwise in case you are not. Indeed, the greatest, most numerous, and most lasting joys of life are bestowed by friends, who can enhance every hour, and who can add their strength to your own in banishing anxiety, sorrow, and pain. Concerning anyone, therefore, you should, if possible, make that person your friend. Even though the cost and trouble of this may be great, the rewards always promise to be greater still. If it is someone who cannot be befriended, because of character, intellectual inferiority, or any other difference that precludes genuine friendship, then you must at least avoid creating an enemy. And if, furthermore, such obstacles to friendship are so great that any contact at all would produce enmity, then at least make the best of that by simple avoidance. Friendship may at times be impossible, but the avoidance of enmity is always within the power of the wise.

JUSTICE AND DUTY

It will be noted that the notions of justice and duty are not prominent in the Epicurean philosophy. Indeed, up to now they have not come into the picture at all. Justice, it is implicit in this philosophy, is no natural good. In fact, it does not even exist in nature. Justice is simply a human contrivance to enable people to live together in a civilized state, and the motive to respect it is a purely self-regarding one. We cannot live well except with others, and justice, which simply counsels us to refrain from injuring each other, is a necessary precondition to such social life. It is therefore a good, because it renders possible a life that is pleasant and, more obviously, free from pain, but its goodness is clearly derived from the natural goodness of pleasure. Thus could Epicurus declare that it is not possible to live pleasantly without living justly, honorably, and well—nor to live justly, honorably, and well without living pleasantly. Such a dictum guarantees a respect for the virtues of justice and personal honor, but it is perfectly clear that what it really extols is the goodness of pleasure.

The Epicureans had an even lower regard for duty, or moral obligation. In fact they recognized no concept of moral obligation at all. Your only "duty" is to fashion a life that is pleasant and free from pain, but this is no duty at all in any ethical sense of the term. It is only a consequence of the claim that pleasure is a natural good, and pain a natural evil. The Epicureans in fact had little use for the idea of performing one's duties to the state, and generally avoided public office. Public office can offer little reward except honor, and to the Epicurean, the desire for honor is no natural desire to begin with. Such office offers, moreover, abundant sources of pain, anxiety, and the alienation of friends, and on the whole, almost nothing can be said in its favor.

The Significance of Epicurus

This philosophy, then, is no philosophy of heroic deeds. It is self-regarding throughout, and even the virtue of friendship, upon which the Epicureans placed so much stress, is recommended solely for its rewards to oneself; you are not expected to love friends for their sake, but for your own. Still, it would be very difficult to dislike a thoroughgoing and consistent Epicurean, and even though the moral ideal he sets himself may seem to fall short of what human nature is capable of, it is not clear that this is so. Perhaps the world has seen enough heroes. Perhaps the words *justice* and *duty* are more often than not camouflages for the conscious or unconscious self-regarding aims of those in whose mouths they take shape. Certainly people have willingly died in their cause, and many have been sent to their deaths. Perhaps we should, then, give the Epicurean his due, in terms of honesty, unashamed love of self, and sincerity. This philosophy may not be profound, it may contain little that inspires, but we should not presuppose from the outset that truth must be either profound or inspiring. It may be that the basic truths of morality are quite simple, and even that the Epicureans really enunciated those truths. It is my own view, as I have already indicated, that this philosophy contains a most serious flaw, which I shall soon point out. It nevertheless appears to me a far better philosophy than the one Socrates wove around his somewhat mystical notions of the soul, or the one Plato derived from a notion of the "good" that is so abstract and detached from the world that only a metaphysician can understand it.

– 7 –

A MODERN VERSION OF HEDONISM

I HAVE DEFINED hedonism as any philosophy according to which pleasure is always good for its own sake, and the only thing that is good for its own sake. One who is by this definition a hedonist need not, of course, maintain that pleasure is the only thing that is good, for other things are good insofar as they are productive of pleasure. But this is goodness in a different sense, being the goodness of a means rather than of an end. However, pleasure is, according to this philosophy, the only thing that is good as an end, or the only thing sought, not as a means to something else, but for its own sake.

J. S. MILL'S HEDONISM

The moral philosophy of John Stuart Mill is by this criterion a philosophy of hedonism. Mill called it utilitarianism, emphasizing the importance he attached to the practical consequences of actions, and also no doubt because of the odious connotations of the word *hedonism* in the minds of his contemporaries. It is, nevertheless, a doctrine of hedonism, as defined here.

For Mill did explicitly declare that pleasure is always good for its own sake, and that nothing else is such. For the most part, he regarded this as so obvious as to require no argument, and he accordingly referred to it as an "ultimate principle." It is, he thought, precisely what everyone means by calling something good; namely, that it is pleasant, or conducive to pleasure. Furthermore, it is the only thing that we universally desire for its own sake, and it must, therefore, be desirable. Many philosophers have wondered whether this last observation does not in fact amount to a philosophical argument, and if so, whether it is a valid one; but we need not go into that. Mill's basic starting point is that pleasure is by its nature good, and that it is the only thing that is good for its own sake.

Mill made two significant departures from the hedonism of the ancients, however. First, he declared that pleasure and human happiness are one and the same thing. To say that you are *happy* is to say, and to say nothing more, than that you are experiencing pleasure; to say that you are *unhappy* is to say nothing more than that you are experiencing pain. This equation of pleasure and happiness seems harmless enough at first but, as we shall see, its philosophical consequences are great.

His second departure, the consequences of which were even greater, was to declare that pleasure is good, no matter whose pleasure it is. The pleasure of your neighbor, or even of the most distant stranger, has precisely the same value as a similar pleasure of your own, and that value is absolute and unqualified. He seems to have regarded this as axiomatic. If pleasure is good by its very nature, then its goodness does not depend on where it is, or by whom it is experienced.

THE GREATEST HAPPINESS PRINCIPLE

This claim enabled Mill to formulate a principle of *duty* that, as we have seen, was quite foreign to the philosophy of the Epicureans. If pleasure is alone good by nature, then it is everyone's duty to maximize it and to minimize pain; and this means to increase to the utmost the total amount of pleasure *in the world* and to reduce to the utmost the total amount of pain. Mill formulated this by saying that it is your obligation to promote the greatest happiness for the greatest number of people; but here we must remember, of course, that by happiness he means pleasure. Thus, where the hedonism of the Epicureans was entirely self-regarding, Mill's hedonism was a thoroughgoing altruism. The Epicureans were mostly concerned with the question "What should I do in order to achieve for myself a life of goodness?" But Mill's question was an entirely different one: "What should I do in order to do my duty?" And his answer was perfectly straightforward: "I shall do my duty if I increase the total amount of pleasure in the world and reduce the total amount of pain." Every act can be tested by this principle. Every act one performs either does, in comparison with the other acts one might have performed instead, tend more to produce that result, or it does not. If it does, then the action is right, or in accordance with duty. If it does not, then it is in one degree or another wrong, or contrary to what is required by duty.

These are the fundamental principles of Mill's hedonism, and his own elaboration of them consisted of devising replies to all the objections he could contrive, and then recommending these principles as a guide to legislation. We can pretty much disregard all this, because it is the fundamental principles that concern us. There are, however, two objections he deals with that we should consider, as they throw considerable light on the basic principles.

DUTY AND MOTIVE

We are accustomed to taking into account motives when bestowing praise or blame; that is, when trying to decide whether someone has succeeded or failed in being dutiful. The question is not, most people think, simply a question of what someone has done. We need also to know what the motive was for doing it, what was being attempted. Kant, of course, had made this perfectly explicit, declaring that the consequences of your behavior do not even enter into the picture in assessing the moral quality of your actions. So long as an agent is guided by a dutiful motive, Kant declared, then his action is possessed of true moral worth, which shines forth, he said, like a jewel, by its own light. And this remains so, according to Kant, even in case the consequences of such conduct are perfectly dreadful in terms of human happiness. Similarly, Kant declared, your actions are without such moral worth in case they are not prompted by the sense of duty, even though their fruits, in terms of human happiness, should turn out to be bountiful. What counts is *why* you act as you do, and not, what is produced by the action.

Now Mill appears to say the opposite: namely, that you perform your duty, in case your actions foster happiness in all who are affected by them, whether this was what you were trying to accomplish or not. If you save another from drowning, Mill said, then it does not matter, so far as the worth of your action is concerned, whether your motive was to relieve the distress of a fellow human being, or to be paid for your trouble. It is in either case the same action, with the same consequences, and it has therefore the same moral value. A consideration of your motive can only be relevant to evaluating, not your actions, but your character, which is an entirely different matter. Pressed on this point, Mill eventually began drawing distinctions between motives and purposes, thus yielding to his critics what they seemed to demand without appearing to abandon his basic position, but it is doubtful whether he succeeded. Whether your action is dutiful must surely be a function either of your motive, or of the actual consequences. One cannot have it both ways, because it is a fact, which no philosophical argument or elaboration of distinctions can banish, that we do not always accomplish what we try to accomplish, and sometimes, quite accidentally, we produce results that are far indeed from what we were attempting. The road to hell, it is said, is sometimes paved with good intentions, and to this we can add that the road to heaven is sometimes paved with bad ones.

Perhaps what Mill should have done was follow the example of the Epicureans and abandon altogether the idea of moral duty. The Epicureans said, in effect: Let us set about making ourselves as happy as possible. Had Epicurus been asked: Do you think *that* is your duty? he would surely have dismissed the question as having no relevance to his program. I am not, he would surely have said, trying to discover what is my moral duty; I am trying to make myself happy, and here is how I propose to accomplish that end. Now Mill could surely have done much the same thing. What he was plainly saying in effect, was this: Let us set about making the whole world as happy as possible. When asked, do you think *that* is your duty, he surely could have dismissed the question as irrelevant, as it quite plainly was. The concept of duty is derived from religion and law, neither of which rests on any foundation of hedonism. There was, therefore, no need whatever for Mill to try to show that his hedonism incorporated the very concept of duty we have inherited from these sources. Here one can hardly help noting that the Epicureans saw things in a much clearer light than did Mill. They said: Let us make our lives pleasant. They then proceeded to show, in useful ways, how this might be done. Mill in effect said: Let us make a happier world. But instead of then proceeding to show, in useful ways, how this might be done, instead of setting forth any significant program for the reformation of society to bring about this result, he labored for page after page to convince his readers of what plainly is not so: that hedonism is what everyone believes anyway, that it is the very basis of Judeo-Christian morality, the basis of law, and that it incorporates perfectly the traditional concepts of duty derived from these sources.

THE QUALITY OF PLEASURE

The other serious objection Mill considered was this: If pleasure is alone the supreme good, the only thing good as an end, does it not follow that one would be better off being a satisfied pig than a dissatisfied Socrates? What this question is meant to suggest, of course, is that if pleasure is the only thing good as an end, then it can hardly matter from what source your pleasure is derived. So long as you are feeling pleasure, then you have attained the ideal state of existence, whatever other goods you may lack; and, conversely, if you are not feeling pleasure, and are in fact perhaps feeling pain, then you have failed to achieve anything worthwhile for yourself, no matter what else you may have. To assert that we should try to increase, to the maximum possible, the total amount of pleasure in the world, seems to suggest that we should convert the world into one vast amusement park, disregarding all those fruits of civilized life that we prize and replacing them with cheap and simple feelings of pleasure.

The Epicureans faced this problem by noting that pleasures differ in numberless ways. Some are more durable than others, some less admixed with pain, and so on. On the basis of such considerations they rejected the Cyrenaic way of life, not as morally inferior, but simply as less pleasant in the long run. Mill, however, took the extraordinary tack of declaring that some pleasures are inherently *better* than others. Thus, the pleasures of literature, art, and those, in general, that the Greeks had called pleasures of the mind, were declared by Mill to be superior in their goodness to such bodily pleasures as pigs and other animals are presumably, together with humans, capable of experiencing. The pleasure of some idle and pointless amusement, for example, might indeed be a pleasure, and might even be a fairly intense one for some persons, but it is much inferior in its quality of goodness to, say, the pleasures of literature, even though these latter might be more feebly felt. Mill even proposed a test by which one can discriminate between these higher and lower pleasures. Consult someone who has experienced both, he said, and it will invariably be found that this person gives his preference to the higher pleasures, rejecting those that are base. It is doubtful whether Mill meant this as an actual empirical test, however, for if you consulted such a person, and were then surprised by his choice of a baser pleasure in preference to one of the pleasures of the mind, this would, I think, only indicate to Mill that this person was not a good judge.

This view of Mill's is, in any case, extraordinary. To say that pleasure is the supreme good, and the only thing good for its own sake, that it is the only thing that lends value to anything else that is good, and then to declare that some pleasures are intrinsically *better* than others, is quite obviously to appeal to some standard of goodness other than pleasure, some standard by means of which even pleasures can be evaluated as better and worse. The claim is just incoherent. It would be no worse to declare that some yardsticks are longer than others. Clearly, if one were to say this, it would imply that there is some standard yardstick in terms of which others could be measured and declared longer or shorter. Of course this might very well be true; but in that case, you could hardly declare that the original yardsticks, now variable in length, were nevertheless an ultimate standard of length. The hedonist cannot have it both ways. Either pleasure is the standard of goodness, or it is not. If it is not, if something other than pleasure is good for its own sake, then of course the basic principle of hedonism is false. But if it is, if pleasure is the only thing good for its own sake and is the standard by which other things are deemed good, as hedonism declares, then no pleasures can be inherently better than others. Pleasures can in this case only differ in quantity, some being more intense than others, or more lasting, and so on; they cannot differ in their quality of goodness. This point was made long before Mill ever wrote about pleasure, for in one of Plato's dialogues[1] Callicles suggests the same point; namely, that some pleasures are better than others. At that point, Socrates declares, quite aptly, that Callicles is treating him like a child! The fallacy here is so obvious that Socrates thought only a child could be hoodwinked by it.

THE PRESUPPOSITIONS OF HEDONISM

It is appropriate now to take a closer look at the basic presuppositions of hedonism. There have, of course, been many other hedonists besides the Cyrenaics, Epicureans, and Mill, but we need not consider any of them. The samples of hedonism we have before us

---

1. Plato, *Gorgias*, trans. W. C. Helmbold (New York: Liberal Arts Press, 1952), p. 72.

are adequate for the present purpose, for I want to consider the basic presuppositions of *any* hedonistic philosophy. These are (1) that pleasure is always good for its own sake and pain always bad, and (2) that pleasure is the only thing good for its own sake and pain the only thing bad in the same way. Both claims are essential to any philosophy of hedonism. For if (1), for example, should be false—if pleasure should sometimes not be good for its own sake—then, contrary to the fundamental injunction of hedonism, it would not always be wise or reasonable to pursue it. And if (2) should be false—if things other than pleasure should sometimes be good for their own sakes—then the same will follow. For it will sometimes be wise to pursue things other than pleasure; namely, whatever other things are good for their own sakes.

It should be emphasized again here what pleasure, or anything else, being good for its own sake or in itself means. It means that it is good, not merely as a means to some end, but as an end in itself. Thus, concerning most of the things in our environment that we deem to be good, such as food, shelter, the various tools that we use, and so on, we can ask: What are they good *for*? This means: To what *end* are they useful as instruments or means? And in the case of most such things there is usually an obvious answer. Food, for example, is useful for nourishment, shelter for comfort and warmth, and so on. Such things, then, are good, not for their own sakes, or in themselves, but as means to certain ends that are good. If we ask concerning pleasure, however, what it is good *for*, then the question appears to be out of place. Pleasure, it is generally thought, is something good in itself, even if it is not good as a means to anything else.

But now let us ask whether pleasure is, in this

sense, always good for its own sake and pain always bad. Suppose that, after a hard day's toiling in the fields, you shower off the dust of your labor, satisfy your hunger and thirst, and collapse into a good bed, your limbs aching with fatigue. Now the bed feels good, and the feeling of what has been wrought, in case it was considerable, is good too. And what about the aching limbs? Might not that very aching, together with the prospect of awakening refreshed, be good too? Is it not something that adds to the total felt goodness of the situation, something that you would, in these conditions, rather have than lack? In short, might not these very aches and pains be felt as good, in the same sense, for example, that the warmth of the bed felt good? If so, then pain is not, contrary to the hedonist's presupposition, always in its very nature something bad.

Here the temptation will be to say that what would normally be aches and pains, and therefore bad, are in these circumstances pleasant and, hence, good. But if you say that, then it is important to note that you are using "pleasant" not as a description of a particular kind of feeling, but as a term of appraisal for any feeling or experience that is liked, and "pain" for any feeling or experience you happen to dislike. The hedonist's presupposition will in that case rest only on a definition of words, and no longer express any fact at all. It is, however, with something that is alleged to be a fact that we are concerned: with whether it is a fact that feelings of pleasure are always good in themselves and feelings of pain always bad.

THE DOUBLE MEANINGS OF PLEASURE AND PAIN

To see more clearly what is at issue here, let us note that the words *pleasure* and *pain*, or *pleasant* and *painful*, each have a double meaning or use. This is, once it is recognized, particularly evident in Mill's philosophy. The plausibility of hedonism will then be found to rest entirely on this ambiguity. For hedonism purports to rest on a fact of experience: There is something that is always found to be good in itself, and something else that is always found to be bad in itself—these being pleasure and pain, respectively; and that, moreover, nothing else in the world is good in itself, and nothing else in the world is bad in itself. Insofar as this philosophy has any plausibility, however, it rests on nothing more than a conventional usage of words: the convention of applying the word pleasant to any experience or feeling (whatever it may be) that one finds to be good in itself, and unpleasant or painful to any experience or feeling that one finds to be bad in a similar way.

Thus, the word *pleasure* is sometimes used as a *name* for a certain familiar sensation or feeling, one that might be described as tingling, for example. Such a feeling can often be induced by mild stimulation of the skin surface, sometimes by certain cadences of music, and the like. It can sometimes be localized, that is, you can sometimes, although not always, say where it is being felt, such as on the back, around the ears, and so forth. Some parts of the body are more susceptible to the feeling than others, of course, and in those parts of the body that lack certain nerve structures, such as the lungs, it cannot be felt at all. Such a feeling has a beginning and a waning, so that you can sometimes say approximately how long it is felt—for about thirty seconds, or three minutes, for example.

Pain, similarly, is sometimes used as a *name* for a certain familiar sensation or feeling, a feeling that might be described as throbbing, or piercing. Such a feeling can of course be produced in numberless ways—by piercing the skin surface, wrenching this or that part of the body, and so on. The feeling can also often be localized—in the head, the back, the foot, the tooth, or wherever—and like the kindred feeling of pleasure, it waxes and wanes, so that you can sometimes say not only where, but for approximately bow long, it is felt. In those parts of the body lacking pain receptors it cannot be felt at all, of course.

This, then, I shall refer to as *sense one* of the word pleasure, and similarly, *sense one* of the word pain. In this sense, the words pleasure and pain serve as *names* for definite feelings.

In what I shall now call the *second* sense, however, pleasure and pain, or more usually their cognates pleasant and painful, are more than nominal. Indeed, pleasant is in this second sense applied to any experience or state you happen to find good, whether it includes any feelings of pleasure, in sense one, or not. Painful, in a similar way, is applied to any experience or state one happens to dislike, whether or not it is painful (includes pain) in the first sense of the term. Thus, you can speak of such very diverse things as a refreshing walk, the reading of a book, a trip abroad, and, so on, as pleasant, in this sense, or of an awkward social situation, a reverse in one's finances, or a difficult day's work, as unpleasant or painful. These words are, in such contexts as these, merely *terms of appraisal*. They are not at all the *names* of anything, much less are they names of particular feelings. They are merely ways of saying, of the experiences in question, that they are liked, or that they are disliked. Other terms of appraisal, having their own nuances of meaning, serve just as well; such as enjoyable, agreeable, boring, and tedious, for example. The most *general* of the appraisal terms, however, are simply *good* and *bad*.

Now it is perfectly obvious that something might be pleasant (enjoyable, agreeable) in the second sense, without involving any *pleasure*, in the first sense, whatsoever. Similarly, something might be painful, in this second sense, without involving any feelings of pain. You might quite truly describe an entire day as pleasant, for instance, without suggesting that you were, throughout that day or even any considerable part of it, experiencing those feelings for which the word pleasure serves as a name. Indeed, it would be perfectly congruous to so describe such a day, even though it contained no such feelings or sensations at all. To describe a day as *pleasant* is only to appraise one's experiences of that day as liked, enjoyed, or experienced as *good*.

Now let us look again at the basic presuppositions of hedonism. The first is that pleasure is always good for its own sake, and pain is always bad. Is this true in the *first* sense of pleasure and pain, the sense in which these words serve as the names of certain feelings? It *may* be that it is, but this is by no means obvious. The ache in one's limbs after a day of successful toil that I described previously is pain in the first sense, for example; but it is not obvious that, in the circumstances described, it is also painful, in the second sense, and therefore bad. One might feel it as good.

Is this presupposition true, then, in the *second*

sense of pleasure and pain? That is, is it true in the sense in which pleasant and painful are not descriptions of feelings, but are instead simply terms of appraisal? Are things that are in this sense pleasant always and invariably found to be good, and are things that are in this sense painful always found to be bad? Well of course they are, but only because this is a tautology, that is, a way of saying the same thing twice over. If calling something pleasant is, in this sense, simply a way of appraising it as good, and calling something painful is just another way of expressing one's dislike for it (and thus appraising it as bad), then it plainly tells us nothing to affirm that pleasant experiences are always good and painful ones bad. This is a necessary "truth," only because it is an empty one.

What, then, of the second hedonistic presupposition; namely, that pleasure is the *only* thing in the world that is good in itself, and pain the only thing that is bad?

Well, if we take pleasure and pain in their first sense, as the names of certain identifiable feelings, then this claim is obviously not true. Ever so many things, besides feelings of pleasure, are good in themselves—namely, absolutely all those things that various people at various times and places *find* to be good for their own sakes, or, in another way of saying the same thing, find to be pleasant in the second sense. The experience of being loved, for example, and of loving, or the experience of seeing the sun set, or the feeling of achievement, and so on, *endlessly*. The things that are good in themselves, or for their own sakes, must indeed be numberless, for they include absolutely everything that anyone ever likes for its own sake; that is, all the things that are ever found to be good and are thus prized, not as means to still other things, but as good in themselves. And you should be most careful, at this point, not to be tempted into thinking that because we have a common term of appraisal for such agreeable experiences—namely, the word *pleasant*—we must after all be talking about just one thing, *pleasure*. For insofar as *pleasure* is the name of just one sort of thing—a certain familiar kind of feeling or sensation—then it is not a term of appraisal, and what it names, even though it is doubtless something good, is assuredly not uniquely so. Most people, moreover, would unhesitatingly deem it not terribly good anyway, something of fairly trivial value in comparison with other things that are prized for their own sakes.

What, then, of pleasure, in the second sense? Is this uniquely good for its own sake? Of course it is, but only, again, because this is a tautology. To describe something as a pleasure, in this sense, is only to describe it as pleasant, which is in turn only a way of appraising it as good for its own sake. So of course we can say of anything that is good for its own sake that it is pleasant—but this is, unfortunately, not to say anything at all.

PLEASURE AND HAPPINESS

The confusion just noted, once it has been appreciated, becomes particularly evident in Mill's system. For Mill says at the outset that by pleasure and happiness he means exactly the same thing. Now clearly, insofar as pleasure is a *name* for a particular kind of feeling—the kind of feeling you experience when the surface of your skin is lightly massaged, for instance—then happiness is not another name for the same thing. You can be perfectly happy even though you are experiencing no such sensations or feelings at all, or even if you experience them only rarely. They are no significant ingredient of happiness for most people.

What, then, is happiness? Essentially it is a certain state, which the Greeks called *eudaemonia*, or well-being. Probably no definition of it could be given, but some sort of description is possible. You are usually (but not always) happy, for example, when, in addition to being in good health and relatively free to pursue your own goals, your interests are flourishing and the objectives you have set for yourself show promise of realization. This is very general, vague, and inadequate, because happiness, or human well-being, is a very grand, vague, and general idea, and the conditions of it for different people are quite variable. The happiness of an illiterate and primitive tribesman is remote indeed from the happiness of a modern European, having nothing in common except that they are referred to by the same word and are found agreeable to their possessors.

Is happiness, then, uniquely good for its own sake, as Mill maintains? Doubtless it is, but it should be apparent by now how empty a claim this is. It amounts to no more than saying that human well-being is uniquely good, or that it *is* human well-being, and that nothing else is such. This, of course, tells us nothing. But Mill attempts to make the claim look like a significant one by identifying happiness with *pleasure*. To the extent that the claim is thus made significant, however, it is also made false—for it is not true that pleasure, in this sense, is the only thing good for its own sake, and it is doubtful whether it is even invariably good. Mill thus weaves his whole moral philosophy around a presupposition that is true, just to the extent that it says nothing. To the extent that it does say something, it is quite plainly false.

– 8 –

KANTIAN MORALITY

THE MORAL PHILOSOPHY of Immanuel Kant represents perhaps the most thoroughgoing expression in modern literature of what I have called true morality. Between the Socratic and the Kantian morality there is very little resemblance in detail, but the basic assumptions are the same, and to understand one is to understand the central point of the other. Kantian moral philosophy can, in fact, be considered to carry out to its logical conclusion the Greek distinction between nature and convention, together with the Socratic conviction that there is a natural or true morality. The differences between Kant and Socrates can be understood largely as a difference between Greek and Christian attitudes, the former stressing the idea of the good, and the latter the idea of the dutiful.

THE BACKGROUND OF KANTIAN MORALITY

By the time of Kant, the assumption that there is a true morality, or a natural as distinguished from a conventional right and wrong, had become so thoroughly a part of philosophical thought that it was rarely questioned. It was just taken for granted. The philosophical task was not, as with many of the Greeks, to establish this distinction, but only to discover the *content* of true morality, to set forth those propositions of ethics that can, like the propositions of any science, claim to be *true*. Philosophers differed as to what is really right and good, but they seldom differed in supposing that there is a genuine right and a genuine good and that these are fixed and quite independent of what are so variously and conflictingly *thought* to be right and good by various cultures at various places and times—in short, that natural and merely conventional morality are two quite different things. Conventional morality is the province of empirical science, specifically of anthropology, a part of whose task is simply to *describe* the conventional practices of various civilized and semicivilized peoples. Such empirical descriptions can shed no light whatsoever upon moral philosophy, however; for moral philosophy is concerned, not with what various people in fact *do*, but with what all rational people *ought* to do. Such, at least, was Kant's presupposition. From time to time he expressed it in various ways as being simply something obvious; he never tried to defend it. His attitude was that this is the starting point of moral philosophy, this distinction between what *is* and what *ought* to be, and that unless you recognize the latter as the province of moral philosophy, you are not on the subject of morals but are instead confusing morals with other things—with anthropology, for example, or perhaps with psychology.

It is doubtless this presupposition of Kant's that has contributed so greatly to his fame as a moralist, for it is one that virtually all thinking people share, although like Kant, they seldom question it. It is probably safe to say that virtually no one thinks in Kantian terms in any of the practical affairs of life, and yet intellectually his moral philosophy touches very deeply things that most persons of our culture hold very dear: the ultimate distinction between right and wrong, the claims of duty, the dignity of man, and so on. Nor is it difficult to see why this is so. Greek moral philosophy, abetted mostly by the efforts of Socrates and Plato, begat the conviction that there is natural morality, a true good, a *summum bonum*, independent of human contrivance. Christianity inadvertently confirmed all this, identifying our duty with the will of God and the good with God's plan. Wherever Christianity had any influence at all, one of its effects was to remind everyone of the distinction between what they may want to do and what they ought to do—namely, God's will. The idea of the divine will pretty much disappeared from secular philosophy—it arises only illustratively in Kant's writings, for example—but the idea of the dutiful certainly did not. Even though duty was no longer thought of in theological terms by philosophers, it nevertheless remained central to their moral philosophy. Divested of its association with the divine will, it survived as a purely philosophical idea. Indeed, it survived as the basic philosophical category of ethics. Few were even willing to ask, as Protagoras had asked concerning the true good, whether there really is any such thing as a moral duty independent of a command of God or some other being. It simply was assumed that there is, that as philosophers we must find what it is, and then as moral beings we must perform it.

THE BASIC IDEAS OF CONVENTIONAL MORALITY

We all have a fairly clear idea of the conventional distinction between right and wrong. It is essentially a distinction, empirically drawn, between two kinds of action: those that tend to help and those that tend to injure and frustrate. Any normal person can tell fairly well, just by considering any action and its probable effects, whether it helps or hurts. No philosophy is needed for this. Some actions, to be sure, are ambiguous; that is, no one can be sure, because of special circumstances, just what their effects will be. This sort of uncertainty, however, accompanies all observation and prediction, and no philosophy can remove it.

Similarly, we all understand fairly well the conventional distinction between good and bad. This is essentially a distinction between things that are good *for* something and things that are not. It is, in other words, a distinction between things that tend to promote and things that tend to frustrate whatever ends or goals we may at one time or another happen to have. And we learn which things are which the same way we learn everything else, by experience. No philosophy is needed to make this distinction, and those who are entirely ignorant of philosophy draw it with about the same reliability as anyone else.

Both distinctions, then—between right and wrong actions and between good and bad things—are relative to our needs, feelings, and desires and have no very clear meaning apart from these. To beings like ourselves, however, who are basically egoistic or selfish and look first and last to the satisfaction of our own wills and desires, but who are nevertheless forced by circumstances to live with others, these are distinctions that come to have great practical, social significance. They come to be represented as uniquely moral distinctions, in order to give them weight and impress them on our minds and hearts. Emotions of approval and disapproval come to be associated with them, religion is enlisted to enforce them, and eventually they cease to seem like relative distinctions. Right and wrong and good and bad come to be thought of as real and absolute distinctions, distinctions existing in nature rather than human distinctions, as things having to do with reason, truth, and reality, rather than as the products of practical needs and feelings.

Laws

Again, we all know what laws are. They are usually prohibitions, promulgated for a variety of purposes, some trivial and some not, but having as a common element the prohibition of actions that are injurious, or actions that are "wrong" in the sense just delineated. Laws, in other words, are "positive" laws, that is to say, prohibitions and injunctions actually promulgated by actual people—by kings, legislators, judges, and others. There is no such thing as "the law" as such, except as this abstract expression is taken to refer to some particular set of positive laws. Those who make these laws are simply those who happen to have the power to do so. It was pointed out in antiquity—by Thrasymachus, for example—that the content of any body of laws or enforced practices can be readily understood in terms of the interests of those who promulgate them, or of that class, economic or social, that such lawgivers represent. And obedience to such laws is obtained, not by some supposed moral truth that they embody, and not by any appeal to the conscience or reason—they would be ineffectual indeed if this were all that supported them—but simply by the threat of penalty that is implicitly or explicitly incorporated in every one of them and by the power that someone has to carry out that threat. Remove either the threat or the power, and the laws become dead and useless. They similarly become dead and useless if replaced by other laws enunciated by people having the power to enforce the new ones. There can, therefore, really be no such thing as an unenforced law; there can only be the empty statement, existing as a curiosity rather than a real law. Laws are, then, in any case, human fabrications, contrived and enunciated at different times and places for a variety of reasons, but usually just for the reason of self-protection or protection of some established order.

Because we live under laws, however, and have instilled in us the necessity of obedience, enforced by threat, we are easily encouraged to think of law as something fixed, as somehow belonging to nature, as the Greeks expressed it, and therefore something to be respected for its own sake. We find ourselves speaking of The Law, or even Natural Law, thereby concealing the purely human origin of laws, as though these pure abstractions stood for something real, something belonging to the very fabric of the universe. Having got to that point, it is then not difficult to speak, as Kant and many others have done, of the Moral Law—something that is not supposed to be the fabrication of men or even of gods. The precise content of such an abstract moral law is of course very difficult to discern, but many philosophers have conceived it as their task to discern it and publish it to all humankind. Few have wanted to believe, with Protagoras, that there may simply be no such moral law, and hence nothing to discern, nothing to publish. The Moral Law is supposed to be there, *above* the human laws that may very imperfectly express it or that may even oppose it; it is supposed to have no necessary connection with anything so mundane and practical as the need to survive and somehow get on with one another. It is a metaphysical thing, part of the invisible fabric of nature and, of course, absolutely worthy of respect. Kant himself declared that this Moral Law, together with the starry heavens above, filled his mind with awe.

JUSTICE

The existence of laws readily begets the idea of justice. Justice, as some of the Sophists quite accurately perceived, originally arose from the necessity imposed on people, unlike most other creatures, to live together in groups, in perpetual contact with each other, their paths constantly crossing, and the threat of injury at the hands of others being therefore always present to each. The idea of justice could never occur to a race of hermits. Yet, we are all more or less hermits so far as our desires, feelings, and wants are concerned, and social beings mainly from convenience and necessity. The desires, aims, and purposes of others do not interest any of us very deeply, except insofar as they have bearing on our own, or except insofar as we can, through human sympathy, identify their feelings and desires with our own. Yet we do have to live together, and justice is simply the name of those practical formulas by which various peoples have managed to do this. In our own culture it essentially means fairness; this, in turn, expresses the idea that a limit is put on the gratification of your selfishness by the need of your neighbor to gratify his. It is a necessary condition of social life that people cannot have everything they want. Justice is accordingly the price, and a fairly onerous one, that they pay for the practical benefits, and indeed the necessity, of living with others whose selfishness matches their own.

Like all moral terms, however, this one too has been moved to heaven from earth, first by Socrates and Plato and then by the generations of theologians, jurists, and moralists who have followed. In most minds, justice no longer stands for anything so mundane as a practical formula for minimizing injury, but for some high abstraction that, although seemingly indefinable, is thought to be absolutely worthy of reverence. Perhaps no word in our language has a more buoyant effect on us than this one. Revolutionaries and conservatives would alike feel disarmed without it, and any man needs only to let it roll off his tongue in some situation in which his desires or ambitions are mightily involved to feel as though he were being borne aloft in a balloon. The laws, originally contrived as practical means to practical ends, now appear to have no such vulgar source, but are instead thought to derive a special and compelling authority from the principle of Justice. But because there apparently exists no such principle, independently of human fabrication, it usually tends to become identified, more or less unconsciously, with whatever some group happens to cherish. The spectre of the judge, armed with the power to punish, is always there to remind us of the awesome authority of this principle and the dangers of defiance.

There is, then, an irresistible tendency to objectify, reify, and weave into some rational or metaphysical system those moral notions that are born of the union between certain human feelings and human needs. Kant's fame as a moralist, like Plato's, derives from his employing his great learning and acumen to persuade us that this extraordinary tendency is absolutely correct, is even required by reason itself, and that the system of true morality constitutes a veritable metaphysics of its own. He even referred to the subject matter of his inquiry as the *metaphysics* of morals. The thing reified in Platonic ethics was The Good. In Kantian ethics, it is the Moral Law.

KANTIAN MORALITY

It is not my intention to give any detailed exposition of Kant's ethical system. I propose instead to discuss certain of Kant's basic ideas in order to illustrate a certain approach to ethics that I think is essentially wrong. For this I could have chosen the ideas of some other modern moralist, but I prefer to

illustrate my points by Kant's thought. I am doing
this first because of his great fame and the reverence
with which many philosophers still regard him, and
secondly because it would be difficult to find any
modern thinker who has carried to such an extreme
the philosophical presuppositions that I am eager to
repudiate. I shall, thus, use some of Kant's ideas to
show how the basic ideas of morality, born originally of our practical needs as social beings and
having to do originally with our practical relations
with each other, can, under the influence of philosophy, become so detached from the world that they
become pure abstractions, having no longer anything to do with morality insofar as this is a practical concern. Philosophical or metaphysical morals
thereby ceases to have much connection with the
morality that is an abiding practical concern and
becomes, instead, a purely intellectual thing, something to contemplate and appreciate, much as one
would appreciate a geometrical demonstration. Its
vocabulary, which is the very vocabulary of
everyday morals, no longer has the same meaning,
but instead represents a realm of pure abstractions.
Intellectually satisfying as this might be, it is nevertheless highly dangerous, for it leads one to suppose
that the problems of ethics are essentially intellectual problems, that they are simply philosophical
questions in need of philosophical answers. The
result is that the eyes of the moralist are directed
away from the world, in which moral problems are
the most important problems there are, and toward
a really nonexistent realm, a realm of ideas rather
than things. The image of philosophical moralists,
who are quite lacking in any knowledge of the world
and whose ideas about it are of the childish sort

learned in a Sunday school, is a familiar one. These are moralists whose dialectic is penetrating and whose reasoning is clear—they grapple with many philosophical problems of morality and have many subtle answers to philosophical difficulties—but they have little appreciation of the pain and sorrow of the world beyond the knowledge that it is there.

DUTY AND LAW

Laws, as practical rules of human invention, find no place in Kant's metaphysical morals. The Moral Law that replaces them is sundered from any practical human concerns, for it seemed to Kant that our practical ends and our moral obligations are not only quite different things but, more often than not, are actually opposed to each other. Obligations, which were originally only relations between people arising from mutual undertakings for mutual advantage, similarly disappear from the Kantian morality, to be replaced by an abstract sort of *moral* obligation that has no connection whatsoever with any earthly good. Duties—which were originally and are still imposed by rulers on subjects, masters on servants, employers on workmen, and so on, in return for certain compensations, privileges, and rights—are replaced by Kant with Duty in the abstract. This abstract Duty is deemed by him to be the sole proper motive of moral conduct; yet, it is not a duty *to* anyone, or a duty to do any particular thing. The notion of duty to sovereign or master has always been well understood, and Christians understand the idea of duty to God. In such cases duty consists simply of compliance with commands. But in

Kant's system, duties are sundered from particular commands, and Duty becomes something singular and metaphysical. We are, according to this system, to do always what Duty requires, for no other reason than that Duty does require it. Beyond a few heterogeneous examples for illustration, we never learn from Kant just what this is, save only that it is the obligation to act from respect for the Moral Law. You must cling to life, for example, and give no thought to suicide—not because any lawgiver or God has commanded it, not because things might work out all right for you if you stick it out a little longer, but just because Duty requires it. You must also help others in distress; not, again, because any man or God has admonished you to, not just because they need you, or because you care for them, or because you want to see their baneful condition improved—indeed, it is best that you have no such feelings at all—but just because it is your Duty.

THE GOOD WILL

It is in such terms that Kant defined the *good will*, declaring it to be the only thing in the universe that is unqualifiedly good. Now we normally think of a person of goodwill as one who loves others, one whose happiness is sympathetically bound up with theirs, one who has a keen and constant desire to abolish suffering and make the lot of neighbors more tolerable than it might be without a helping hand. Not so for Kant. Indeed, he dismisses the actions of such persons, "so sympathetically constituted that . . . they find an inner satisfaction in spreading joy, and rejoice in the contentment of others which they have made possible," as devoid of any moral worth. Human conduct, to have any genuine moral worth, must not spring from any such amiable feelings as these; these are, after all, nothing but human feelings; they are not *moral* incentives. To have genuine moral worth, according to this moralist, our actions must spring from the sense of Duty and nothing else. And you act dutifully if you act, not from love or concern for others, but from respect for the Moral Law.

THE CATEGORICAL IMPERATIVE

The Moral Law assumed, in Kant's thought, the form of an imperative, or command. But unlike any command that was ever before heard on earth, this one issues from no commander! Like a question that no one ever asks, or an assertion that no one ever affirms, it is a command that no God or man ever promulgates. It is promulgated by Reason. Nor is this the humble rationality of living, mortal beings; it is Reason itself, again in the abstract. And unlike what one would ordinarily think of as a command, this one has no definite content. It is simply the form, Kant says, not of any actual laws, but of The Law, which is again, of course, something abstract. It has, unlike any other imperative of which one has ever heard, no purpose or end. It is not the means to the achievement of anything; and it has no relation to what anyone wants. For this reason Kant called it the Categorical Imperative, a command that is supposed to command absolutely and for its own sake. The Categorical Imperative does not bid us to act in a manner calculated to advance human well-being, for the weal and woe of human beings has for

Kant no necessary connection with morality. It does not bid us to act as we would want others to act, for what people want has no more bearing on morals than what they happen to feel. This Imperative does not, in fact, bid us to do anything at all, nor, indeed, even to have any generous or sympathetic motive, but only to honor some maxim or rational principle of conduct. We are, whatever we do, to act in such a manner that we could, consistently with reason, will this maxim to be a universal Law, even a Law of Nature, binding on all rational beings. Kant does not ask us to consider how other rational beings, thus bound, might feel about our maxims, for again, how anyone happens to feel about anything has no bearing on morality anyway. It is Reason that counts. It is not the living and suffering human beings who manage sometimes to be reasonable but most of the time are not. It is not our needs and wants, or any human desires, or any practical human goods. To act immorally is to act contrary to Reason; it is to commit a sort of metaphysical blunder in the relationship between one's behavior and some generalized motive. Human needs and feelings have so little to do with this that they are not even allowed into the picture. If someone reaches forth to help the sick, the troubled, or the dying, this must not be done from any motive of compassion or sentiment of love. Such love, as a feeling, is dismissed by Kant as "pathological," because it is not prompted by that rational respect for Duty that filled Kant with such awe. Indeed, Kant thought that such human feelings as love and compassion should not even be allowed to cooperate in the performance of Duty, for we must act solely *from* Duty, and not merely *in accordance* with it. Such

feelings as love, sympathy, and friendship are therefore regarded by Kant as positively dangerous. They
incline us to do from sheer goodness of heart what
should be done only from Reason and respect for the
Moral Law. To be genuinely moral, you must tear
yourself away from your inclinations as a loving
human being, drown the sympathetic promptings of
your heart, scorn any fruits of your efforts, think
last of all of the feelings, needs, desires, and inclinations either of yourself or others and, perhaps de-
testing what you have to do, do it anyway—solely
from respect for the Law.

RATIONAL NATURE AS AN END

This Moral Law is otherwise represented by Kant as
respect for Rational Nature, something that again,
of course, exists only in the abstract but is, presumably, somehow exemplified in humanity and, Kant
thought, in God. Indeed, it is the only thing in us
that Kant considered worthy of a philosopher's
attention. Because we are deemed to embody this
Rational Nature, human nature is declared to be an
End in Itself, to possess an absolute Worth, or Dignity. This kind of absolute End is not like ordinary
ends or goals, something relative to the aims or purposes of any creature. It is not anything anyone
wants or would be moved to try to achieve. It is, like
so many of Kant's abstractions, an absolute end.
And the Worth that he supposes Rational Nature to
possess is no worth *for* or *to* anything; it, too, is an
abstract or absolute Worth. Kant peoples a veritable
utopia, which he of course does not imagine as
existing, with these Ends in Themselves, and calls it

the Kingdom of Ends. Ends in Themselves are, thus, not to be thought of as those human beings that live and toil on earth; they are not suffering, rejoicing, fumbling, living, and dying human beings; they are not beings that anyone has ever seen, or would be apt to recognize as human if he did see them, or apt to like very much if he did recognize them. They are abstract things, reifications of Rational Nature, fabricated by Kant and now called Rational Beings or Ends in Themselves. Their purpose, unlike that of any creature under the sun, is not to sorrow and rejoice, not to love and hate, not to beget offspring, not to grow old and die, and not to get on as best they can to such destinies as the world has allotted them. Their purpose is just to *legislate*—to legislate morally and rationally for this rational Kingdom of Ends.

THE SIGNIFICANCE OF KANT

Kant's system thus represents the rational, logical conclusion of the natural or true morality that was begotten by the Greeks, of the absolute distinction that they drew, and that people still want to draw. This is the distinction between what *is*, or the realm of observation and science, and what *ought* to be, or the realm of obligation and morals. No one has ever suggested that Kant was irrational, and although it is doubtful that his ideas have ever had much impact on human behavior, they have had a profound impact on philosophy, which has always prized reason and abstraction and tended to scorn fact. Kant's metaphysical system of morals rests on notions that are still a part of the fabric of our intellectual culture and inheritance. His greatest merit is that he was consistent. He showed us what sort of metaphysic of morals we must have—if we suppose that morality has any metaphysic, or any logic and method of its own. He showed what morality must be if we suppose it to be something rational and at the same time nonempirical or divorced from psychology, anthropology, or any science. That general conception of morals is, of course, still common in philosophy, and still permeates judicial thought, where it expresses itself in the ideas of guilt and desert. A man is thought to be "deserving" of punishment if he did, and could have avoided doing, something "wrong." Our basic moral presuppositions, in short, are still very much the same as Kant's, and Kant shows where they lead. We still assume, as he did, a basic dichotomy between what in fact *is* and what morally *ought* to be, between what the Greeks called convention and nature. Like the Greeks, and like Kant, we still feel a desperate need to *know* what, by nature or by some natural or rational moral principle, *ought* to be. Kant was entirely right in insisting that no knowledge of what in fact is—no knowledge of human nature, of history, of anthropology, or psychology—can yield this knowledge. But Kant did not consider, and many philosophical minds still think it somehow perverse to consider, that there may be no such knowledge— and not merely because no one has managed to attain it, but because there may really be nothing there to know in the first place. There may be no such thing as a true morality. Perhaps the basic facts of morality are, as Protagoras thought, conventions; that is, the practical formulas, some workable and some not, for enabling us to achieve whatever ideals and aspirations happen to move us. In the Kantian scheme, such considerations have nothing to do with morality, which is concerned, not with what is, but with what morally ought to be, with what is in his strange sense commanded. According to the Protagorean scheme, on the other hand, such considerations exhaust the whole subject of morals. Here we are, human beings, possessed of needs, feelings, capacities, and aims that are for the most part not of our creation but are simply part of our endowment as human beings. These are the grist, the data, and the subject matter of morals. The problem is how we get from where we are to where we want to go. It is on our answer to this question that our whole happiness and our worth as human beings depends. Our problem is not whether our answers accord with nature or even with truth. Our problem is to find those answers that do in fact work, whose fruits are sunlight, warmth, and satisfaction in our lives as we live them.

– PART TWO –

GOOD AND EVIL

~ 9 ~

GOOD AND EVIL

I T HAS, AS we have seen, been fairly characteristic of moral philosophers to begin with an assumed dichotomy between what *is* and what *ought* to be. Having turned their backs on the former as having little relevance to philosophical ethics, they have proclaimed the content of the latter as the unique realm of ethics. Some, in fact, have declared it a fallacy even to attempt to derive any philosophy of what ought to be from what in fact is, which pretty much amounts to declaring that facts can have little bearing upon ethics. One result of this is that moral philosophy has all too often resembled declamation. The advocates for the various and conflicting programs have had little to appeal to other than their own intuitions of things, these being sometimes baptized as the deliverances of "practical reason" and the like.

I am now going to remove this distinction between *is* and *ought*. More precisely, I shall show that all moral distinctions, beginning with the basic distinction between good and evil, are based entirely on certain facts and, in particular, on facts concerning human nature. It is because we are the kind of beings we are—namely, what I have called conative beings—that the distinction between good and evil arises in the first place. Once this has been seen, we can see what good and evil in fact are. This basic distinction then having been made clear—and having been based not on intuitions and sentiments or abstract reasoning, but on a certain conception of human nature—we can derive the further distinctions between moral right and wrong and give a fairly clear content to the idea of the common good.

CONATIVE BEINGS

Human beings are rational or cognitive, but to say this is very far from stating the whole truth about them. So far as ethics is concerned, it leaves entirely out of account the most important fact about us, that we are desiderative or conative beings as well. I have already explained what this means, but it needs to be briefly reiterated here, as it is crucial to establishing the distinction between good and evil.

To describe us as conative is not to say anything at all abstruse or metaphysical, as this bit of terminology might suggest. It is only to call attention to a fact of human nature with which everyone is perfectly familiar: we have needs, desires, and goals; we pursue ends; we have certain wants and generally go about trying to satisfy them in various ways. Psychologists, metaphysicians, and others might have conflicting theories concerning how this fact is to be understood and explained, but the fact itself is hardly open to any question. It is more obvious that we are, in the sense just explained, conative beings, than that we are rational ones. There are people whom one might genuinely doubt to be rational, but it is doubtful whether anyone has ever seen a living person who could be suspected of having no needs, desires, or wants. Such a being would be totally inactive and resemble a statue more than a person.

Thus, when a man is seen doing anything, it can generally be asked why he is doing it, what he is doing it for, or what he is trying to accomplish. This need not suggest that his behavior is not caused in the usual way, although some might want to maintain this. What it does mean is that there is some point to what he is doing, some outcome that he intends. It implies nothing more.

For example, a man is seen operating a typewriter. Why is he doing that? Perhaps he is writing a letter, or an editorial, or something of that sort. In short, he has some purpose, and his typewriting activity is his means to fulfilling it. Or a woman is seen running. What for? Perhaps to get to a store before it closes, or to catch a bus. Again, she has some purpose and is trying to fulfill it by running. Or once more, a man is seen walking toward a pump with an empty bucket. What for? Presumably, to fill the bucket (a goal) to enable himself to drink, wash, and so on (further purposes or goals).

I have used these exceedingly commonplace examples of human activity to illustrate three points. The first is that voluntary or deliberate human activity is generally interpreted as goal-directed. When we ask why some man is doing whatever it is that he is doing, we are usually seeking some explanation in terms of what he is trying to accomplish by that activity. This presupposes something about us that is universally taken for granted: we have goals and purposes and wants and desires, and we generally act in ways we consider appropriate to fulfilling them. It presupposes, in fact, that we are conative beings or, as I shall sometimes express it, that we are beings having desires and wants.

The second point is that, in speaking of goals or purposes, one need not be referring to some *ultimate* goal or even to any that is very important. The goal of one's activity might be exceedingly trivial and of only momentary significance, as in the foregoing examples. It could hardly be one's ultimate goal, or the goal of one's lifetime, to fill a bucket with water or to catch a bus. Yet, that might be precisely the goal then and there. Of course most do have larger, more long-range goals. We spend years struggling in pursuit of some important objective, such as a degree in medicine, or perhaps fame as an author. Some devote the better part of their lives to ends having that kind of personal importance. In speaking of human behavior as goal-directed, however, I do not have this sort of thing primarily in mind, even though I include it. What I am calling attention to is much simpler and more commonplace. The conative aspect of human nature is as well exhibited by munching an apple or swatting a fly as by someone devoting a lifetime to a great ambition.

And the third point is that reason appears to enter into our purposeful activity primarily to devise the means to attain the ends and has little to do with ends themselves. Thus, if you want to fill a bucket with water, it is in the clearest sense rational that you should carry it to the pump, as the most elementary reason or intelligence indicates that this is the appropriate means to that end. Merely wishing that the pail might become filled, or trying to find some way to bring the pump to the pail, would be unreasonable, precisely in the sense that these are not means that give much promise of working. There is not, however, any reason for filling the pail in the first place. There is, to be sure, some further purpose that can thus be fulfilled—the purpose of drinking, for example, or of washing—but this only indicates that filling the pail, which is the immediate purpose, is in turn a means to still some further purpose. It is, for example, neither rational nor irrational that you should want to drink; it is merely an expression of the fact that you are thirsty. In the same sense, it is neither rational nor irrational that you should want to swat a fly, or catch a bus, or become a physician, or attain fame as an author. These are simply statements of your aims or goals, both trivial and great, and they have nothing to do with reason. How they are to be reached, on the other hand, has a great deal to do with reason, for in general, you can set about trying to accomplish whatever it is you want to accomplish in either an intelligent and rational way or otherwise. To say you are pursuing goals in an intelligent way is only to say, as an inference from experience, that the means you adopt have some promise of succeeding.

CONATION AS THE PRECONDITION OF GOOD AND EVIL

With these rather commonplace observations in mind, let us now ask what conditions are necessary in order that any distinction between good and evil and between right and wrong can be made. That is, what must be presupposed in saying of something that it is good, or that it is bad, or in saying of an action that it is morally right or morally wrong?

Unthinking people have a tendency to assume that some things are just naturally good and others bad, and some actions right and some wrong, and that we need only to discover which are which. Even some of the most thoughtful philosophers, as we have seen, have started out with the same assumption. Thus, it is supposed that we are born into a world in which these distinctions already hold. Many have insisted that these distinctions cannot either have been contrived or have awaited the invention of laws, conventions, and customs. Ever so many things are man-made, including laws and moral customs; however, it is often thought that we cannot suppose the ultimate distinctions between good and evil or right and wrong to be such, for this would render all ethics, all justice, and all morality entirely relative. Indeed, most philosophers have thought that the problem of the moralist is simply to discover the true nature of goodness and rightness; they have disagreed not on whether such things exist independently, but on what *is* truly good, and what is truly right.

But now let us note that the basic distinction between good and evil could not even theoretically be drawn in a world that we imagined to be devoid of all life. That is, if we suppose the world to be exactly as it is, except that it contains not one living thing, it seems clear that nothing in it would be good and nothing bad. It would just be a dead world, turning through space with a lifeless atmosphere. Having deprived our imagined world of all life, we can modify it in numberless ways, but by no such modification can we ever produce the slightest hint of good or evil in it until we introduce at least one living being capable of reacting in one way or another to the world as that being finds it. Thus, we can imagine on the one hand that it is filled with things satisfying, lovely, and beautiful—with sunrises and sunsets, pleasing sights and sounds and fragrant odors, and with all such things that beings like ourselves would find necessary and agreeable to life. Or we can imagine the opposite—a world that is dark and cold, filled with nauseous smells and barren of anything that would redeem such bleak aspects. But so long as we suppose that neither of these worlds does contain any being like ourselves, or any sentient being whatever, then neither world is *better* or *worse* than the other. Each is simply a world of facts, neutral with respect to good or evil, and destined to remain so until we suppose at least one onlooker capable of some sort of reaction to such facts.

Next we note that, if we begin to add inhabitants to this world who are, like ourselves, more or less rational, intelligent, and capable of perception but who, unlike ourselves, have no needs, purposes, or desires, the distinction between good and evil still does not arise. Imagine, for example, a whole colony of machine-like beings, living together and interacting in various ways. These beings, we can suppose, can perceive what is going on around them, distinguish between true and false, and make various inferences; but they are machine-like in that nothing matters to them, nothing makes any difference so far as their needs and purposes are concerned, because they have no needs or purposes, they do not care about anything. If it is raining, they observe that it is raining, but they seek no shelter, for they have no interest in being dry. If it is bitterly cold, then again they note this fact, but make no attempt to warm themselves because they care not whether they are warm or cold. If one of these beings observes another moving with great speed and force toward itself, it infers that a collision is impending, but makes no attempt to step aside, because it has no purpose that would be frustrated by such a collision. It has not even the desire to perpetuate its own existence, because it has no desires whatever. Having then been run down and broken by the onrushing being, losing a few limbs perhaps, it simply notes that this has happened, but it does not retaliate, because it had no interest in preserving any of its limbs or other parts anyway; and so on.

Such beings are, to be sure, difficult to imagine, for if we suppose them to be capable of perceiving, then we seem to imagine them to be living things, and it is difficult to imagine *any* living thing having no interests or purposes whatever, not even an interest in self-preservation. But of course we need not imagine that they are living things; we can instead suppose that they are enormously complex computers, if that makes it easier. And then we need only suppose that they share with certain living things, such as ourselves, the capacity to perceive what is going on and to draw certain conclusions from what they perceive, but that they do *not* share with other living things, such as ourselves, any interest in what is going on. They are, in short, possessed of some degree of intelligence, but of no will whatever.

Now I think it is clear that a world inhabited by such beings would still be a world devoid of any good or evil. Like the first world we imagined, which did not even contain any beings of the most elementary intelligence, this one might contain anything we care to put into it without there arising the least semblance of good or of evil—until we imagine it to contain at least one being having some need, interest, or purpose. It would not matter to the beings just described whether their world was one filled with sunlight, warmth, and beauty, or dark and cold and filled with nauseous smells, because nothing would matter to them. They could tell the difference between sunlight and darkness, between warmth and cold, but they could in no way tell the difference between good and bad. Such a distinction would in fact have no meaning to them, and if they found their world dark, smelly, and cold they would have no basis for pronouncing it bad, simply because they would have no preference for any other kind of world.

THE EMERGENCE OF GOOD AND EVIL

Thus far, then, there is no good and no evil; there is nothing but bare facts of this kind or that.

But now let us suppose a world, much like our own, except that it contains throughout its vastness just one sentient being, a man who, like ourselves, cannot only perceive what is contained in the world around him and make certain inferences, but one to whom what he finds makes a difference. Suddenly, with the introduction of just one such being, certain things in the world do acquire the aspect of good and evil. Those things are good that this one being finds satisfying to his needs and desires, and those bad to which he reacts in the opposite way. Things in the world are not merely perceived by this being, but perceived as holding promise or threat to whatever interests him. Thus, the things that nourish and give warmth and enhance life are deemed good, and those that frustrate and threaten are deemed bad. The distinction between good and evil in a world containing only one living being possessed of needs and wants arises, then, only in relation to those needs and wants, and in no way existed in their absence. In the most general terms, those things are good that satisfy this being's actual wants, those that frustrate them are bad.

Now, with this picture still before us, let us note two things that are highly significant for the problems before us. The first is that the judgments of this solitary being concerning good and evil are as *absolute* as any judgment can be. This man is, indeed, the measure of all things: of good things as good and of bad things as bad. Whatever he finds and declares to be good *is* good, and what he similarly finds to be evil, *is* evil. No distinction can be made, in terms of this solitary man, between what is merely good *for him* and what is good *absolutely*. Whatever is good for him *is* good absolutely; there is no higher standard of goodness. For what could it be? If good and evil in this world arise only in relation to this being's wants and needs, then what could it possibly mean to say that something satisfies these but is nevertheless bad, or that something frustrates them but is nevertheless good? There simply is nothing else, apart from these wants and needs, in terms of which good and evil can possibly be measured, or even exist.

The second thing to note is that, even though good and evil have emerged with the appearance in this world of a single man having wants and needs, no moral obligation has similarly arisen. The distinction between moral *right* and *wrong* has not yet come into the picture at all. That such a being should find something useful and agreeable and subsequently seize it, or find something threatening and shun it, is neither right nor wrong. Whatever he finds and wants is his for the taking, by a kind of natural right that is nothing but the absence of any natural wrong, and he cannot possibly have an obligation to undertake what would injure him, or even so much as make him the least uncomfortable. Although he can in this moral solitude create good and evil for himself, merely by his own declaration of what he finds things to be, he can in no way inflict them. For who could be his beneficiary or victim, besides himself? To whom could he owe any obligation to do anything? And by what standard, other than good and evil themselves, over which he is the sole judge, could any action of his be deemed right or wrong? He could, to be sure, fail to act in his own best interest, or even injure himself through neglect or stupidity, but this would be no wrong. It would only be neglect or stupidity, for which he would be accountable to no one. It would be as inappropriate to ascribe any moral responsibility to this solitary being as to the merest insect crawling through the grass.

Our next step, then, is to add another being like ourselves, another man with his own feelings, wants, and interests, and to suppose that the two who now inhabit our world have some interaction with each other. No new distinction between good and evil is introduced with the introduction of this new inhabitant, for that distinction emerged, complete and perfect, as soon as we assumed the existence of but one such inhabitant. With this small plurality of beings, it remains just what it was before. The first inhabitant deemed those things good that he found agreeable to his needs and purposes, and those things bad that threatened the opposite, and in this judgment he was absolutely correct. For him, the good and evil of things consisted of precisely such promise and threat to his interests. Such, accordingly, will it also be for our second sentient and goal-directed inhabitant. Those things will be good for him that promise fulfillment of his aims, whether grand or trifling, and those that threaten the opposite will be bad. In this judgment he, too, cannot err. For this will be precisely what the distinction between good and evil will mean to him, as it is what it means to the first; it will be the condition, and the only condition, of such a distinction being drawn by either of them. And we are not, it should be noted, here supposing any power of reasoning in either of our two beings. We do not suppose them to be appraising the various features of their common environment in terms of what they promise or threaten, and then *inferring* from such features that they have the moral qualities of good or evil. We do not even assume these two beings to be rational, though the picture is not altered in case they are. We only assume them to be sentient beings with needs, or in other words, beings who desire and shun, and can feel it when their needs are fulfilled, and when they are not.

THE EMERGENCE OF RIGHT AND WRONG

There was, we noted, no place for such ethical notions as right and wrong or for moral obligation, so long as we imagined a world containing only one purposeful and sentient being, although the presence of such a being was enough to produce good and evil. With the introduction of a multiplicity of such beings, however, we have supplied the foundation for these additional notions, for they are based on the fact that the aims or purposes of such beings can conflict. Thus, two or more such beings can covet the same thing. In that case each will deem it a good, but it can easily arise that not both can possess it, that its possession by one will mean deprivation for the other. The result is a conflict of wills, which can lead to a mutual aggression in which each stands to lose more than the thing for which they are contending is worth to either of them. Such a situation can produce a threat to life itself, for example, and without life all good and evil are reduced to zero.

There is, moreover, another side to the coin. For just as the wills of two purposeful beings can conflict, in the manner just suggested, so also can they coincide in a very significant way. That is, situations can arise in which each of two such beings needs the help of the other in order to attain what it wants, or to ward off some evil. They may, for example, be threatened by some force, animate or inanimate, that the strength of neither is sufficient to overcome, but from which their combined strength offers some hope of safety. Or again, each may find that he possesses in excess of his own needs something that the other requires. One, for example, may possess an excess of food, of which the other has none, while the latter one possesses an excess of the requirements for shelter, entirely lacking to the former. The possibility of mutual giving and taking thus presents itself, wherein each can benefit greatly at small cost to himself. Or again, two such beings may have some common end, such as the begetting of children, for which some sort of cooperation is needed by the very nature of things, and so on.

The supposition of a multiplicity of beings, each with its own needs and purposes, presents, in short, numberless possibilities for (1) conflict, and (2) cooperation. Possibilities of the first kind are loaded with the threat of evil, and those of the second kind with the promise of good, still thinking of good and evil in the sense already adduced—namely, as that which satisfies or fulfills, and that which frustrates felt needs and goals.

RIGHT AND WRONG AS RELATIVE TO RULES

If needs are to be satisfied and goals fulfilled, however, then situations of conflict and, particularly, situations of cooperation must be resolved in the context of *rules*, using the notion of rules in an extremely broad sense that encompasses any regular and predictable behavior. Thus, it becomes a "rule" that two or more such beings, faced with a common threat, shall abstain from attacking each other until that threat is overcome. It becomes another rule that they shall meet the threat together by combining their resources, inasmuch as acting in accordance with such rules will enable each to avoid what appears as an evil. When two such beings each covet the same thing, and not both can possess it, it may become a rule that it remains with him who first possessed it. The underlying basis for such a rule is that, if it is deregarded, the coveted thing may end up in the hands of neither, and that evils even greater than this, such as mutual injury or even death, may follow instead. When each of two such beings possesses an excess of what is sought by the other, a rule of trading becomes obviously advantageous to both. Through such behavior, the good of each is enhanced at no significant cost. The alternative is combat, in which each would be faced with the possibility of total loss.

Now it should be clear from this that by rules I do not mean rational principles of conduct, in the sense that it would require any powers of reason to discover them, much less do I mean principles that are set forth in any coherent writing or speech. They need not be things that are formulated at all. Rules, in the sense that I am now considering them, are nothing but *practices* or ways of behaving that are more or less regular and that can, therefore, be expected. They are, on the other hand, rational in this sense: such behavior offers promise, to those who behave in the manner in question, of avoiding evil and attaining good. Mutual aggression, for example, always presents the threat of great and unpredictable evil to each aggressor, and the possibility of such evil is almost certain to outweigh any possibility of good. To the extent, therefore, that some good can be ensured by a certain mode of behavior or, as I am using the term, by action in accordance with a rule, and that such behavior will remove the threat of evil contained in any situation of combat, then action in accordance with the rule is better than combat. In that sense, but only in that sense, is it more rational.

Suppose, for example, that among a certain people the practice arises that men, on approaching one another, extend a forearm with the palm of the hand open and exposed to view, each thus indicating that he is unarmed.

The gesture is recognized and acknowledged by each then grasping the other's open hand, that is, by shaking hands. Now here, clearly, is a rule, as I am using the term, even though it does not need to be formulated or embodied in any code. It is simply a regular mode of behavior. It has as its obvious purpose the avoidance of evil and the advancement of good and is in that sense, but that sense only, rational. It would be most treacherously violated by one who, extending his open hand of friendship, assaulted his greeter with a weapon concealed in his other hand. The treachery of this would consist in using the rule to promote the very evil the rule was meant to avoid.

THE WORLD AS IT IS

We have been imagining, then, a world, at first lifeless and barren, that gradually becomes occupied with beings having needs, feelings, and purposes. Until the appearance of the first such being that world contains no hint of good or evil, but both arise the moment he comes into the picture. With the multiplication of such beings, the possibilities of further goods and evils arise with the appearance of situations of cooperation and conflict. Good is increased and enhanced by the former and evil by the latter. Cooperation, however, and the safe resolution of conflict obviously require certain regular modes of behavior, or what I have called rules. These notions having been made tolerably clear, we can now refine and elaborate on the imaginary picture with which we began until it begins to resemble the world in which we actually live.

Thus, we can suppose that the multiplicity of sentient and purposeful beings by which our imaginary world is inhabited are people like ourselves, for we, too, are sentient and purposeful beings. We can suppose that those modes of behavior required for cooperation and the resolution of conflict situations become actual precepts, conveyed by one generation to the next, and that the most important of them come to be rules embodied in traditional literature for which people have a certain awe. They are, thus, passed from generation to generation, like the Ten Commandments of Scripture. Others come to assume the form of written laws, and various practical means are hit on for securing, as nearly as possible, the adherence to them on the part of all. Groupings are formed for the attainment of the maximum of good for some or all and the minimization of evil. Thus do societies arise, by their common adherence to rules that become more elaborate as the societies themselves become larger and more complex. The behavior required by such rules rises, by some degree or other, to that level we call civilized conduct; but the basic principle of those rules remains exactly what it was from the outset: the minimization of conflict and its consequent evil, and the maximization of cooperation and its consequent good.

All this is, of course, but a sketch, and a very superficial one, but no more is really needed for our present purpose, which is to explain good and evil and moral right and wrong.

How, then, do moral right and wrong arise? The answer is fairly obvious in the light of what has been said. Right is simply the adherence to rule, and wrong is violation of it. The notions of right and wrong absolutely presuppose the existence of rules, at least in the broad sense of rule with which we began. That two beings should fight and injure each other in their contest for something that each covets, and thereby, perhaps, each lose the good he wanted to seize, is clearly an evil to both. But in the absence of a rule of behavior—that is, some anticipated behavior to the contrary—no wrong has been done; only an evil has been produced. Given such a rule, however—for example, given the simple and rudimentary expectation that the thing in question shall be his who first took it—then a wrong is committed by the one who attempts to divest the holder of that good. The wrong comes into being with the violation of the rule, and in no way existed ahead of the rule. The same is, of course, true of right. If, for example, we presuppose no expectation that a good may be enjoyed in peace by whoever first seizes it, then, if another nevertheless, in the absence of any such rule, abstains from seizing that good from its first possessor, this potential aggressor has clearly fostered a good, simply by eschewing an evil. But he has in no way done "the right thing," for the notion of *right* conduct can have no meaning in the absence of some sort of rule. If you are tempted to say that this would-be aggressor has done something morally right, then you will find that all you mean is that you have produced an effect that was good. That is something entirely different. You also may be reading into a situation, in which, by hypothesis, there is no rule to which to adhere, certain rules of right and wrong that you have learned to respect.

– 10 –

THE COMMON GOOD

SINCE THE BIRTH of philosophical ethics, the aim of moralists has been to identify the greatest good for humanity, the *summum bonum*, and we have seen the results of some of these efforts. But instead of speaking of the greatest good, perhaps we might get further by considering what is the common good for actual people, that is, for groups of people living together. Such a group might be small or large, but it must in any case contain a multiplicity in order for the idea of a *common* good to have meaning. There is, in fact, no reason why it should not comprise everyone.

Goodness, itself, it has been suggested, is simply the satisfaction of needs and desires, or what can generally be described as the fulfillment of purposes. The *greatest* good for any individual can accordingly be nothing but the total satisfaction of his or her needs, whatever these may be. William

James expressed the same idea by saying that the greatest good for an individual man would be the satisfaction of every claim that he makes, the moment he makes it. Now this can of course be misleading, for it gives rise to the image of a man all of whose desires are fulfilled at once without requiring any effort or struggle on his part. What this overlooks, however, is that one need that virtually everyone shares is the need to struggle for whatever they achieve. A life of idleness, in which every wish was fulfilled the moment it was made, would not be a worthwhile life for the very reason that most of us need the kind of satisfaction that comes only as a result of our own effort. Taking this into account, however, the formula is quite unexceptionable. If, as it appears, good is whatever does in fact satisfy your feelings and felt needs—whatever these may be— then the greatest good can be nothing other than their total satisfaction, if this were possible. But because this is not possible, then your greatest *possible* good can be nothing else than the satisfaction of your desires, that is, of all your aims and purposes, to the extent that this is possible. The greatest good for humanity, in turn, will be the maximum satisfaction of everyone's desires, to the extent that this is possible. This is what is ultimately meant by the common good, and it suggests something at least more down to earth than the greatest good or the *summum bonum*.

Several things are to be noted in rendering this idea more clear, and the first is that desires are exceedingly variable. Beyond a few basic desires that are commonly shared, such as the almost universal desires for life, love, approbation, and so on, together with the elementary desires for nourishment, physical comfort, and the like, people have all sorts of different aims and purposes, both great and trivial. One, for example, wants to clear a woodland for its timber, whereas another wants to preserve it as a sanctuary for wildlife; one wants noise and music, whereas a neighbor craves quiet for reading and thought; one wants the warmth and affection of a family circle, whereas another cherishes the freedom of a single state; and so on, endlessly. As such examples show, our purposes are not only drastically diverse, but some are in mutual conflict, or are such that they can be satisfied only at the expense of another's dissatisfaction.

We shall consider the implications of this last point in a moment, but for now the next point is to be made that desires themselves, considered apart from their possible conflict with others, are neither good nor bad, and are therefore without moral significance. This is, of course, only a consequence of the conception of good and evil that has been set forth. If the goodness of anything consists of its capacity to satisfy any desire or purpose, and the evil of something of its capacity to frustrate such desire or purpose, then desires or purposes themselves can be neither good nor bad. The mere fact that a desire exists, that something is wanted, or that something is regarded as a goal, entails that the desire should be fulfilled or the goal achieved; that is to say, that such satisfaction would be a *good* for him who wants it. It matters not in the least what the desire is. It might be, as James expressed it, a desire for "anything under the sun."

CONFLICTS OF AIMS

But now we come again to the point just turned aside; namely, that actual felt desires or wants may conflict, and the possibility of such conflict can arise in several ways. First, two or more people might want the same thing, which might be such that not all can have or even share it. For example, two or more men might want to marry the same woman, or to possess the same house, or be chosen for the same office. Secondly, the fulfillment of one person's purpose might require the frustration of another's, even when their desires are not shared. Thus, one man may want to practice on his tuba, while his neighbor wants quiet for reading; or one may want to use a tree for its wood and another for its shade. And finally, a given person's desires may conflict with each other. Thus, a man might want to marry both Susan and Jane, but he cannot do both; one desire must yield to the other, or both be forfeited. Similarly, a man might want a home and family and at the same time crave the freedoms of bachelorhood. Or he may want to become an attorney, but begrudge the years of study needed to do so—and so on. There are doubtless numerous other ways in which desires may conflict, but these three are fairly obvious and will serve to illustrate the point that is to be made.

That point is just this: As soon as the conflict of desires of the sort just illustrated is taken into account, then it becomes possible to supply what was missing before, namely, a means of evaluating desires themselves as good or bad. For, clearly, those desires that can be satisfied at no cost in terms of frustration of other desires—or in other words, desires that in no way conflict with others—ought to be satisfied forthwith. The satisfaction of any desire being good, the satisfaction of such a desire is an unqualified good. This of course does not mean that it is a *great* good, for it may be quite trivial. It is, nonetheless, admixed with no evil. What, then, of desires or aims that conflict? Should these in every case be disregarded and, thus, remain unfulfilled? Clearly not, for the frustration of anyone's aim is precisely of what evil consists. Moreover, such conflict is usually between desires of different strength or importance, in which case the more pressing should be fulfilled at the cost of the lesser one. The reason is the same as before: such will result in a good, which is the satisfaction of desire, although in this case not an unqualified good. The desire of a family to dwell in safety, for example, may conflict with the desire of one of their children to play with explosives. The latter is plainly the lesser desire, as it conflicts with others of far greater importance; these, accordingly, should be fulfilled at the cost of the other. The desire of the child, although in no sense either bad or wrong in itself, is bad in relation to the more pressing desires of others, with which it conflicts. And to say that these other more pressing desires "should" be fulfilled means, as before, that more good will result from their satisfaction than from their frustration. The general principle remains the same if we consider other ways in which desires may conflict; for instance, the desires of one and the same man. Thus, a man who prizes life and health and has a keen wish to perpetuate them in himself may nevertheless have a felt desire for something that might gravely injure him. The example we have used before, of a thirsty man standing before a well that happens to be poisoned, is a case in point. It is perfectly clear, in such a case, which desire should yield and which should be fulfilled, the principle being, as before, the maximization of good at the least cost of evil. For it *is* an evil that anyone's thirst should remain unquenched, but a greater evil that life itself should be lost. These, it might as well be noted once more, are evils only in relation to his desires themselves.

THE NATURE OF THE COMMON GOOD

With these considerations before us, we can formulate better the concept of the common good. It is clearly what Mill had in mind by the greatest happiness for the greatest number, but that formula is defective in two serious respects: First, it suggests that there is some one thing called happiness, and even Mill identified this with pleasure. Happiness, if it is anything at all, is at least the satisfaction of one's aims and purposes, or what I have for brevity been calling the satisfaction of desire. It is, in fact, much more than this, as we shall eventually see. Desires themselves, however, are diverse and various beyond description, and so, accordingly, must your happiness differ from that of your fellows. Secondly, Mill's formula, as thus expressed, presents an ideal that is not even attainable. The greatest happiness of some might entail the very greatest misery of others, due to the type of conflict of aims that we have been considering. A better formulation of the idea of the common good, although still very general, would be this: The maximum fulfillment of all those aims that different people actually have, and the maximum satisfaction of their felt desires, whatever these may be, at the least cost—that is, with the minimum frustration of precisely the same aims and desires. This way of expressing it, it should again be noted, does not require us to appraise individual desires themselves with respect to whether they are good or evil, which no one has ever done or will ever be able to do. Concerning such desires we need only to know first, that they do in fact exist—that is to say, that some people actually have them—and secondly, whether they can be fulfilled without frustration of other actual desires that are felt even more pressingly.

This formulation enables us, as others, I believe, do not, at least to make some sort of beginning in appraising various institutions and states of affairs with respect to whether they do, or do not, promote the common good. For we can now approach such questions at the level of experience; we can look at various practices or institutions and, with some semblance of knowing what we are talking about, say whether they do or do not promote the fulfillment of the aims people actually have. We need at no point resort to any intuitions of good and evil, for these are defined in terms of actual aims and desires whose existence can to some extent be ascertained empirically. We need introduce no abstract considerations of duty, human dignity, and the like, for the concept of the common good is formulated entirely independently of these. We need not even take into account considerations of moral right and wrong, for these can be defined in terms of rules, and the presence or absence of rules is again something that can be empirically discovered. Rules themselves, moreover—that is to say, established and predictable practices—can be assessed with respect to the question whether or not they are in accordance with the common good. And finally, even though we must take into account the aims and desires we actually have, we are spared the impossible task of trying to distinguish, at the outset, which of these are and which are not morally acceptable or worthy. The determination of this becomes a *result* of our inquiry, empirically arrived at, rather than being a datum with which we begin, established by some kind of esoteric moral intuition or Platonic insight.

THE MORAL EVALUATION OF INSTITUTIONS

This can be illustrated with the example of slavery in America, familiar to all. The first thing to be observed, even by the most fervent opponent of slavery, is that this practice was a good, although not an unqualified one. The satisfaction of *any* interest or desire is a good—indeed, this is precisely what the goodness of anything is—and slavery did in fact promote the aims and interests that large numbers of men actually had. If this had not been true, the practice would never have taken root in the first place, nor would it have found any defenders when it was attacked. On the other hand, it was also an evil, although not an unqualified one. That is, it simultaneously served to defeat the aims and interests that large numbers of other men actually had, most manifestly those who were enslaved. If this had not been true, the practice would never have been attacked or even questioned. The picture that presents itself, therefore, is one of a conflict of interests, exactly of the sort already illustrated. The aims that men actually had were served by the practice, but only at the expense of the aims that other men actually had. The result is that slavery, like nearly all institutionalized practices, produced a mixture of good and evil. The next task is to try to ascertain which effect overbalanced the other.

Nothing is to be gained at this point, it should be noted, in appealing to any considerations of the moral rightness or wrongness of the practice. That is the lazy way out and solves nothing. The moral rightness or wrongness of anything is entirely relative to accepted rules of behavior, and without meaning except in relation to such rules. And there were, in fact, generally accepted, although incompatible, rules according to which each side to the controversy could and of course did legitimately claim the moral rightness for its position. In the first place, the institution of slavery was itself governed by an elaborate structure of rules, many of them embodied in valid civil law, and some even claiming the authority of religion and long-standing tradition. On the other hand, the institution stood condemned by other rules, which also claimed the authority of religion and of a long-standing tradition of democracy and egalitarianism. It was, then, perfectly hopeless to appeal to questions of rightness and wrongness, as this could settle nothing without an ultimate recourse to bloodshed, in which every participant would be driven to slaughter by a perfectly rational conviction of the rightness of his position and the moral blindness of his opponent. The view people took on this issue, with respect to moral right and wrong, was simply a function of which set of rules and traditions they chose to honor. And this, in turn, was decided for them by their antecedent conviction that their position was morally right.

They were, in short, not assisted at all by appealing to rules, but were instead blinded by them, and there then remained nothing to do but fight.

The task all the while, however, was simply to weigh good against evil to see which overbalanced the other. This, admittedly, is not simple, but it is at least an approachable task that presents some promise of shedding light on things.

The first step in the determination of this is of course simply to *count*, something that can be done without flaming oratory and without precipitating civil strife. That is, one can form some approximate idea of the numbers of those whose interests are served by the practice in question, and the numbers whose interests are foiled. This might not of course settle the matter, but it is an intelligent start. It might not settle the matter, because even if those whose aims are served should turn out to be more numerous, their aims themselves might be of lesser importance than the aims that are foiled. If, on the other hand, it is found that those whose aims are served are more numerous, and that these aims are in fact of equal or even greater importance than the aims that are frustrated, then this *does* settle the matter. The practice does produce more good than evil. That is its justification, the only justification it needs, and the only justification that can be given.

If, on the other hand, it is found that those whose aims are served are less numerous and, moreover, that these aims are themselves of smaller importance than the aims that are suppressed, then again the matter is settled. The practice produces much more evil than good, and in the face of this, no tradition, no rules, no laws, no men, and nothing under the sun can possibly justify it.

Or finally, let us suppose it is found that the number of those whose interests are served is very large in comparison with those whose interests are frustrated, but that the interests of the larger number are of small or even trivial importance in comparison to those of the smaller group. Here the outcome is far less clear-cut, but we are not left in total darkness. If the interests of the larger group are truly trivial in comparison to those of the smaller one, and if, in particular, the aims that are thus sacrificed are those that all or most people would recognize as the primary aims of everyone, then again it appears that the practice that produces such a result thereby produces more evil than good and is without adequate justification.

Other combinations are of course possible, and it cannot be denied that with respect to some it is far from clear what is the balance of good and evil. But it is not hopeless, for we are at least dealing with facts and not just with slogans and precepts. People can be counted, but their aims and desires cannot be weighed in any objective way, nor their relative strengths clearly assessed. Still, some judgment can be formed even on these matters, and that is at least better than importing into the picture absolutes and abstractions and appeals to moral imperatives, which can only lead to deadlock or war.

With respect to the example of American slavery, for example, it can be conceded at the outset that those whose interests were in some way or other served by the practice vastly outnumbered those whose interests were sacrificed. The former included everyone who benefited from it, however slightly. But when we look at those whose interests were disregarded, namely, at the slaves themselves, we see that their interests included their very basic and supreme ends: the interest in dwelling in freedom, in self-determination and inner pride, in founding a family that cannot be sundered at the will of another, of enjoying the fruits of one's own labor, and so on. It thus becomes fairly clear that, in terms of good and evil, the practice is not worth what it costs, taking all its effects into account. That is its evil, and the whole of its evil.

– 11 –

SOME FUNDAMENTAL QUESTIONS REVISITED

AT THIS POINT we should reconsider some of the basic questions that presented themselves earlier, to see whether the account thus far sheds more light on them than we were initially able to summon.

NATURE VS. CONVENTION

Probably the fundamental question of ethics concerns the status of its basic ideas. Are the distinctions between good and evil, right and wrong, and just and unjust discovered in the same way we discover the difference between hot and cold and male and female? Or are they, unlike these, simply distinctions that are invented, like the distinctions between married and unmarried, free man and slave, ruler and ruled? Human beings, we know, create

189

their own laws and customs and, no doubt, their religions—in short, their conventions. Are these modeled on any real distinction between right and wrong or between good and evil, or are these merely derived from the conventions?

The Greeks, as we have seen, never answered this question with one voice, but they certainly understood with enviable clarity what the question was and why it was important. Modern moralists, it seems fair to say, have with few exceptions done less well, most of them merely assuming an answer to it without really addressing themselves to the question. G. E. Moore, who for decades set the intellectual tone of philosophical ethics in several nations, declared the question "What is good?" to be the most fundamental and important question of moral philosophy; and after many pages of subtle distinctions he delivered his answer to this great question. The good, he gravely declared, is simply, *the good*, and that is the end of it.[1] It is probably fair to say that even the least moralist of antiquity had a better grasp of the problem than is displayed in that tautology.

If good and evil are natural qualities of things, then, as Plato rightly perceived, they must be highly elusive ones, yielding themselves to human understanding only after the most difficult and painstaking philosophical inquiry. Plato embraced this conclusion, and in his *Republic* he permitted students of philosophy to consider goodness and justice only after many years of philosophical training. Until then, he thought, they were insufficiently equipped with the knowledge and understanding to perceive them.

---

1. G. E. Moore, *Principia Ethica* (Cambridge University Press, 1956), pp. 3–14, 59–79.

The thing to see, however, is that both answers to the question are wrong. The distinction between good and evil is not a natural one that merely awaits discovery, nor is it purely conventional, in the sense that it is arbitrarily created by this or that culture. Good and evil, as such, form no part of the framework of nature, as do darkness and light, for they would find no place whatsoever in a world devoid of any living thing. At the same time, however, they do result, in a perfectly natural way, from certain facts of human nature that are evident to anyone, and along with them emerges every other moral distinction, such as right and wrong and just and unjust. And although these distinctions—right and wrong and just and unjust—do to some extent depend on human contrivance—because they arise only with the appearance of rules, which are man-made—they are not created capriciously or arbitrarily. They are always tailored, badly or well, to our perception of good and evil. And that distinction is not, even by the broadest meaning of the term, a human fabrication. Man is not the measure of *all* things, because he is not the measure of himself. That we are the kind of beings we are is a fact of nature, and it is from that fact that good and evil arise.

For it is a fact that we are, as I have expressed it, conative beings. It is a fact that, by nature, we have nerves, and are therefore capable of feeling; that we have desires, wants, and needs; and, in short, that we pursue ends of all sorts, both trivial and great. Virtually every moment of anyone's activity is aimed at something or other—at getting food, comfort, enjoyment, at building and removing, at getting something done. This is, indeed, the very nature of human activity.

When obstacles and threats to our activity are

encountered, we deem them bad, and when things that assist in our goal-seeking are discovered, we deem them good. The objects of our desires are also deemed good, as the objects of our aversions are deemed bad. There is, moreover, one general purpose that everyone normally has, and that is self-preservation and the enhancement of well-being in numberless ways. There is, perhaps, no metaphysical reason *why* any beings should be of this nature, but it is a fact that we are. Our activity is directed toward this persisting goal and, together with it, toward numberless subordinate goals that are exceedingly diverse from one person to another. And it is just in the light of this fact that we draw the distinction between good and evil in the first place. We regard those things as good that satisfy our conative nature, and bad, those that frustrate it. This is all that the distinction originally means, the very basis for even making the distinction to begin with. The distinction between good and evil could never have occurred to a race of beings incapable of pursuing any ends, who had no desires or aversions, and who had not, for example, even an aversion to the feeling of pain. To such beings, everything would appear simply as given, not as something to shun or pursue; and this, it should be noted again, would remain true, no matter to what degree they might be endowed with reason and intelligence. Reason, by itself, can discern no good or evil in anything, but the will detects it at once.

At this point it may be enlightening to contrast again the two crude pictures of human nature with which we began. Figure 2 roughly portrays human nature as the moral rationalist and defender of a true morality conceives it:

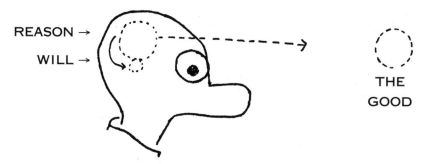

FIGURE 2. MORAL RATIONALISM

In this figure, your reason has a two-fold function. In the first place, it understands nature, which simply means that it is by your reason that you understand what is true, to whatever extent you do understand this. And incorporated in this understanding is the perception, however fallible, of the difference between good and evil. Thus, perceiving which things are good and which things are not, you direct your will to the pursuit of those that appear good and away from the things that seem bad. And this expresses the second function of reason: to *govern* the appetites and desires or—which is the same thing—the will, keeping it aimed at the good, insofar as this is possible, and away from the bad, to which it naturally tends. As we have seen, Socrates considered this conception of human nature so true and admirable that he deemed a man *unjust* to the extent that he lapsed from it. He supposed that the natural objects of appetite or desire are more often than not *bad*. The same idea is found in traditional Christianity and also was monumentally reinforced by Kant. Kant declared that nothing can be really morally worthwhile if it is at the same time satisfying to the will. The idea has, ever since, turned most moral philosophies quite upside down and seriously infected the attitudes even of people who are good.

Figure 3 crudely portrays human nature as I have described it, and I have called it the conception of moral voluntarism:

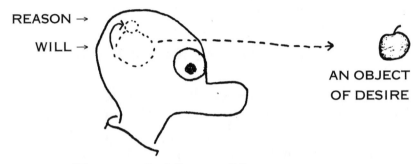

REASON →

WILL →

AN OBJECT
OF DESIRE

FIGURE 3. MORAL VOLUNTARISM

According to this picture, too, it is by your reason that you understand what is true, to whatever extent you do understand this. But embodied in such understanding are no *a priori* truths of morality. In fact, the understanding alone finds no distinction in nature between things that are good and things that are bad, because no such distinction exists independently of the will. Reason, accordingly, can in no way govern the will, directing it toward the attainment of what it perceives as good and away from what seems evil, for it lacks any such perception to begin with. As Figure 3 further shows, however, we will certain things; that is, we have desires and aims. There is no indication of why this is so; the picture only suggests that it is. And what we then perceive as assisting the will—that is, as satisfying our desires and aims—we pronounce good, and things that promise the opposite, we pronounce bad. But far from the reason *directing* the will toward whatever object it has—for example, toward self-preservation and the enhancement of one's well-being—the will by its very nature is directed to these things. No reason whatever can be given why it should be. It just is. And to the extent that anything can even metaphorically be described as being governed here, it is clearly the reason that is governed by the will. For it is the will that determines what you will declare to be good, and what you will pronounce evil. The end or goal of activity is set by the will, for to say that anything *is* your goal or the object of your desire is simply to say that it is willed. In this a man's reason has no voice whatsoever, and surely no power of veto. It is instead reduced to the humble office of devising the means to its attainment. If you are at all tempted to doubt this, ask yourself at what point in your life you first rationally derived the conclusion that the preservation and enhancement of your life was a thing to be desired—thus making your first discovery of this hitherto unsuspected good—by what line of reasoning you were led to that conclusion, and approximately how soon thereafter you enlisted your will to the pursuit of that goal. And then, having seen the nonsense of this, ask the same question concerning the rest of your interests, desires, and goals—your recurring interest in eating, for instance, or in sex, or your persistent desires for possessions, status, or power, in case you have any obsessions with these. It was surely with such considerations as these in mind that Hume made his famous and sometimes reviled comment that reason is, and ought to be, a slave to the passions and can pretend to no other office.[2]

---

2. David Hume, *A Treatise of Human Nature*, ed. L. A. Selby-Bigge (Oxford, 1888), p. 415.

JUSTICE

Socrates evidently thought that justice is something one should aim at, as a good in itself, and quite clearly repudiated the suggestion that the practice of justice might be honorable only as a means to avoiding evil. Plato thought in similar terms, considering it of subordinate importance that those who are just are also, as it happens, fairly happy. We have seen the same idea expressed by Kant, who claimed that a will governed solely by the sense of duty is an unqualified good, and the only unqualified good in nature, even though such a will may at times produce great sorrow and grief. At the extreme opposite in their opinions have been those many thinkers who have maintained that justice, and morality generally, are simply the products of convention and, hence, entirely relative to this. The justice of one society is the injustice of another, they have observed, and there is no true or natural justice against which such diverse conceptions of it can be measured.

It is important to note that my own account of things does contain a conception of true justice. But there is nothing particularly abstract or metaphysical about it, and far from its being any presupposition with which I begin, it is a result. It is not pretended that justice is anything good for its own sake. On the contrary, it is good as a means to the avoidance of evil and the pursuit of goodness, and that is the whole of its worth. It is conventional in the sense that it cannot exist apart from rules of behavior; but such rules are not arbitrarily made, nor do they spring ready-made from any god or king. They are themselves rules for the minimization of evil and the growth of goodness, and justice is simply the name for the most general principles embodied in such rules. The actual practice of justice can and does vary enormously from one culture to another, because the rules of conduct themselves vary, but from this it does not follow that justice is itself purely relative. For the rules of conduct, however variable, have generally the same purpose, which is primarily the avoidance of evil. This is something that is felt as the same everywhere, at least to the extent that we share common desires and aims.

We have noted that, although good and evil spring into being as soon as we assume the existence of sentient and purposeful beings, right and wrong do not. Right and wrong are distinctions that apply only to conduct, and such conduct must of necessity be conduct in relation to others. A solitary individual can neither commit any wrong nor perform any duty, for there is no one to hurt but himself, and similarly no one to benefit. If a solitary man injures himself, he acts from folly, imprudence, or stupidity; but he can hardly thereby commit any wrong. If he promotes his own well-being he acts from intelligence, prudence, or perhaps sheer good luck, but he can hardly be deserving of praise. It is perfectly obvious, however, how entirely this picture is altered as soon as his behavior affects *others*. As soon as we suppose people living together, so that what each does can affect the weal and woe of the rest, there arises the need for some kind of regular conduct, the very minimum expectation of which will be that each will refrain from injuring the rest. *Injury* does not consist merely in the infliction of bodily wounds, however, any more than *helping* consists merely in administering to the wounded. You are injured just to the extent that someone imposes obstacles to the pursuit of your needs and purposes; similarly, you are helped to the extent that someone renders positive assistance to these. The preservation of bodily integrity and physical well-being is an aim that virtually everyone shares but obviously it is not the only aim anyone has. If it were, then there would be little to distinguish us from amoebas. The satisfactions we seek, especially in a civilized society, are numerous and diverse beyond counting, and it is in terms of all of these that good and evil must be conceived. As human associations become larger and more complex, then, expanding from families to tribes and eventually to whole nations, rules of behavior become similarly more numerous and complex, but they continue to spring from the same source. That source is the human perception of the utility and, up to a certain point, the absolute necessity of the governing principle: *Do not hinder, but help.* This, accordingly, is the principle of justice, which has both a negative and a positive content. It is a natural principle, in the sense that it is not the mere product of convention, or one that could just as easily have been otherwise. Far from being the product of convention, it is the foundation and source of convention itself—that is, of the written and unwritten rules by which this or that society is governed. Without it there could not even be a society, or even so much as a family. Hence, without it, there could be no social conventions. It is not, however, a natural principle in the sense that it exists as a part of the fabric of nature, independently of human nature, waiting only to be found by philosophers. For apart from the fact that we exist and have needs and desires, it would have no meaning at all.

From this we can see, too, how the practices of different groups can differ so greatly without our being tempted to conclude, as some persons have, that the basic principles of justice are similarly diverse and purely human inventions. For, in general, there are often numerous means to one and the same end, no matter what it is, and when the conditions under which such an end is pursued are extremely different from one place and time to another, the means to its attainment are often of necessity different. Thus, from the fact that we all seek nourishment, it hardly follows that we must eat the same things; and if, moreover, the same food is not available to all, it follows that of necessity we will not. In a similar way, different cultures have evolved quite different means of pursuing what they variously conceive as the common good, some of which, of course, work better than others. Hence, one cannot consider practices and rules, independently of their intended results in terms of a whole society, and simply pronounce them just or unjust, morally right, or morally wrong. That a given society should, for example, destroy its own members when they have reached an advanced and feeble age is, in itself, no more just or unjust, right or wrong, than that the same society should subsist largely on the fat of sea mammals. The question of whether such a practice is just relates to whether it does or does not promote the common good of that society. The answer to the question may not be obvious, but the chances are that it does serve the common good. Otherwise, one would need to find some adequate explanation for the survival of the practice. In any case, it is no abstract question of philosophy, but a straightforward question of fact.

The answer to it is to be found, if at all, not in any *a priori* theory of morals or any abstract system of the principles of justice, but more likely in the researches of social anthropology.

CAN VIRTUE BE TAUGHT?

Socrates often questioned whether virtue can be taught, and even though most of his interlocutors seemed to think that it can, he was greatly puzzled not to find established teachers who were recognized experts in the subject. He seems to have decided that although it cannot be taught in the ordinary way, it can be learned by a process of remembering the true principles of justice that were divinely imparted during the prenatal existence. Plato somewhat modified this conception of things, but not altogether. He appears to have believed that although ordinary people can acquire the unreflective habits of just conduct, the ultimate principles of justice are vouchsafed only to philosophers, from whose ranks rulers must accordingly be drawn. And thinkers have been enchanted by this fond notion ever since. Kant believed that the metaphysical principles of morality are knowable *a priori* and, hence, within the ken of every rational being. He seems not to have been particularly struck by the fact that these metaphysical principles, as they unfolded themselves to his own rational faculty, had a marked resemblance to the austere principles of Christian morality that he had derived from his mother in childhood. Mill thought that the principles of morals and justice pretty much followed from what he took to be the fact that pleasure is alone good for its own sake. Learning virtue, then, is essentially a matter of seeing that this is a fact—that is, of removing the prejudices that blind men to its truth. I think it is not unrealistic to say that none of these thinkers had a very convincing answer to the question whether virtue can be taught.

So let us address ourselves anew to this question, in the light of what has been said. Can virtue be taught? If this means can people learn to live according to the principle of justice, then the answer is that they can, because most in fact have, at least to some degree. That is to say, people can learn to abstain from injuring their fellows and, on top of this, learn to help them, and this does express the fundamental principle of justice. We see, then, that on this question, Protagoras was at least on the right track. Justice means, first of all, certain ways of behaving, and such behavior is indeed learned. It is not imparted by nature, for human beings have, by nature, a certain tendency to behave in contrary ways. And they learn such behavior in the way Protagoras described: by precept and example, praise and blame from others, reward and punishment, and by the traditions of their culture by which they are constantly nourished. If we fail to find the teachers of virtue or justice, then the reason is, as Protagoras suggested, not that they do not exist, but that they are everywhere. The basic principle of justice, however, together with all the numberless principles and practices to which it gives birth, is no arbitrary fabrication. On the contrary, it has its root in nature itself; that is to say, in certain features of human nature that no one ever contrived, but that are simply given. The basic fact of human nature that gives rise to this principle is that we are, by nature, appetitive or goal-seeking beings for whom, because of this, things in the world can take on the aspects of good and evil.

This view of things is no doubt oversimplified, but it is important at least in what it denies. If by the principle of justice you mean some rational principle, the apprehension of which will enable us to direct our energies to its realization in the world, then it would appear that no such principle can be learned, even by philosophers, because it evidently does not exist. We can learn, and act on, certain particular rules and principles for the avoidance of evil and the enhancement of good—the Ten Commandments, for example, and other general precepts that have been found in time to work well. But we cannot in any similar way learn good and evil ourselves. These we can only find. We find them through our experiences of satisfaction and rejoicing, on the one hand, and frustration and pain on the other; they can in no way be spelled out in advance by philosophy and thereby imparted to minds that do not know them. A philosopher like Mill might think that, in the light of this, he can declare satisfaction and rejoicing to be good and pain and frustration evil, as though these were things existing in their own right, but this is really no achievement at all. It only calls attention to the fact that we react to what we find in the world, this fact then being formulated in a general philosophical proposition that appeals to the reason.

Two Shortcomings

It should nevertheless be noted, and in fact emphatically declared, that the account of things thus far is by no means complete. Indeed, it has left virtually untouched two things that it is imperative to know if we can. The first is the answer to the question "What is a genuinely moral person?" And the second is the answer to the question "What is our true good?"

It might appear that what I have said rules out any answer to these questions, but in fact it does not. Both questions can, I think, be answered in terms of the theory of good and evil that I have outlined. In fact, I think that they can be answered in no other way.

It is not enough to know, in the general way I have so far proposed, what justice is. We need also to know, if we can, what human virtue is, and what ideal of human nature we should set for ourselves. That is, we need to know what is a truly good person—whether, for example, such a person is one whose inner life is a harmony, as Socrates sometimes suggested; or one who is prompted solely by his perception of duty, as Kant thought; or one who is altruistic, as Mill supposed; or something else. The clue to this, I suggest, lies in what I briefly alluded to as our capacity for what I called sympathetic projection.

Again, it is not enough to know only in the general way I have outlined what good and evil are. We need also to know, if we can, what is really good. It clearly is not enough to say that this is what we find satisfying in relation to the goals we happen to have; for we can still ask, "What does yield such satisfaction? Is there anything that, if we but possess it, our life is filled with goodness, and if we lack it, our life is empty?" The hedonists thought pleasure to be such a thing, but they were, as it seems to me, quite mistaken. Kant thought that a dutiful will is the thing we should aim at, but this, too, seems quite wrong, for all the reasons I have given. I do still believe, however, that there is such a good.

These two questions will be central to all the discussion remaining. What has been said up until now is in fact an extensive introduction to them, for these are the ultimate questions of ethics: What is human virtue? What is our highest good?

PART THREE

HUMAN GOODNESS

– 12 –

CASUISTRY

I F THERE IS a true morality, embodying true general principles of right and wrong, then it ought to be possible to apply them to particular actions to see whether such actions do or do not possess the moral quality of rightness. Thus, if among the various alternative actions open to one, the *right* action will be the one that will, more than any of the others, promote the greatest happiness for the greatest number, then we can determine which is the right action by seeing, as best we can, which has that tendency. Or on the other hand, if a right action is one that is prompted by duty, and it is one's duty always to so act that one could will the maxim of his action to be a universal law for all rational beings, then again, one can determine whether his action is right by seeing whether it is so motivated; and so on.

This is the procedure of *casuistry*, which can be

defined as the determination of the moral quality of particular actions by the subsumption of them under true general rules or principles of morality. It is almost invariably the approach most persons take to moral problems, whether they know the name for it or not, and most moralists seem to presuppose its legitimacy. Most moral philosophers seem to think it extremely important to find and enunciate some ultimate principle of moral rightness, the implication being that such a principle can then be used as a criterion for the moral praiseworthiness or blameworthiness of particular actions.

Here I am going to show that such a procedure is quite impossible, and that the customary approach to moral decisions is, therefore, fundamentally mistaken. What are appealed to as moral principles are usually rationalizations for courses of action decided on quite independently of any such principle. Casuistry is, in fact, always a putting of the cart before the horse, for the general principles in terms of which people try to justify their conduct are themselves only justified by the assumed rightness of that conduct itself. There seems to be no exception to this. It becomes perfectly evident when we discover that in case of a clear conflict between a given course of action that seems wholly right and proper on its own merits and some principle that we had hitherto thought to be true and unexceptionable, it is the principle that is modified or abandoned, rather than the action itself.

More particularly, we shall see that:

1. There is no general moral principle declaring a certain kind of action to be always right or always wrong that cannot be shown to have an exception, even in the eyes of those who declare their allegiance to that principle.

2. Such an exception to the principle cannot (obviously) be made on the basis of the principle itself and must, therefore, be made either (a) on the basis of some still higher principle, or (b) on some other ground.

3. It cannot be made on the basis of some still higher principle, for such a principle will itself, under (1), admit of exceptions, even in the eyes of those who uphold it.

4. Exceptions to general principles are, therefore, made on some other ground, and that is what I shall call ordinary human feeling.

5. Because such ordinary human feeling is, therefore, what finally settles the matter anyway, the moral principle was superfluous from the outset, contributing nothing to the judgment of whether a given course of action is right or wrong.

That, somewhat formally stated, is the thesis, and it now needs to be filled out and made clear.

THE FUTILITY OF JUSTIFYING CONDUCT

In the meantime, the importance of this claim should be well understood. For if what I am saying is correct, it follows that the usual, typical, and normal approach to questions or morality is basically wrong. When a man appears, perhaps to himself as well as to others, to have given a moral justification for a certain course of conduct by showing that it accords with some general principle of rightness, he has in fact done nothing of the sort. The principle to which he appeals is itself in need of justification, and (here is the rub) nothing under the sun can possibly justify that principle unless the course of action in question is itself seen to be right independently of that principle. When one appeals to a moral principle in justification of his decision, he only succeeds in changing the subject; he in no way justifies anything. He changes the subject to the principle itself, which now comes under scrutiny, and if, as is typical, this principle is "justified" by still another principle, then he only manages to change the subject still another time. This, I believe, is the basic reason why discussions of morality are so invariably inconclusive and no one's mind is really changed about anything. They involve a perpetual jump from one subject to another, getting farther and farther away from the issue originally raised, without hope of settling anything. We can also find here the basis for a very common illusion about moral problems: namely, that the answers to moral problems are very difficult to reach. Indeed they are, if they are sought in this way, for *that* kind of answer does not even exist. Still, people simply assume that the only allowable moral justification of an action must be in terms of some moral principle, and plenty of philosophers reinforce this assumption. Moral discussion therefore weaves tortuously from principle to principle, going about in circles, getting increasingly remote from the issue at hand, in a vain search for "the answer." Insofar as the answer exists at all, however, it lies right under one's nose, in the very action itself, and cannot possibly exist anywhere else. It is as if a man were to set forth from his cottage in search of his son, getting farther and farther away and still with nothing but misleading clues, until he finally gave up and came home to find the youngster in bed.

SAMPLES OF CASUISTRY

Let us consider some typical examples of casuistry.

Sample 1. A man of military age decides to resist a summons to serve; he will go to jail first, or perhaps flee the country. Why? "Because killing is wrong" (the appeal to a principle). Does he mean *all* killing is wrong—for that is what the principle seems to assert—such that one may not innocently swat a mosquito that is biting him, for example? This he dismisses as pettifogging. Obviously, what he is talking about is killing *people*. This is what is wrong, and because serving in war might oblige him to do it, he will, in obedience to his conscience, resist serving. (Here, it will be noted, "conscience" comes into the picture and plainly means nothing more than allegiance to a principle.) So the principle— and it is a slightly new one—is that it is always, without exception, wrong to kill any *person*. Then one may not drive a car, even with due care, over any considerable distance on crowded highways, or build great bridges or tunnels for human convenience, or fly in airplanes, because all such activities clearly risk life, and in fact take great tolls of it each day? This he again dismisses as pettifogging—he was not talking of that sort of thing. What he meant was the *deliberate* taking of human life—shooting at people, and that sort of thing. That is what is morally wrong, and is always so. So the principle, it must not be overlooked, has been changed still again. At this point the discussion can go in either of two directions, each of which will, in its own way, get us a bit further from the question at hand. First, one can seek a definition of "deliberate," which will conveniently serve to rule out what the man wants

to rule out while preserving what he wants to preserve—a definition, for example, that will enable one
to say that driving down crowded highways is not
deliberate, whereas marching off to boot camp, the
alternative being jail, is. Or secondly, one can skip
all that and look at the new principle here. Suppose
we go in the second direction. Here someone will
say, "What if a madman is approaching your wife
and children with a knife, bent on cutting them to
pieces, and you can only stop him by shooting at
him?" Or, perhaps, "What if your wife were pregnant, but in such a way that her life could only be
preserved by an abortion?" Or other cases of that
sort that are, of course, proposed as the *deliberate*
taking of human life. Now the challenge is to modify
the principle still once more, thus producing what is
really a new principle—and so on and on. But here
is the thing to note: At every stage of this attempted
justification, a moral principle, already enunciated,
is modified for the obvious purpose of *ruling out*
those cases to which it *does not apply*. And why does
it "not apply" to these? Not, obviously, because
they do not in fact fall under it, for they do. If
killing is wrong (period), then killing a mosquito is
wrong. The principle is thought not to apply to
these cases because they are *not* considered morally
wrong. It is thought to be no sin to kill a mosquito,
drive a car with due care, or (perhaps) even permit
an abortion in some circumstance. The principle
was not *meant* to cover things of this sort. What it
was *meant* to cover is the thing with which we began:
going off to war. But now look at what has happened. It is assumed that we already know, without
appealing to any principle, that certain things are
not wrong. Moreover, someone seems to be assuming,

before he even has any principle to justify it, that something *is* wrong, and the only job then is to tailor some principle to show why it is wrong. This is the whole course of the discussion. Something is just assumed to be wrong and other things not wrong, quite independently of any principles of right and wrong, and then the whole discussion is aimed at finding some principle that will *fit* what is thus already assumed. This is not the justification of anything. It is at best a game of definition, and at worst, pure rationalization.

At this point the question should honestly be faced: If we already know that certain things are *not* wrong, and if someone thinks he already knows that something, not agreed to by others, *is* wrong, then just how are these things known? Not, obviously, by the light of any moral principles, for no principles were suggested, and certainly none were needed, for the former, and every principle proposed for the latter was immediately proved to be inadequate. Indeed, what the whole discussion turned on was not the justification of any course of action in the light of some principle, but the very opposite; that is, the justification of the principle itself by whatever modifications and amendments seemed required, in the light of various actions antecedently thought to be right or wrong.

Sample 2. This time we shall start, not with some proposed course of action, but with a moral principle that is thought to be fairly secure. We shall then see what happens to the principle when the attempt is made to apply it to difficult cases. Here the point will be to illustrate how a principle, which is supposed to provide the very criterion of right and wrong, is admitted to have exceptions, even by those sworn to uphold that principle. If this is so, then it will show that some criterion *other* than the principle is the one that is really at work.

Let the principle then be the commandment "Thou shalt not kill." Let us grant at once that what is intended by this principle is that one may not, without moral guilt, deliberately and with premeditation take the life of another human being, and furthermore that no considerations of practical advantages to others can morally justify such an act.

Now it is pretty clear that such a principle, if rigidly adhered to, is going to have some very real and large consequences in some situations. Let us consider, then, a hospital administered by a church that is sworn to uphold that commandment—not merely to respect it, in the sense of paying lip service to it, but actually to decide difficult cases by applying the principle without any exception. In such a hospital no nurse or physician will intentionally administer to any patient any substance that might precipitate or hasten that patient's death. Now if a medication seems called for that might, admittedly, shorten life, but it is administered for some other purpose—for the alleviation of pain, for example—then such a course is perhaps not forbidden, because the purpose or intention of the medication is not to hasten death, but rather, to alleviate pain, which is a permissible end. What is forbidden is the deliberate hastening of death, even though the interests of others and even those of the patient might greatly be served by such action. One could not, for example, take the life of a patient in order to relieve the workload of the nurses. And of course a terminal disease will provide no exception. If a patient is clearly approaching death day by day, and there is no hope whatsoever of reversing this course, then his family might, indeed, wish profoundly that the disease and its suffering might not be prolonged. But if such a wish is expressed as a request that his life be shortened, it cannot be honored, and the moral justification for refusal will be the principle: One may not deliberately take the life of another, even if the interests of others would greatly be served by such action. In short, murder is wrong. And finally, of course, abortion of pregnancy is ruled out on the same principle. Even though the pregnancy may have resulted from rape or from incest, or there may be clear evidence that it is seriously abnormal, such that the resulting birth will be grossly deformed, the prohibition of murder will be followed. A child, although unborn, is already human. It does not await the light of day or the first drawing of breath to become a human being, although of course it is not fully developed. The rule thus becomes, in such cases, that one may not deliberately take the life of the child, even though the interests of others—of the mother herself, for example—would be greatly enhanced by that step.

The principle appears, then, to admit of no exception. It can be applied in all situations, and what is forbidden will stand out very clearly as morally wrong. One will, accordingly, have a *moral* justification for his conduct whenever it falls under that principle, and the principle is adhered to.

So it seems, but now let us look again. Suppose the hospital is subjected to aerial bombardment; is one not permitted to shoot back? Well, it will be said, this (obviously) puts the whole thing into a new dimension. The principle was not meant (note) to condemn war, as such, nor was it meant (note again) to apply to every case of self-defense, or the defense of things one is sworn to protect. Now it will be noted that already exceptions are being made, but what must be particularly noted is that they are *not* made on the basis of that principle. How can they be, when they are exceptions to the principle? What has happened here is that a certain course of action is assumed to be permissible, quite apart from this or any other principle, and it is then simply declared that the principle was not *meant* to rule it out. Of what final use, then, was the principle anyway? And may not one then declare, with equal justification (and lack of it), that the principle was not meant to rule out abortion or euthanasia either?

Let us, then, stay within the dimension in which the principle is declared to have no exception, the relatively narrow dimension involving only the care of persons consigned to hospital treatment. We suppose a case of ectopic pregnancy, in which the embryo becomes lodged, and begins to develop, within the fallopian tube. Now in such cases the fetus cannot develop and be born; it will inevitably die and abort itself, sooner or later. In the meantime, however, there is grave danger to the mother, for she is exceedingly likely to perish unless an abortion is performed promptly. *Now* what shall we do in the light of the principle that one may not deliberately take the life of another, even though this would greatly serve the interests of others, or in the light of the more particular principle, that one may not take the life of the unborn child?

The course of action actually taken in such cases is, of course, abortion, although this was allowed to become a policy only after the most tortuous casuistry of theologians, who were confronted with the impossible task of maintaining the authority of a principle while declaring that it does not always apply. What actually determines that this type of case constitutes an exception to the principle is no moral principle at all, even though one could perhaps be contrived. It is nothing but ordinary common sense and human feeling. If the result of doing nothing is going to be the loss of *two* lives, whereas one life can be saved by taking the other, soon destined to be lost anyway, then one needs no moral principle to discover the course of action to take. Common sense produces its verdict, and no moral principle whatever, from whatever source it may issue, overrules it. On the contrary, as soon as the principle is discovered to conflict with what is so plainly seen to be not wrong, then it is the principle that yields. If one then contrives some still "higher" principle that will reconcile the contradiction between moral principle and common sense, then he does not, as he may imagine, preserve moral principles after all; he only conceals his rejection of them.

Sample 3. I shall now render two descriptions of the same case. The first description will be a general one, in which a series of events is correctly described, but not in detail. The second will simply fill in the details.

The general description is this: A man came into possession of a very small human being. He nurtured it for a time, with great devotion and care, but then after a while discovered that it was developing quite abnormally, whereupon he deliberately destroyed it.

Now, with only that before us, let us ask: Did the man commit a murder? Did he do something morally wrong? It seems quite clear that, if the description of what happened is true, the first answer is Yes, and most persons would be inclined to answer the other in the same way. Now why? Because the action fits the definition of murder, and there is a general moral principle that murder is morally wrong.

The more detailed description of the same set of events is this: A medical researcher succeeded in fertilizing a human ovum in his laboratory, in a dish. The ovum began to develop, in a quite normal way, and this development proceeded for a considerable time, upward of three weeks, at which time serious abnormality became quite apparent under magnification. The researcher then flushed the contents of the dish into the sink.

Now the answers to our two questions are not so apparent. Hardly anyone will say that a murder was committed, and hence a moral wrong, even though some might object to such an experiment being undertaken to begin with, which is of course another question altogether.

What is significant, however, is the reasoning by which people are now apt to counter their original verdict. It was not, they say, really a human being at all. It was not large enough. Or it was not conceived in a natural way. Or it did not look like the usual human being. Or it had not yet begun to draw breath, or to move, or whatnot. But here the thing to note is that an effort is being made to *define a term (human)* in such a way as to preserve the second verdict of innocence of murder, without in any way appearing to unsettle the moral principle that gave rise to the first verdict. (It is perhaps worth noting that, even in the first very general description, it was conceded that the human being was "very small," and nothing was said concerning whether it was or was not normally conceived or how it looked to the eye.) Surely it would be more honest to put the matter like this: Technically, a living human being, although a minute one, was deliberately destroyed; hence, technically, a murder was committed, according to a perfectly good definition of murder. Under these bizarre circumstances, however, murder is not really wrong, notwithstanding the moral principle.

The other approach, involving finding a definition of human that will enable us to arrive at what is for all practical purposes the same conclusion while still appearing to preserve the moral law, is the one most persons feel somehow obliged to pursue, and it is not hard to see why. It is simply assumed that the moral principle has got to be true, and that no exception should be granted. One thus feels compelled to find some way of describing the exception, so that it will not be an exception.

It will not work, however, as can be seen from the following. Let us suppose that the abnormality is discovered a bit later on. Suppose that this child, conceived in a dish, develops fairly normally for about three hundred days and then begins to draw breath. It turns out to be a boy, and a few months later the first tooth appears, a few months after that he begins to walk, and to say a few words—"daddy" and that sort of thing. But *then*, at that still undeveloped stage, abnormality is discovered—one ear is found to be very distorted, and he appears deaf in that ear. So at that point, being still very small, he is destroyed. *Now* who will say he was not "really" a human being—that he was too small, or not conceived in a natural way, or did not look (quite) like normal human beings? Here, surely, our original verdict still stands. A murder was done, and the size, shape, manner of conception, and so on, of whoever was killed are quite plainly irrelevant. They were as irrelevant before. A human life was taken in either case, even though, in neither case, was it a life that was fully developed. But in the first case this was not, as then seemed quite obvious, morally wrong. Of course some would, at this point, revise this verdict and conclude that even this was murder *and hence wrong* after all. This shows how desperately one wants to cling to a moral principle, at whatever cost.

THE SIGNIFICANCE OF THESE EXAMPLES

Now it is important not to lose sight of the philosophical issue these examples were meant to exhibit. What we are concerned with is not whether it is sometimes morally permissible to take human life. We are not discussing the morality of war, abortion, or the like. In fact, the issue before us now is no moral one at all. It is a purely philosophical one, expressed in the claim that there is no moral principle, whatever it might be, that will not be admitted to have some exception, even by those sworn to uphold it. Such an exception is made, it appears, not on the basis of the principle itself, which is plainly impossible, nor on the basis of any other principle, but on the basis of common sense or ordinary human feeling. More specifically, it is made in the light of the practical consequences of one's actions, and how these affect the deepest interests of those involved. Nor is this to propose still another criterion of morality: namely, that an action is right if its consequences are good. No such claim has been made. On the contrary, I have suggested that there is *no* principle, generality, or rule whatever that will guide one to the "right" action. Even to put matters in those terms—in terms of what is the right as opposed to the wrong action—is to invite all over again an exercise in casuistry, and it is the entire enterprise of moral casuistry, on whatever terms it is conducted, that is declared to be impossible. The very nature of such an approach precludes its ever giving any knowledge of what is right or what is wrong, for it must at every step presuppose that we already know this, at least in certain clear and "obvious" cases.

THE FUNCTION OF PRINCIPLES

From this it of course does not follow that moral rules and principles have no function or use, or that they should be scorned. It only follows that they cannot be used in the way that is so often attempted: to grind out "answers" to moral problems. It is not merely that, when so used, they work badly; they do not work for that purpose at all. The question of whether a given course of conduct is or is not morally right—that is, does or does not conform to a moral principle—is not, contrary to what is generally supposed, the basic question at all. It cannot be, because it cannot be answered. You can find, quite easily, whether a given action does or does not conform to a rule; but this never, by itself, tells you whether the action is morally right, wrong, or indifferent. The principle itself can find no justification except in the rightness of the actions that fall under it, and when tested in that way, no such principle is unexceptionably true. We must always, in any case, first find what we should do, and after that see whether this does or does not agree with any principle. The principle, accordingly, can never tell us what we should do. If we did not somehow know that already, we would have no way whatever of knowing what principles to embrace.

Moral principles are nothing but conventions, but they have the real and enormous value to life that conventions in general possess. They help us to get where we want to go. Without them social life would be impossible, and hence any kind of life that is distinctively human. Their justification is, therefore, a practical one and has nothing to do with moral considerations in the abstract. The moment such a principle ceases to have that value, the moment its application produces more evil than good, then it ceases to have any significance at all and ought to be scorned. Nothing is achieved, other than those dexterous feats of intellectual dishonesty called casuistry, by paying homage to the principle while redefining all the terms necessary to abate its effects. It is far simpler and more honest to declare: Here the principle ceases to work; let us cast it from view; we owe it nothing, and it is not going to coerce us.

The purely practical basis and the justification of rules of conduct are very obvious in the case of those that have not been so hallowed by age as to acquire in our minds the status of moral principles. Rules governing the movement of vehicular traffic are good examples. There is, for example, no ultimate moral principle from which it can be derived that cars should proceed on the right lane rather than the left of the highway. Countries that follow the opposite practice are not censured in our eyes. All that matters is that there be *a* rule, and the reason it matters is very obvious. General adherence to the rule enables people, quite literally, to get where they want to go. The rule minimizes hindrances, obstacles, and danger. It is for this reason, and this reason only, that it ought to be followed; its practical justification is its moral justification, and the whole of it. When, accordingly, circumstances arise such that adherence to the rule would cause more harm than good, its whole basis is swept away and it ought then to be disregarded. This is recognized by all in the case of an ambulance, under certain conditions, on an urgent mission. The driver of such a vehicle would be a fool who deemed it an unexceptionable principle to drive always in the manner prescribed by the rule, even though it was obvious that, in some situations, this would produce great harm. He would be no less a fool if he cast about for some higher principle to justify every departure from it. The only "principle" involved is a practical concern for human welfare. It is the only justification for the rule to begin with, and no other justification is required for departing from it, provided such a justification for the departure actually exists.

The case is no different with what we have come to think of as *moral* rules and principles, except that these are much older, have acquired the venerability bestowed by time, and have for the most part become embodied in religion. The rules against murder, adultery, bigamy, and so on have an obvious practical basis. Like traffic rules, they enable people to get where they want to go, with the minimum of hindrance and danger, although in not so literal a sense. "Enabling people to get where they want to go" means, here, enabling them to fulfill their various aims and purposes in such a way as to hinder as little as possible the pursuits of others. All such rules prohibit certain ends, or the means to them, in order that other more widespread and important pursuits may flourish. The general utility of the rule against murder, for instance, is too obvious to belabor. The utility of the prohibition of adultery and bigamy is hardly less obvious. Such rules tend, although not infallibly, to protect home life, in which most people have a deep interest, as well as the interests of children. As with all rules, however, they do not always work. Adherence to them can sometimes produce more harm than good, and in such circumstances the basis for adherence evaporates. It is probably the reluctance to face this fact that has led people to suppose that such rules have some origin other than practical utility. It is, once one has become accustomed to it, easier to follow the rule than to depart from it. It gives you a sense of security and innocence and relieves you of the necessity to think or to make difficult decisions. People accordingly invent other sources for the rules, saying, for example, that they are delivered by God, or that they are derived from some eternal Moral Law.

Does a wise person, then, deal lightly with rules and conventions, following or departing from them as he or she pleases?

Surely not. A general adherence to rules that is not slavish, unthinking, and mechanical, even in situations in which there seems to be no practical point to it, is perhaps a virtue, although certainly a minor one. It is by such general adherence to rules, just because they are rules, that social life is made regular and predictable, and this is itself a considerable source of security. If the members of any group know what the rules are and in general comply with them, then human relationships are enlivened and relieved of friction and uncertainties. This does not imply, however, that rules, even though one chooses to view them as principles of morality, are to be respected for their own sake and adhered to mechanically; for it always remains possible that the violation of a rule on a given occasion—the violation, if one likes, of a "fixed" moral principle—will still produce more good than harm. Putting the matter graphically, you should really think twice before committing a murder, just as you should think twice before going through a red light. Someone of very dull understanding might take this to mean that murder is considered to be no more significant than a traffic violation, but one of more sense will not fail to see its true meaning. The rules involved here have, certainly, not the same importance, but the justification of both is identical, and in neither case does that justification always hold.

There is a strong tendency in people, particularly in those who think a great deal, to prize consistency above ordinary human goodness. Such persons are apt to extend consistency beyond thought and opinion to conduct itself, and then, almost before you realize what has happened, you find them *equating* human goodness with consistency of behavior—that is, with acting on principles. It is in such a mind that casuistry flourishes, in spite of its inherent defects. Moral principles can become, in such a mind, veritable tyrants, guiding one into courses of conduct in which no fine conscience or

good sense can find the slightest merit. The actions
of such a person have in their favor only this, that
they are *consistent* with the rest of his actions, or in
other words, that they fall under some rule. But
clearly, it is perfectly possible for a truly good person
to pursue one course of conduct one day and the
very opposite course the next, enhancing the goodness in the world both times. It is hardly a justification for any action that it resembles one that was
done yesterday, or indeed, that it resembles those
one has done all his life. Suppose one were to say,
"Yes, I can see that what I am about to do might be
a bit cruel on this occasion, if one puts it in those
terms; still, there *is* the moral principle to consider,
and it clearly obliges me to act in this way." Surely
one does not detect here any expression of human
goodness. One detects only consistency.[1] Worse than
this, such devotion to moral principle easily provides
rationalization and excuse for conduct that one
could not, without the principle, possibly approve.
More than one abominable cruelty has been committed in obedience to the most high-sounding principle, more than one vicious truth has been uttered
out of respect for veracity, and plenty of people have
been needlessly punished for breaking rules that
needed breaking. A decent and sensitive person does
not, in any case, imagine that the sweet and considerate things he does stand in need of the guild stamp

---

1. Compare Mark Twain's remark: "I am persuaded that the
world has been tricked into adopting some false and most pernicious
notions about consistency—and to such a degree that the average
man has turned the rights and wrongs of things entirely around, and
is proud to be 'consistent,' unchanging, immovable, fossilized, where
it should be his humiliation that he is so." *The Complete Essays of Mark
Twain*, ed. Charles Neider (Garden City, N.Y.: Doubleday & Co.,
1963), p. 583.

of any moral principle. Their goodness is apparent in the actions themselves; or if it is not, then no moral rule will bring it to light. On the contrary, when someone is found justifying his conduct by citing principles and rules, it is not unreasonable to suspect that he is excusing himself—that he is doing what would never occur to any really decent person—and then making it look all right by its conformity to principle. Moral principles, if conscientiously applied, sometimes enable one to get through life with the minimum risk of censure, but by themselves they tend to deaden rather than enliven the heart. Even though they sometimes serve to minimize evils, if not applied too rigorously, they rarely give birth to genuine goodness.

– 13 –

JUDICIAL CASUISTRY

CASUISTIC REASONING IS part of the very essence of juridic thinking. Indeed, it is probably from the legal tradition, conditioned by religion, that most moral philosophers have unconsciously derived their own habits of thought, as can be seen from the way judicial thinking typically proceeds.

A judge is someone called on to settle a dispute between litigants. Ideally, he turns to a law applicable to the case in question and derives from it the respective rights of the litigants. Such a law is a *positive* law, that is to say, a law that is promulgated and normally written. It has the status of law by virtue of its source. That is, it is either promulgated by some sovereign authority—king or legislature, for example—or it forms a part of the rules and principles evolved over the course of time by judges themselves and is thus deemed the *common* law. But the thing to note, first, is that a judge, wherever possible, points to some *existing* law as the source of his decision. It is not assumed that either he, or the litigants, necessarily approve of the law, nor need it embody any moral principle. To be a law, it needs only emanate from a conventionally recognized source.

Moralists as Lawmakers

Insofar as moral philosophers try to emulate this procedure, in trying to determine the moral (as distinguished from the legal) rightness or wrongness of a given course of conduct, then they labor under an obvious disadvantage, for the moralist, unlike the judge, cannot cite any actually existing law as the basis for his decision. The moralist can, of course, *concoct* a law and baptize it a moral principle, or he can borrow such a principle from his religion, but he must then depend entirely on the acceptance of that "law" on the part of those for whom he presumes to speak, in which case, of course, he settles nothing. Such a procedure gets nowhere, because the moralist lacks two things that are absolutely essential to a judicial decision: some existing law and the power of enforcing his decision. Many moralists have tried to overcome at least partially these seemingly fatal difficulties by postulating an *unwritten* law they can cite and calling it either natural law or, with Kant and others, the Moral Law. This creates the impression, even in their own minds, that their moral reasoning has the same force, validity, and authority as judicial decision—indeed, perhaps even more—and under the influence of such philosophy ever so many people go about thinking that they can distinguish a moral element in some rules and principles that is lacking in others. It appears, however, that the unwritten law to which the moralist appeals—which he claims not to invent but to discover through philosophical reasoning—is merely a thing of his own contrivance, postulated precisely to supply something that is absolutely essential to a juridic approach, namely, some kind of law.

Not all the difficulties lie on the side of the moralist, however; judicial reasoning and decision, being casuistic by their very natures, are infected with the limitations of all casuistry. One would suppose that, the laws on which they are based being promulgated and capable of being known to all, judicial decisions could be ground out quite automatically and with fair certainty by any intelligent judge who knows what those laws are. This is far from true, however, because virtually all positive laws, and certainly all that are basic and important, admit of exceptions, and these are often exceptions that cannot be made in terms of any written laws themselves. This difficulty is exactly the one encountered before, with moral principles. It is in response to this difficulty that the common law—that is, judicial decisions that are rendered on the basis of no prior enacted law—has come into existence and survived in some societies, whereas others have tried, without much success, to elaborate systems of *code* law sufficiently comprehensive to cover every issue that can arise. Neither is really workable, because of the difficulties inherent in casuistry, but the common law tradition is *made* to work by enabling judges to invent new laws, as the circumstances require, and at the same time to conceal fairly adeptly the fact that they do so. If this were not possible, it would not be possible to have a viable judicial system. The system involves, in short, a kind of hypocrisy and dissimulation; but it is hypocrisy and dissimulation that are absolutely essential to a decently ordered social life. Consider, for example, such situations as these.

Example 1. A statute prescribes the method of composing a valid will, and stipulates that no court shall modify or revoke such a will except under certain conditions that are specifically set forth: coercion of the testator, insanity, and so on. A case comes before a court in which the conditions of a valid will are met, but it turns out that the legatee under the will has in fact murdered the testator, precisely in order to speedily gain his inheritance. The statute says nothing about this sort of thing, and in fact specifically forbids any court to revoke a will except under certain defined circumstances that do *not* include this one. What is the court to do? Should it follow the law and lend its support to this murderer's scheme? What one court in fact did when confronted with this kind of case was to revoke the will, in violation of the written statute, believing, and doubtless correctly, that had the authors of the law thought of this possibility, they would surely have included it as a basis for revocation.

Example 2. A statute of New York provided that adultery was to be the only ground for divorce. It then turned out that thousands of persons living in that jurisdiction had obtained divorces in Mexico. The divorces were obtained on other grounds, without taking up any real residence in Mexico but, on the contrary, while homes and businesses were being maintained in New York. The parties in many of these divorces had, moreover, remarried and had children by their new marriages. The courts then had two options when these divorces were challenged: First, they could, in keeping with the plain language and purpose of the law—which quite clearly aimed at limiting divorce to cases of adultery—declare that these thousands of people were not really divorced, that those who had remarried were therefore bigamists, in violation of the law, and that their new children were all bastards. Or secondly, they could simply accept the Mexican divorces, in violation of the language and spirit of the law. The latter is of course the choice the court made.

Example 3. The statutes of a certain state made no provision for an action in court on behalf of a child tortuously injured before birth. According to the one clear precedent of this jurisdiction such an action could not be sustained, the reasoning then being that no one exists until born, and that some-one injured while still in the womb therefore has no standing to sue. Such a suit was nevertheless brought on behalf of a child who was born maimed as a result of a fall by its mother while pregnant, the accident resulting from the negligence of her land-lord. The trial court dismissed the suit on the basis of the precedent in question. The first court of appeal upheld the decision of the trial court. When appealed still further, however, to the court of last resort, the decision was reversed, it being declared that the child did have standing to sue after all, and a considerable sum was awarded.

Now we are not concerned here with whether decisions such as these are just, proper, or wise. The question is rather: Why did the courts decide as they did? Not, plainly, on the basis of the law that was given to them, for each of these decisions represents in one degree or other a *rejection* of the written law. And not, equally obviously, on the basis of some higher unwritten law, vouchsafed to reason or to philosophers. Decisions concerning the legality of Mexican divorces, for example, could hardly have been derived from such a source, even if anyone had presumed to know what it is. Quite clearly, the courts decided as they did because they thought it would do more harm than good to follow the explicit provisions of law. Most judges, like other people, have a certain degree of common sense and are accustomed to applying it to all sorts of problems day after day. They have also a sense of the ordinary feelings and values that most people share. When, accordingly, applying the letter of the law to a given situation violates that common sense, when such a course would appear to damage more interests than it would serve—when, in short, it would evidently do much more practical harm than good—then the law is no longer deemed sacred, to be followed at all cost. Laws, like moral rules and principles, have a purely practical basis and purpose. Their purpose is, generally, to serve the interests of people, to enable them to get where they want to go with the minimum of hindrance and danger. For the most part laws tend to achieve that purpose, but sometimes they do not. When they quite clearly do not, and in fact have the opposite effect in an intolerable measure, then they no longer bind anyone, including judges. Their basis is swept away, even in the eyes of judges sworn to uphold and apply the law, and with it is swept away our allegiance to them. If this were not so, then social life, which is difficult in any case, would be rendered harsh and painful indeed, and civilized life would be altogether impossible.

JUDICIAL DECISION BY PERSUASIVE DEFINITION

Another feature that judicial reasoning shares with casuistry generally is the tendency to *define* crucial words in such a way as to yield the answers desired. We noted the great temptation to define words like *human*, *murder*, *deliberate*, and so on in just such a way as to rule out the things one wants his principle to exclude, while preserving its application to the things one wants to condemn. For example, murder is always wrong—but not always abortion, because an unborn child is not "really" human. Or again, murder is always wrong—but war is not necessarily so, nor capital punishment, nor killing in self-defense, because these are not "really" murder; and so on. How you react to the definitions that yield such conclusions entirely depends, of course, on how you feel about such things as abortion, war, and the like. No facts are ever changed by the way we choose to use words. All that happens is that we are led, or misled, into seeing the facts in a different and sometimes strange light.

Suppose, for example, a man is charged with murder, even though it turns out that his victim's heart is still beating, this having been removed by a surgeon and transplanted, still pulsating, to a heart patient, who survived. Was the man whose heart was still beating when removed really dead? Or should the surgeon, perhaps, be charged with the murder? The answer will turn on how one chooses to define death.

Or suppose a man who has been shot and is dying then cuts his own throat. Was he really murdered? Or did he commit suicide? This will depend on how one chooses to define the "cause" of his death.

Or again, statute declares that the financial responsibility for a child rests on his natural father. This appears perfectly clear-cut and unambiguous. But what of a child who is artificially conceived, with the consent of the husband, using a donor? Do we still want to use "natural father" in the same sense as before?

Again, it is a provision of law that United States jurisdiction extends only three miles beyond its continental shore. An enterprising man selects a shoreline where the water is exceedingly shallow for many miles out, carts a quantity of rubble and sand to a spot five miles out, and declares his new island to be a sovereign state. Is this really an island, or is it perhaps only an ocean bed? Here we need a fresh definition of "*island*" that will yield the conclusion desired.

Is a contract *delivered* when mailed, or when received? Where is a child *born*, when born in an airplane on an intercontinental flight? Has a document signed with disappearing ink really been *signed*? Is a pushcart a *vehicle*? Is a seaplane a *vessel*? Judicial decisions often turn on answers to questions like these, to which the written law provides no clue whatsoever. They are usually represented as problems of *interpretation*, but this is highly misleading. It suggests that there is one underlying meaning to the crucial word that only awaits ferreting out by the judicial mind. In fact, the more precise meaning is not *found*, but *bestowed*, and such bestowal is not aimless. It is entirely governed by the conclusion, already arrived at, that the new meaning will tend to support.

There is, then, a certain dissimulation here. One appears to be arriving at a conclusion by following an exact process of reasoning and discovery of obscure meanings, when in fact the meanings are largely invented to support the conclusions desired. It is, however, a kind of dissimulation or pretense that is useful. Just as people like to think of moral principles as having an authority of their own, rather than as rules made up as the occasion requires, so also they like to think of the law as something that is already there, defining our obligations in advance. The alternative is to suppose that laws are to some extent made up as we go along, by judges themselves, and worst of all, that they are to that extent made up *ex post facto*. This is of course exactly what happens in cases of the sort just considered. The man who built his island off the coast did not learn that it was *not* an island when the judge decided it was an ocean bed; he learned that, for the practical ends that the law pursues, it was going to be so regarded, and at that point the word *island* acquired, at the judge's hand, a more specialized meaning than it had before. When the laws, as they stand, fail to promote the public good, or lend themselves to possible interpretations that would do more harm than good, then a court is inclined to interpret them in a way that will improve things, even though this sometimes means creating what are in effect new laws. A certain sense of security is preserved, however, if this procedure is kept out of sight by the appearance of applying laws that existed all the while and needed only to have their true meanings discovered.

MORAL AND JUDICIAL CASUISTRY COMPARED

Moral principles and positive laws thus have certain similarities, and they give rise to similar reasoning. The crucial difference is that positive laws actually exist, and there are procedures for determining whether a given course of conduct is lawful. Moral principles, on the other hand, appear to be generalized expressions of sentiments that some or most people happen to have, and there is no clear procedure for determining whether a given course of conduct is moral. Moral disputants can only wrangle; litigants can put their question to a judge and be certain of receiving an answer. Judicial reasoning is, like moral reasoning, essentially casuistic, but this is not utterly self-defeating in law, as it is in morals. Every moral principle admits of an exception, even in the eyes of those dedicated to upholding it, and from this it follows that no moral principle can, by itself, determine the moral rightness or wrongness of any action. If a course of action is morally wrong, this can never be because it is condemned by a principle, for the principle itself is abandoned or modified as soon as it is found to prohibit an action that is seen to be morally permissible. The moral principle or rule derives any merit it has from the moral qualities of actions it covers; they do not derive their moral quality from it. In law the situation is in some ways analogous, but it is not quite so bad. There may be some positive law governing conduct that, just as it stands, admits of no exception whatever, but most laws do, even in the eyes of judges. In that case the existing law is modified—that is, it is in effect replaced by a slightly different law—through judicial interpretation. Still, it is the actually existing law, in whatever way it is interpreted, that creates the distinction between conduct that is and is not *lawful*. This marks a significant difference between the claim that, in the light of a rule, a given act is unlawful, and the claim that, in the light of a rule, a given act is immoral. No rule can confer on an act its moral wrongness, whereas nothing *but* a rule can confer on it its illegality.

– 14 –

THE INCENTIVES OF ACTION

WE HAVE SEEN how the distinction between good and evil arises as a reflection of our conative or appetitive nature, and solely as a reflection of this. If there existed no beings having desires, aims, and purposes, then nothing would be good and nothing evil; all things would be neutral with respect to their worth. As soon as just one such being is postulated, however, then the distinction between good and evil emerges, and it emerges as *complete*. Such a being regards as good those things that are desired, together with whatever promises to assist in attaining them, and as evil those things that are shunned, together with whatever threatens to inflict them.

The distinction between justice and injustice, on the other hand, presupposes the existence of a multiplicity of such beings, and it is a distinction that applies, not to the things we find in the world, but to our behavior with respect to each other. Things, states, and events, such as food, shelter, sickness, health, strength, bloodshed, and so on, can be described as good or as evil—that is, as things that we seek or shun; but they can never in themselves be described as just or unjust. It is not until one views them as products of human action that this latter distinction becomes applicable. Thus, no injustice is involved in the bare fact that a given man is, say, hungry or bleeding, although such a state of affairs will surely be viewed by him as an evil. As soon as we add, however, that he is hungry because he is the victim of theft and bleeding from the wounds of an assailant, then it is appropriate to say he has suffered injustice. Here, quite plainly, the notion of injustice applies to someone's act and only derivatively to its effect. An unjust wound can only be one that is inflicted unjustly. You suffer no injustice, only injury, if you stumble and run into a post; but you suffer both if the same wound is inflicted by somebody else.

Now there is obviously no difficulty in understanding what incentives we have to pursue good and shun evil, so long as these notions are understood in their basic sense. For things are, originally, good precisely because they are sought, and evil because they are shunned. The seeking and shunning is what gives rise to the distinction between good and evil. It is, therefore, an empty injunction to say that we *ought* to pursue good and avoid evil, as this amounts only to saying we should seek what we seek and avoid what we avoid. For a similar reason, as we have seen, it is quite pointless to assert, as Socrates did, that no man can knowingly and voluntarily pursue evil. The claim is not false as it stands, but it becomes false as soon as one interprets it as saying something about human ability.

THE INCENTIVE TO JUSTICE

There is a difficulty in understanding how anyone could have any incentive to justice, however, and the more so when we consider that the principle of justice has both a negative and a positive content. Negatively, the principle is simply to refrain from injuring others; positively, it is to help others. The whole basic principle is expressed, then, by saying: Do not hinder, but help.

Now what incentive can anyone have to behave in the manner suggested by this? Why should anyone refrain from injury to others, in case it would advance his own good? And why, indeed, should anyone positively assist others in the attainment of what they seek, in case this can only be done at the expense of his own aims?

The first thing to do when confronted with such a seemingly simple question as this is to scorn the easy answers to it. Otherwise, you will entirely fail to see that any significant problem has been raised. It is of absolutely no use to say, for example, that the principle of justice counsels such behavior. That is already given, and it only returns us to our original question framed somewhat differently: Why should anyone honor the principle of justice? We cannot here simply *assume* that justice is a good, and that we ought, therefore, to pursue it. That may be wise counsel, but it is no answer to our question; it is only an exhortation. It can, moreover, be doubted whether justice is even a good. If it is, then this must be shown; it cannot simply be taken for granted.

It is not too difficult to see, up to a point, how we might have an incentive to adhere to the negative side of this principle; how, in other words, we might find it worthwhile to refrain from injury to each other, even though this might be at some cost in terms of our other aims. Imagine, for example, two or more men confronted by a common threat of such magnitude that only by standing together has any of them any hope of surviving. In such a situation, an injury to any is a threat to all; each man has, therefore, the clearest incentive, just in terms of his own interests, to refrain from hurting his fellows. No one needs to be told why he should avoid evil to himself, and in any situation in which injury to another, even though it might advance some interest of his own, would threaten an even greater interest, such injury would clearly be hindrance to himself.

Up to a point this sort of picture can be generalized, and philosophers have never hesitated to pursue it as far as they could. We can next, for example, imagine a multiplicity of men living in proximity to each other who do not share any common threat from outside. They are, nevertheless, a threat to each other, for so long as each has only the incentive to pursue his own good and avoid evil to himself, and they are governed by no principle of justice, then each has the power of life and death over the rest and nothing at all to restrain him. If a threat to my neighbor is no threat to me, and his life and well-being are no interests of my own, then there will frequently arise situations in which these may be quite properly disregarded in advancing my own good. If, for example, he possesses a field, or anything else that I covet, and if this can be mine simply by my abolishing him, and if, moreover, this can be accomplished fairly effortlessly and without danger, then I have the clearest incentive to behave in the manner suggested and no apparent counterincentive. If we look at the situation again, however, we can perceive an incentive to justice, for it can be seen that, just as I am a threat to my neighbor, so also is he a threat to me. It is not difficult to suppose, then, that a basic pattern of cooperation might arise between us, wherein each refrains from injuring the other, in the hope that he will himself remain uninjured. Now, of course, such a hope is not worth much until supplemented by some genuine assurance, and this can only take the form of coercive power vested in some additional law enforcing person or group. Thus, it has often been supposed, does a civil society arise, or a society under the governance of men and rules.

This was, in substance, the theory of Thomas Hobbes, and with numerous variations it has been embraced by many others. It is not to our present purpose to ask whether such a view, however elaborated, is adequate as a theory of government, for that is not the question before us. The question we are now asking is what incentives there are to adhere to the principle of justice, and insofar as we have an answer before us, it appears to be this: It is to your own advantage, considering only your own possible well-being, to refrain from injuring your fellows and, moreover, to attempt to help them.

Is this, then, true? Let us assume a universal and unqualified selfishness on the part of all, meaning by this that people devote themselves solely to those pursuits that will benefit them. Assuming this to be so, can we then account for the justice that is displayed in the behavior of most people much of the time? Is it, in fact, normally to your own interest to refrain from injuring others and, beyond this, to help them?

Often it undoubtedly is, as in situations of the type just described. When a group is attacked by a common foe it may be to the interest of each to cooperate with the rest, ignoring for the while any advantages he might gain from them. Beyond this it cannot be denied that the lot of any individual is improved by a social life and, hence, by those conditions of peace and security that render such life possible. It is, nevertheless, evident to anyone, save only those to whom a low and brutish conception of human nature seems inherently more plausible, that we are capable of a degree of mutual help and forbearance far *exceeding* what self-love alone would explain. We need now to see that this is so, and then to explain it. The explanation, I believe, will reveal to us not only how justice and injustice are possible, but how human virtue and vice, in their purest meanings, are possible too. We shall see what human nobility is, what human depravity is, what are the conditions for both. We shall see what it is that we share with the angels or the kingdom of light, and what with the kingdom of darkness.

THE INCENTIVE OF COMPASSION

If our voluntary and deliberate behavior is always at bottom self-regarding or aimed at our own well-being, then there can be no explanation of anyone knowingly forfeiting this out of a concern for the well-being of another, particularly if that other should be some being with whom we share no common enterprise and whose welfare cannot in any clear way enhance our own. Similarly, there can on this supposition be no explanation of our ever knowingly forfeiting our own well-being in order to injure another, in case such injury can in no way redound to our own good. Yet, we do find clear instances of both, and although such strictly *unselfish* behavior is admittedly not what is usual, it is also not so rare as to be a source of astonishment.

Thus, there are people who, having paid all their debts, will reach still further into their stores, even though these may be meagre, in order to relieve the hunger of others who are perfect strangers to them, and who are so distant that their paths can never cross. You can say, if you like, that such beneficence is practiced in the expectation, on the part of the giver, that he too will be similarly treated in his own days of want; but this is hollow and contrived. Surely the best assurance anyone can have against his own distress is to guard what he has against the evil day—and what we find is someone doing precisely the opposite. Again, a whole continent can be caught up in the drama of the attempted rescue of some child who has fallen into a deep well. Machines are brought up and hordes of rescuers set aside their own cares and concerns in a long and desperate effort to bring the child up alive, while a nation watches and listens—all this, even though the child was entirely unknown to them a few days ago, will not be heard from again, and can have not the slightest influence on their own fortunes. Or again, there are people who sometimes drop what they are doing, leave family and children behind, and go to some distant place, sometimes at considerable peril, to help exploited people win a better life for themselves. One can indeed say that they are only trying to combat a distant evil before it approaches their own doorstep; but if we look again we see that these people are not threatened at all. They are people to whom the evil they combat presents no threat whatever. If one supposes that they must, then, be moved by aspirations of glory, political power, or honor, then the explanation is altogether too thin for belief; for in fact, these are sometimes the very first things they ruin forever. Or again, there can be found people who, when they could be using their time to augment their own share of the world's goods, are instead seen going to considerable trouble to relieve the distress of dumb animals, and this in the hope of no praise or gain, and in response to no plea. This case is perhaps the clearest of all, for although one can always, with sufficient ingenuity, make it appear that all people are of at least some speculative use to all others, and represent this as the underlying motive for helping them, a similar case can in no way be made out for the seemingly spontaneous sympathy that is sometimes extended to suffering or threatened animals. There is hardly anyone who will not lift a young bird back to its nest, even though the bird is a pest; many men, who seem otherwise bereft of sentiment, have nearly smashed their cars in a spontaneous and unthinking effort to spare a dog or a cat in the road; and sometimes construction representing a considerable value is held up in order that a common robin, nesting in the path of the work, might see her fledglings into the world.

Examples like this could be multiplied endlessly, and while they are not samples of the kind of behavior we have learned to expect from men automatically, they do exist and are not rare. They may even appear banal, hardly worth the notice of philosophy; certainly a man who took the trouble to nourish an abandoned young bird to maturity would not make it the boast of his lifetime. Nevertheless, such behavior is of the most profound significance to morals, for it, and it alone, provides the basis for claiming that human life has a moral dimension, as we shall see.

THE INCENTIVE OF MALICE

There is another side to this disregard for themselves of which people are capable, and that is the selfless pursuit of and natural satisfaction in injury to others. We tend to hide this from ourselves, as it is so shameful in our own eyes, just as we tend to disregard and treat as of little significance our capacity for unthinking kindness. It nevertheless must be grasped, and not forgotten, and its significance must not be diminished in our minds. Every man, as Mark Twain once remarked, is like the moon: he has a dark side that he never shows to anyone. And to this we can add that every man tries to conceal it from himself as well. Nothing is accomplished by portraying ourselves only in flattering lines, however, and we do no justice to ourselves or to truth by proclaiming that we are created in the image of God, as though the Prince of Darkness could have had no hand in the work.

Thus, a man will sometimes set aside the urgent concerns of the day, in order, at considerable trouble and expense to himself, to see someone get hanged. Hardly anyone would admit to deriving inner satisfaction from seeing such cruelty to another, but the fact is that when such a spectacle is put on for the public it draws unprecedented throngs. Indeed, as this is written, newspapers carry an account of a half-million people turning out in the public squares of Iraq to watch men get strangled. The motive of cruelty is generally camouflaged, of course, theological reasons being invented for the burning of witches and the like, but the camouflage need not be very artful; anything will do. If a man indicates from the height of a tall building that he intends to leap to his death, it is only moments before a crowd gathers to watch, and if he shows hesitation, their voices soon unite in exhorting him to jump. This is not something that has been learned, for it is not sufficiently frequent in the life of anyone. It is the expression of a deeply hidden but dreadfully real malice that taints everyone's soul. Children, of course, are less abashed in their expression of it, having not thoroughly learned that it should be concealed as something shameful. Hence, an insect or small animal can hardly fall into the hands of boys without being tormented, tortured, and killed, its manifest helplessness hardly availing to save it. It is no wonder that the other side of our nature of which I just spoke has prompted us to charter and endow societies for the prevention of such cruelty, for it is ever present. Almost anything will serve as the object of cruelty, provided only, of course, that it is capable of suffering, for otherwise there would be no sport in it. Thus, a child who stutters, or is dirty, is wide open to unmerciful teasing and taunting from all the rest, until grownups step in to put an end to it. We try to minimize the significance of such conduct, describing it, most significantly, as *thoughtlessness*, instead of giving it its true name. Although, in many people, it is eventually quite overwhelmed by the softer side of our nature, it is doubtful whether it

is ever entirely erased in any of us. Plato was aware
of this dark side, and noted that it finds its way into
our dreams when it is given no other chance of
expression. And surely we have seen, and continue
to see, how it can boil up with almost earthshaking
power as soon as the dams are removed that society
has slowly erected against it. Millions instantly face
the threat of death, with no genuine excuse being
required, the moment the bonds to human malice
are sundered. A man, whom we can scarcely imagine
slapping a child or abusing a dog, seems to us trans-
formed when a club is put in his hand and he is given
some sort of official excuse or permission to use it.
We greatly mislead ourselves if we say that he is a
cruel man, for it is enough to say that he is a man.
Both sides of human nature are mingled in all of us,
and each of us is, indeed, like the moon.

EGOISM

It was with such considerations as these in mind
that Schopenhauer discerned three quite distinct
human incentives: egoism, compassion, and malice.
It is not supposed that these are the only incentives
to which we ever respond, but there is something
quite basic about these. They are, moreover, particularly significant for ethics. We need to understand
this significance, and in doing so I am going to draw
quite freely on Schopenhauer's thought. I shall then
relate these ideas to the theory of good and evil and
the theory of justice outlined before.

   All human action has for its general objective the
weal or woe of some being. Normally, of course, it is
aimed at the well-being of the agent himself. This is

so normal that some have supposed that no one ever acts from any other incentive, or in other words, that all voluntary activity is egoistic or self-regarding. Without for now deciding on the truth or error of this latter claim, let us at least understand just what is meant by egoism, and see that it is, at any rate, the usual incentive to action.

Egoism is simply self-love, and behavior that is prompted by egoism is simply behavior that is self-serving. Now there can be no doubt, in the first place, that everyone is, normally, absorbed in self-love. This only means that they have a profound regard for themselves. Indeed, everyone, without reflecting on it or forming any theory about it, tends to think of himself as a center of everything, around which everything else turns. How can it be otherwise when everyone is to himself a center of awareness, to whom everything else in the universe is something *other*? If you fail to note this, it can only be because it is so common and prevalent that, like the air we breathe all the time, it tends to go unnoticed.

Thus, upon hearing some news, you think first of how it affects you, of its bearing on your own interests. If a fire is reported, you think first whether it might be your house. If there is news of war, you think first of your own possible involvement, or the involvement of those dear to you. This does not mean that these are the only things you ever think about, but this is always what you think of first. If, in the hubbub of conversation in a room, your name is mentioned, it immediately registers with you, even though all the rest drifts by without your picking out a single other intelligible sound. It is as though your ears were minutely tuned to pick out anything that has to do with you, as in a sense they are. If you are

presented with a group photograph containing a sea
of faces, you at once seek out your own, all the rest
having only subordinate interest, if any. You are
likely to have more concern for a broken tooth than
for a distant famine that engulfs a whole nation. This
does not mean that you will declare the latter to be of
less importance, for you readily admit that it is not,
and that your tooth is trivial in comparison; but it is,
nevertheless, the tooth on which you bestow your
first and real concern. And, in general, people go
about day after day with these questions, although
unformulated, always before them and always
needing to be answered: How am I faring in all this?
How do I stand with the rest? How do these things of
mine look in comparison? And what promises or
threats to me do all these things hold? All of these, it
can be seen, are variations on the same question, and
their essential element is the dear self.

With this in mind it seems banal even to ask who
it is that you try to serve by your activity. People
seek honor, position, possessions, reputation—indeed, they seek all sorts of things. For whom? You
normally feed yourself first, and if you are a farmer
you feed others as well—but for this you are paid.
You clothe yourself and build your house—or make
it worthwhile to someone else to do this for you. The
point is really too obvious to belabor. It is a principle, the principle of self-seeking, that is so thoroughly taken for granted in all human relations that
it is, quite rightly, not questioned. When a man is
seen busily laboring it is quite naturally assumed
that he has some stake in the outcome of what he is
doing. When things, occasionally, appear to be
otherwise—when it appears that he is sweating for
the well-being of someone foreign to him—we are

struck with some surprise and admiration. It is not quite what was expected. But no one has ever been surprised to see a man thus laboring to obtain some benefit to himself, and willing to move heaven and earth in order to have it.

None of this means, of course, that people are exclusively selfish and uncaring of others, or that in their self-seeking they take no account of others. The point is rather that egoism is the normal incentive, and surely the one that generally prevails. To deny something so obvious would, I think, only reflect a misunderstanding of what was said.

THE MORAL NEUTRALITY OF EGOISM

Considering its pervasiveness, then, it is not surprising that philosophers such as Hobbes should have supposed that egoism, or self-love, is the only incentive to which we are capable of responding and the only one, therefore, that philosophical ethics should take into account. I believe one can, up to a certain point, set forth the broad outlines of justice and injustice on the supposition that human conduct is without exception self-regarding, and I have done this myself. One can see, in other words, how a multiplicity of men, each having a sole regard for himself, might live together in peace and even achieve a degree of mutual cooperation. But even so there comes a point at which what I have called sympathetic projection is required, in order that the interests of others might be taken into account even when those interests are opposed to one's own. At that point one ceases to be an exclusively self-regarding being. Even apart from this, it soon becomes clear that the incentive of egoism, although it may enable us to see an elementary distinction between justice and injustice, allows us to draw no distinction whatever between virtue and vice, between what is morally praiseworthy and morally blameworthy, or what I shall simply call *moral* good and evil. Egoism, as such, is neither a moral, nor an antimoral incentive; it is simply *amoral*, or without any moral significance at all.

That you should act in such a way as to benefit yourself is, considered by itself and independently of its effects, no more praiseworthy nor blameworthy than that you should walk on two legs rather than four, or that you should be born and then die. It is simply a fact. To regard anyone as blameworthy or praiseworthy for this is as pointless as it would be to praise or blame someone for having a mother. Acting from self-interest is something all men have in common, not only with each other, but with everything that breathes. We can note with despair the ravages of a weasel in a henhouse, but we can hardly condemn the weasel as morally guilty of anything. In the same way, we can note with satisfaction the advantages conferred on others by the self-regarding industry of some, but this, by itself, evokes no moral praise. Self-seeking, insofar as it is just that, is morally neutral in both animals and men.

In this Kant seems to have been dead right. The incentive of egoism, he maintained, is without real moral significance, whether it produces evil or good. There are purely practical reasons for combating it in the one case and encouraging it in the other, but this has nothing to do with morality. Thus, a merchant may be ever so careful in his weights and measures, adhering scrupulously to the rule of honesty, but as soon as we see that his reason for this is purely prudential, that his honesty is only calculated to preserve his good name and thus enhance his business, we find no special basis for praise; he is only following a sound business principle. Again, we may find a man who devotes his whole life and energy to relieving the sufferings of others—giving to the poor, perhaps, or helping the sick. But suppose we then discover that behind this behavior is his conviction that this is the pathway to heaven, that he is enduring deprivations for himself in this life only in order that he may be repaid, manyfold, in a life that will come later. We may still rejoice that he has that conviction, when we view the advantages it yields, but his efforts produce in us no particular moral approbation. He is only trying to get in on a good thing, taking whatever disagreeable steps appear to him necessary to come out as a winner at some future date. We get the same result if we consider a man whose actions, unlike these, produce sorrow and pain. Thus, if we think of a man who, in his quest of glory, spreads misery around him, our urge is to confine his zeal and reduce the effects of it; but his behavior itself, considered apart from these effects, stirs in us no real moral condemnation. He is not aiming at the misery of others, but only at his own glory, and there is nothing so unusual in that. We can accordingly describe him as overzealous, intemperate, too hungry for glory, and as uncaring of others; but that does not quite reach condemnation of him as morally depraved. Moral praise and condemnation express a quite different sentiment and should not be confused with such sentiments as hope or fear, gratitude or resentment, or the felt promise of good or evil in any of its many forms.

Now Kant, as we have seen, thought that the missing element, the element needed to confer on actions any moral significance, was the sense of *duty*. He looked at the starry heavens, and his mind was filled with awe. He then looked within himself, thought that he found there the sense of duty, and his mind was again filled with awe. He thereupon proposed this as the element needed in order to make any action fit to be described as having genuine moral worth. In this, I think, he could not have been more totally wrong, and it is to be regretted that, after such a good start, his theory should end up that way. It can in any case be seen that he was wrong, for the incentive of duty has no opposite. Moral appraisal, however, expresses itself in opposite ways, as moral approbation and moral condemnation. If someone is morally praiseworthy for acting from the sense of duty, for what can one be morally blameworthy? Not for acting from self-interest, surely, because this is not the opposite of acting from duty; it is, in any case, a morally neutral incentive. Yet, there is such a thing as moral condemnation. Genuine wickedness, along with pale and common selfishness, is something real. It has, therefore, a corresponding incentive, just as does moral virtue. What this is we shall shortly discover.

THE UGLINESS OF EGOISM

Egoism, then, can sometimes evoke in its beholder gratitude and resentment, hope and fear, as well as other response; but by itself it does not evoke that peculiar feeling of approbation or condemnation that is a uniquely moral one and to which we attach the notions of virtue and vice. It should perhaps be noted, however, that it is something aesthetically repellent, and we should not be surprised to discover that elaborate conventional measures are taken to keep it decently concealed. For, in general, we keep out of sight those things to which the mind reacts with disgust. We bury the bodies of the dead, for example, instead of leaving them about where they will be perpetually assaulting our senses, and almost anyone would find it enormously difficult to go about in a place where this was not done. We similarly move refuse and offensive things to the periphery of things to be out of reach of our eyes. We even cover our nakedness. Having been divested of any coat, and in this respect being quite unique among mammals, we now view the result and find it ridiculous, mortifying, and somewhat repellent. Some like to deny this, out of conceit, I think, for their own species and a felt duty to praise everything human. Such persons are apt to suppose that the use of clothing is but an arbitrary convention that might easily be cast aside without loss. I believe anyone having that view could be promptly disabused of it, however, by performing a simple experiment in two parts. The first part consists of entering a crowded bathhouse and really taking the whole thing in, exactly as it presents itself to the eyes, without romantic embellishment. The second part consists of entering a crowded social gathering, in the garden or parlor of some prominent person, for example, and imagining the scene of the bathhouse suddenly repeated there—in other words, everything would be as it is, but unadorned by any clothing. It is impossible to suppose that this would present no significant change to the mind, equally impossible to suppose that the scene now presented to the imagination would be an enhancement of the reality before the eyes, and finally, I think, quite impossible to suppose that one's comparison of these two scenes is entirely the product of arbitrary convention. Convention it is, but it has its roots deep in aesthetic sensitivity. It is, nevertheless, worth remembering that all of us are still naked beneath our clothing. The point of this trite comment is that even though we improvise curtains and raiments to conceal, interposing aesthetically acceptable veneers, no one for a moment doubts the undiminished reality of what is thereby put out of sight. Clothing is, accordingly, a kind of hypocrisy, and a necessary one, by which we present ourselves to the world as something different from what we really are. But the hypocrisy misleads no one.

Do we not, then, find an exactly analogous concealment for the egoism that is ever present in everyone, and is it not covered over for just the same reason? For why else do we create and cultivate the art of *gentle manners*, wherein we see precisely the same kind of hypocrisy as before that is, like the other, absolutely essential to civilized life? By gentle manners, by utterances that are not meant and not interpreted as sincere, by feigning responses that are not felt, and not taken as felt, we partially conceal the boundless love for ourselves that, if deliberately exposed, would render us so offensive as to be cast out from society. The speech of the parlor and social gathering, the amenities between people, the contrived queries about the health and well-being of those we encounter, and even about the health and affairs of persons unknown to us, in which we pretend an interest, the solicitousness we bestow on those in whose company we are thrown: what are these manners but a clothing to our egoism? Like our other clothing, however, they only conceal, without for a moment really denying. No one ever supposes your love for yourself to be suddenly *abolished* by the things you have learned to say and the manners you have learned to adopt. Gentle manners are, accordingly, a hypocrisy that merely conceals, for decency's sake, the underlying egoism in all its nakedness. It is a hypocrisy by which no one is really taken in, no one really fooled, and one which, like the rest of our clothing, is absolutely essential, not to our existence as human beings, because other animals can exist without manners, but certainly to our existence as civilized beings. One might sooner strip people of their physical garments than of the garments by which they cover over their self-love, for although both conceal a kind of ugliness, the ugliness of an honest, unabashed, and exclusive concern for one's own dear self is ugly beyond bearing. And all this remains true, even though our egoism, like our physical nakedness, is quite without moral significance. Like the absence on him of any natural coat, one's self-love is a fact that, although repellent to the sensibilities, is morally neutral.

FOUR POSSIBLE INCENTIVES

It is quite otherwise when we consider other incentives, however. But first, in view of the undoubted dominance of self-love in our nature, it must be shown how any other incentives are even *possible*. Having seen the possibility of them, we can then see that, although rare, they are real, and that the rarity of some of them corresponds exactly to the rarity of true human virtue and genuine vice.

People are, we have seen, like all living things, constantly in the quest of something or other, a fact I have expressed by calling them conative beings. They are constantly active, and the activity of a person is always (or nearly always) directed to some end or goal, to the fulfillment of some need or desire. It is, in a word, purposeful. This does not, of course, mean that there is some *one* end or goal that all share. Even though many philosophers have supposed this must be so, and have sought to discern what that ultimate goal might be, it is doubtful whether there is any such. We have purposes that are numerous and varied beyond any possible enumeration. I do not mean to go into the metaphysics of this or to raise problems concerning the reality of final causes and the like; I only mean to call attention again to the fact, however it might be analyzed by the metaphysician. And that fact is, simply, that human activity has a point to it, something that is aimed at, something that the agent is trying to accomplish. It is a fairly obvious fact, and a correct moral philosophy would, I think, be impossible without taking it into account.

If this is so, then we can see that, logically, there are four possible basic incentives to action, or four possible objectives that an agent might try to achieve. These are (1) one's own well-being, (2) one's own injury, (3) the well-being of another, and (4) the injury of another. These incentives we can accordingly call, respectively, the incentives of (1) egoism or self-love, (2) self-hatred, (3) sympathy or compassion, and (4) malice.

It is obvious that all these incentives are logically

possible. We need only to consider now whether or not all are incentives on which we actually act. Any action can obviously have a bearing on the weal or woe of someone; that is, it can be constructive or destructive either to the interests of oneself, or of others. Which of these, then, serve as the actual aims or objectives of our actions; or which, in other words, are incentives that we have?

There can hardly be any doubt concerning the first. We do in fact act in such a way as to benefit ourselves, and this is sometimes precisely what we are trying to do. Indeed, it is obvious from general experience and from what has already been said that this is the normal incentive, so normal that it can easily be doubted whether there is any other.

SELF-HATRED AS AN INCENTIVE

What, then, of self-hatred? Men often injure themselves inadvertently when trying to accomplish something else, but can we easily imagine a man doing so on purpose?

Schopenhauer apparently thought not. The incentive of self-love seemed to him so great and powerful that he evidently could not persuade himself of any genuine case of the opposite. Still, we should not be surprised to find that it is real. The logical possibility of it is perfectly clear, and I think we need not search too far to find real examples. It is doubtful, for example, whether *every* martyr has embraced painful death for just the reasons professed. Given any man who harbors a deep hatred for himself, an opportunity such as this to redeem one's miserable existence would be tempting beyond all control. A less dramatic example will be better however. Consider a man who has been despised and rejected by all from the day of his birth, who has never tasted the smallest drop of love and warmth and who, moreover, finds this reaction on the part of others entirely justified in his own eyes by what he takes himself to be. Such a man is not likely to *say* that he hates himself, or even, perhaps, to admit it to himself. Even a man who loves himself, as most do, is not likely to say so, and the inhibitions to admitting self-hatred are even greater. Nor is such a man likely to see his own behavior as self-destructive, even though it sometimes is; he has more reasonable explanations for all the mishaps of his life, and perhaps enough of these are sufficiently plausible to convince even himself of the rest. Thus, in one of his typical adventures, he undertakes a camping and canoe trip with some business associates, this promising, as he resolutely affirms, to be an exhilarating experience. Hardly have they set out before it rains, and while he curses the heavens, the rest overlay their frustration with general merriment. He then discovers that he has "forgotten" certain items essential to the trip, such as a sleeping bag, and is reduced to borrowing equipment from his associates, to his bitter humiliation. At every turn he finds fresh sources of pain and discomfort, which the others manage to take in stride. His anguish only deepens under their ingratiating banter. He finally falls into the water, ruining not only valuable equipment, but the only matches possessed by the group. Driving home at last, he smashes the car, through (as he says) no fault of his own, and so on.

In this picture one recognizes a familiar type. It is someone driven by self-hatred that is concealed even—indeed, particularly—from himself. The blows that rain down on him are always from distant and uncontrollable sources, as it seems to him, when in fact he perpetually maneuvers himself into their path. He seems, like others, to pursue his own good, but he can be depended on to spoil any chance of attaining it, even displaying a considerable ingenuity at this. Whatever goodness others can find is always, for him, loaded with evil. His own woe is the objective that he hides from himself, the incentive that moves him, and for the very clearest of reasons: his despised self is the object of his own enmity.

This incentive seems to me perfectly real, although fortunately not so common or normal as its opposite. Like egoism, however, I think we must say that it is without moral significance. A man is no more morally blameworthy for hating himself than for loving himself. It is far more apt to describe him as sick. You can view the fruit of self-hatred with dismay; you can pronounce it unreasonable; you can avert your attention, and perhaps try to conceal it, as you would do with something unclean; but no such reactions amount to moral condemnation. Such a man is at best a fool and at worst pathetic, but he is not yet a satan.

– 15 –

THE VIRTUE OF COMPASSION

EVEN THOUGH SELF-LOVE and self-hatred seem to have no uniquely moral significance, it will appear otherwise when we turn to the remaining two incentives, malice and compassion. Here we find that the distinction between moral good and evil, which is the basis of *moral* praise and blame, arises for the first time. If we leave these out of account or treat them as of secondary significance, as I am afraid most philosophers have, and treat people only as self-serving beings, then we can render a plausible account of how justice and injustice come into the world, but we derive no clues with respect to genuine moral distinctions. Even with respect to justice and injustice we cannot go very far without introducing compassion, for as soon as justice is conceived in the light of the common good we find egoism entirely insufficient for it. A society that honors the common good has to be one whose members, or a significant number of them, are capable of treating the interests of others as though they were their own. Not only does egoism not enable one to do this, it positively inhibits him.

That malice and compassion are real incentives that we occasionally act on has, I think, been sufficiently shown. Some deny the reality of malice, but only, I think, out of that familiar conceit for one's own species to which I have already alluded. If you once grant that people sometimes act from sheer malice—that they sometimes aim at another's woe without expectation of reward to themselves—then you at once suggest that you are yourself capable of this. There are very good reasons why you should not wish to think of yourself in such terms. But we find no similar obstacle to thinking of ourselves as capable of compassion.

The logical possibility of all four incentives is obvious. If action usually or always has for its object the weal or woe of some being, then no reason can be given why that being might not be, in either case, oneself, or another. All that is needed, then, is examples of behavior that fit all four descriptions, and these, I think, have been abundantly provided. No one will doubt the reality of egoism, or aiming at one's own weal. Self-hatred, or aiming at one's own woe, might be doubted, but that need not concern us, for it is not a morally significant incentive anyway. We are left, then, with compassion and malice. Both will be amply described and illustrated. If the examples are rejected as not really illustrating these two incentives, then one will be obliged to provide a better explanation for the behavior in question. And it must be noted that such an alternative explanation must be better not merely on *a priori* or philosophical grounds—as enabling one to preserve egoism as the only possible incentive, for example—for we have seen that all four are *possible* incentives. The alternative explanation must be a more accurate *description* of the behavior in question; and this, I think, no one can give.

It remains, then, only to show that malice is the antimoral incentive *par excellence*, that it is the presence of this element that confers on one's action its ultimate moral blameworthiness and stamps its author with the mark of vice. Conversely, it must be shown that compassion is the moral incentive *par excellence*, the presence of which confers on one's action its ultimate praiseworthiness and stamps its author with the mark of genuine virtue. We shall do this empirically, by reviewing in turn actions that appear in varying degrees to spring from these two incentives.

MALICE: THE FIRST CLASS OF ACTIONS

Let us first, then, bring to our minds actions of the following sort, beginning with fairly insignificant ones so that we can see moral good and evil, whether small or great.

Story 1. A boy, strolling over the countryside on his way from Sunday school, came across a large beetle lumbering over the ground. Fascinated by its size and beauty, he took a pin from his pocket, stabbed the insect through the back, ran it up to the head of the pin, and impaled it on a nearby tree. Several days later, having forgotten this, while he was going about his daily play, the boy found himself again in the same place and curiosity led him again to the tree. There was the beetle, its legs still moving, although very slowly, against the empty air.

Story 2. A group of boys, wandering aimlessly about in search of amusement, found a dirty and emaciated old cat asleep in a barn. One of the boys was sent off with a tin can for some kerosene while the others tied the cat up in a bag and sat around waiting. The kerosene finally supplied, it was sprinkled liberally over the squirming animal, precautions being taken not to get any into its face and eyes, and then a match was applied to the tail. The effect was spectacular: a howling torch, streaking over the field, culminating in a series of wild gyrations and leaps, and finally into a twitching mass whose insides burst forth in wet sputters, the eyes bulging to the size and brilliance of agates.

Story 3. A trio of soldiers, ragged and bearded and evidently a long time away from home and hearth, was wending its way back to its encampment in recently conquered territory. The surroundings, as far as vision could see, bore the marks of recent incredible devastation by war. Coming upon the remains of a shack, they were surprised to see signs of life. They threw open what served as a door to find a bearded old man huddled in the corner, trembling from fear and cold. A Star of David inscribed on one of the walls was more than sufficient incitement for what followed. The old man was goaded outside with rifle butts, was made to scrape a crude hole in the ground, and was then bludgeoned into it with rocks and sticks. A bit of dirt was finally shoved over his still quaking body. When the soldiers had finished this work and resumed their trek a faint wail betrayed that there was an infant still in the shack. They found her at once, and soon managed to replace her crying with giggling by dangling bright objects in her face and tickling her toes. When her giggling and the laughter of the soldiers flowed freely, her skull was blown open with a single bullet, and what was left of her small body was added to the grave already dug.

Now, with the passing reminder that things of this sort happen, and with fair regularity, we must ask: What is it in stories like this that sickens and evokes revulsion?

Shall we say, with Protagoras, that man, after all, is the measure of all things, that the insensitivity or depravity that some might think they detect in these illustrations really exists only in the mind of the observer, and that modes of behavior simply differ from one group to another? Surely that is not insight, but blindness, and it adds no enlightenment to remark that some courses of conduct are *better*, in terms of their consequences. It is not the *consequences* of actions like this that appall, but what is in the hearts of the agents.

Shall we then, with Socrates, say of the soldiers, for example, that they have acted from ignorance, choosing the lesser in preference to the greater good? That is altogether too tepid, and only manages to assimilate such actions to those of the fool who fails to look before he leaps. It is not the mere folly of these men that produces horror, or their inability to distinguish better and worse. It is something of a different character altogether.

Shall we say then, with Plato, that the agents whose deeds we consider have evidently failed to preserve a harmony between the rational and the appetitive parts of their souls? This seems a bit better, but it still falls far short of explaining our revulsion, which cannot have very much to do with what we take to be the inner arrangements of some-one's mind or soul.

Perhaps we should say, then, that the behavior of these agents is ill-calculated to advance the max-imum of pleasure for the maximum number. It is, in-deed, but what has that to do with moral revulsion?

Perhaps, then, they have all acted from their inclinations rather than from duty, and what they should have done was remind themselves of this maxim, clear to any rational being: So act, that you can will the maxim of your action to be a universal law, binding on all rational beings. Surely that is pedantic. What if they had so acted? Perhaps then they would have done the same things anyway, but with a bit more ceremony and rationalization. It is difficult to see, in any case, what is *irrational* about pinning an insect, or dispatching a stray cat or a starving old man and infant. Surely the words one wants here are not irrational or undutiful, but some-thing like heartless or cruel.

Then maybe we should say that such agents evi-dently overlook the theological consequences of what they do. People may be lax in their laws and punishments, but the eye of God never sleeps. We should remember that great happiness awaits those who conduct themselves properly, and great pain awaits those who forget. But this is only to say that they may be missing out on a good thing and taking a needless risk of going to Hell. Maybe so, but are they condemned in our eyes for *that*?

The recital of answers could go on, Aristotle per-haps noting that all these actions betray a disregard for that golden mean between excess and deficiency that honorable men prize; James observing that we should include in our accounting all of the interests and claims that are made (including, no doubt, the "claims" insisted on by the cat); and so on and on.

But clearly, all we *need* to say about these things is that they are wantonly *cruel*. That is the whole sum and substance of them all, and it is the perception of sheer cruelty or malice, of the intended infliction of injury and the delight derived from it, that fills us with that peculiar revulsion that is moral. Our perception does not stop at the irrationality of such agents, nor at their folly, imprudence, lack of wit, or intelligence. It hardly notices these things. We are not at all tempted to weigh interests against interests, to make summations of pleasures and pains, reserving our verdict until we are sure that none of these features has been overlooked. Even generally considered, it is not the consequences that gives them their moral significance. It is no disaster to the world that an insect should die, or a cat, or even an old man and baby who were destined to soon die of starvation anyway. That such things should result is doubtless an evil, but this is not what gives these actions the stamp of moral evil or distinguishes their authors as vicious. The moral perception goes straight to the heart, to the incentive that produced and was indeed aimed at producing those evils, and the one thing it sees, overriding everything else, is malice.

COMPASSION: THE SECOND CLASS OF ACTIONS

We can now compare the foregoing with deeds of a very different kind.

Story 4. A boy, poking around in a loft where he

had no business to be and looking for something to steal, came upon a cupola that had been screened off with chicken wire to prevent pigeons from roosting and nesting inside. Twenty or so of the birds were inside, however, having somehow gotten trapped there. They presented a lamentable appearance, some crawling about on the filth-encrusted floor, their wings half outstretched, and others lying about dead. They had evidently been there a long time. The boy resisted the temptation to tear off the screening and release them, for it had been put there by the owner; it would only be replaced eventually, and he might get himself into serious trouble by tampering. So he left things as they were. But that night he awakened with an image in his mind of the dumb birds up there in the dark loft, and particularly those too weakened to fly any more. He told his father about it the next day, but was firmly reproved for his trespassing and was given an unqualified order not to do it again, along with remarks about pigeons as a nuisance. He felt profoundly guilty, and the whole thing was put out of his mind until the next night, when his sleep was disturbed even more by the same images of suffering and death. Finally, on the third night, he slipped from the house before dawn armed with a flashlight and, although frightened to the bones of the darkness, he picked his way up to the high cupola. There, one by one he liberated each bird through a hole he tore in the screen, with many painful pecks to his hands and much flapping and commotion bringing constantly closer the possibility of attracting the attention of the owner or the police. He repaired the hole, and gathered the birds that were too weak to fly into a bag and carried them tenderly home. The next morning they betrayed the boy's disobedience to his father, and for this he was beaten, but with only a few deaths he nursed the sick pigeons back to strength and let them go.

Story 5. A man deeply conditioned by the traditions of his local culture was deputized as a sheriff, along with dozens more from the same community, in order to cope with the growing civil rights menace there. Like most of the others, this man thoroughly respected the law and the orderly traditions he swore to uphold. He had always respected, too, his fellow men, black or white, and his firm adherence to the conventions of separation could not fairly be ascribed to any hatred for anyone. Blacks had always worked for him and received decent wages, although he had never seen any reason to treat them as equals and had been taught from childhood not to. He was, therefore, appalled at the thought that they should vote and perhaps even hold elective office. The menace to his settled world came not, it seemed to him, from the local black community, which was peaceful enough, but from outsiders, black and white, who had for months been arousing people at mass meetings, hiring lawyers from outside, goading blacks into disregarding all the legally erected symbols of segregation and, it seemed to him, threatening to turn a peaceful community into a jungle. Matters became intensely critical with the scheduling of a massive parade onto the town hall, in defiance of the law, at which time, it was threatened, all the blacks willing to do so would register as voters. This man, together with a massive force of sheriffs and deputies, went forth heavily armed to repel that assault, and a scene of violence was quickly enacted, blacks falling bleeding by the road, but getting in a few wounds of their own with rocks and pop bottles and whatever came to their hands. Restraint on both sides disappeared entirely when one sheriff and two blacks got killed. Our deputy then managed to seize at gunpoint one of the blacks who was obviously a leader, and an outsider. Throwing him into his own car, which was to serve as a paddy wagon, he drove for about half a mile and stopped. Red and sweating with fury and screaming "nigger," his gun in his victim's face, he began beating him about the head and face with his weapon. Then suddenly the deputy fell to the seat, tears streaming from his eyes. Sobbing like a child, and muttering epithets mingled with abject apology, he helped the beaten and astonished black from the car, wiped the blood and sweat from his brow, and gave him a drink of cold water and a clean handkerchief. Then he drove home and got drunk.[1]

Story 6. Two soldiers found themselves marooned on a tiny island in the Pacific. One was an American marine, the other a Japanese, and for a day or so neither suspected the presence of the other. The Americans had, they thought, killed or captured every one of the enemy, who were not numerous to begin with. The marine had been left behind when he was knocked out and lost, but not otherwise seriously wounded, during the fighting. It was the American marine who first discovered the other, and discovered too, to his dismay, that his foe was armed with a rifle, luger, and knife, while he had only a large knife. From then on he lived only by stealth, hiding during the day, meagerly sustaining himself by

---

1. This story is suggested by, but is not intended as an account of, an episode described by Dick Gregory in *Nigger: An Autobiography* (New York: Pocket Books, 1968), pp. 171–72.

silently picking about in the darkness and covering all his traces, for he knew he would be hunted as soon as his presence was known, and that he would die as soon as he was seen. He soon began to feel stalked, a naked and helpless animal for whom no concealment was safe, and he could sleep only in brief naps, when exhaustion forced sleep upon him, not knowing but that his enemy might at that moment be at his back. He knew that the bullet that was going to kill him would be in his skull before he would hear it, and he lived almost moment to moment expecting it. He began to contrive schemes for ambushing his hunter, who he knew must have learned of him by now, but the odds were so against him in all of these that he abandoned them as futile and lived furtively, certain that it could not go on indefinitely. Thirst, hunger, and exhaustion had after many days magnified his terror and helplessness. He clutched his knife day and night, and his enemy became to his imagination a vast, omnipotent, and ineluctable spectre. But deliverance came suddenly one day when, in the early light of dawn, he stumbled upon the Japanese, lying in profound sleep, both guns at his side, and a huge knife laid out on his belly. His role as the hunted was ended, and with a single lunge he would abolish the source of his terror. His own knife raised high, he was ready to fall on his foe, when he began to shake and could find no strength in his limbs. Thus he remained for some seconds, until the knife fell from his hand. The other leaped awake, and each stood staring into the terrified face of the other. The Japanese reached slowly for his weapons, pushed them violently out of reach of both men, and then, hesitating, let his knife fall, harmless, beside the other.

THE SIGNIFICANCE OF THESE STORIES

There are no heroes in these stories. No one has earned any medal of honor, any citation from any society for the protection of animals, or any recognition from any council on civil liberties. Goodness of heart, tenderness toward things that can suffer, and the loving kindness that contradicts all reason and sense of duty and sometimes denies even the urge to life itself that governs us all are seldom heroic. But who can fail to see, in these mixtures of good and evil, the one thing that really does shine like a jewel, as if by its own light?

Are we apt to learn anything by reviewing these things in the light of the analyses moralists have provided? Who acted from a sense of duty, or recited to himself the imperative of treating rational nature as an end in itself, or of acting on no maxim that he could not will to be a law for rational beings, and so on? Nothing of this sort was even remotely involved in anyone's thinking. Nor can we talk about consequences very convincingly, or the maximization of pleasure, or of competing claims and interests, or of seeing the good and directing the will to its attainment, or of honoring a mean between extremes—in short, there is not much that is strictly *rational* in any of these actions. We are not at all struck by the philosophical acumen that somehow led these people to see what was "the right thing to do." Insofar as they thought at all about what they were doing, or consulted their duty, or weighed possible consequences, they were inclined to do precisely what they did not do. We have in all these cases a real war between the head and the heart, the reason and the will, and the one thing that redeems them all is the quality of the heart, which somehow withstands every solicitation of the intellect. It is the compassionate heart that can still somehow make itself felt that makes men's deeds sometimes noble and beautiful, and nothing else at all. This, surely, is what makes us akin to the angels and the powers of light, and snuffs out in us the real and ever present forces of darkness and evil.

If someone were to say, "This is a good and virtuous man—although, of course, he has a rather pronounced tendency to cruelty and is quite unfeeling of others," we would at once recognize an absurdity. It would be quite impossible to pick out any morally good person under a description like that. Similarly, if one were to say, "This is a truly vicious man, wholly bereft of human goodness—although he has a good heart, and is kind to all living things," the absurdity leaps up again. Virtue and vice are not evenly distributed; no doubt all of us have some of both, and one or the other tends to prevail in everyone. Most, however, seem to know just what human goodness is when they see it, whether they have read treatises on morality or not, or whether or not they have tried to fathom its metaphysical foundations. For the fact is, it seems to have no such foundations, and no treatises on morals or disquisitions on the nature of true justice make it stand forth with more clarity than it already has. It would be as odd to suppose that one must become a philosopher before he can hope to recognize genuine moral good and evil, as it would to suppose that no one can be overwhelmed by a sunset until he understands the physics of refraction.

THE SCOPE OF COMPASSION

It will, of course, appear that genuine morality is not, by this account, confined to our relations with human beings, but extends to absolutely everything that can feel. Why should it not? What but a narrow and exclusive regard for themselves and a slavish worship for rational nature would ever have led moralists to think otherwise? That humans are the only beings capable of reason is perhaps true, but they are surely not the only things that suffer. It seems perfectly evident that morality is tied to the liability to suffer rather than to the strictly human capacity for science and metaphysics and similar expressions of reason.

It makes no essential difference to morality, but only a difference of degree, that in my stories it was an insect that was impaled, a cat that was burned, and common pigeons that were liberated. The incentives were quite plainly identical in my first three stories, and identical again in the latter three, and it is quite obviously this malice in the former and compassion in the latter that stirs the moral sentiment. Something very precious is lost when people die at the hands of others, but that is not the reason for its moral evil. It is perhaps far less bad that a cat should die, and almost insignificant that an insect should perish; yet, the quality of moral evil remains essentially the same in all these cases. Similarly, we can surely say of our marine in the last story, struggling to keep living and finding suddenly the threat to his life lying helpless before him, that he had a good heart. Do the words lose one bit of their force or meaning if said of the boy and his pigeons?

Human beings have always recognized their kinship with the rest of creation and their responsibility to other living things, in spite of the fact that moralists in our tradition hardly so much as mention it. When the question comes up for philosophers to consider, they more often than not relegate it to a footnote or an appendix, thinking it quite ancillary to any serious moral considerations, even though it has as much seriousness and urgency as any moral problem that can be raised. Enthralled by rational nature, and finding no sign of it among what are fondly referred to as the brutes, philosophers and moralists have tended to dismiss the latter as mere *things*. Descartes even went so far as to call them automata, implying that they do not even feel pain— an idea, one would think, that could never find lodgement in the mind of anyone who had seen animals bleeding in traps. Nor has religion, in our culture, done much to offset such an error. The Christian religion, indeed, compares most unfavorably with others in this respect, and in not one of its creeds will you find the least consideration of animals generally. The theological emphasis, to be sure, is not on the rational mind, but on the soul, which other animals are somewhat arbitrarily denied to possess. The result is the same as before, however; animals are thought of as mere things to be treated in any way that one pleases. One can hear a thousand sermons, or study the casuistic manuals of an entire theological library, without finding a word on the subject of kindness to animals. When, in fact, it was proposed to establish in Rome a society for the prevention of cruelty to animals, the effort was vetoed by Pope Pius IX on the ground that we have no duty to them.[2] His reason and theology were

---

2. Edward Westermarck, *The Origin and Development of the Moral Ideas*, vol. 2 (London: Macmillan, 1917), p. 508.

without doubt correct. It can be doubted, however, whether the abstract kind of duty be bad in mind is owed to anything under the sun. Yet, it cannot be doubted that animals suffer exactly as men do, and they suffer unutterably because they cannot protest, cannot make their "claims," of which William James spoke, very articulate. The heart is no less evil that takes delight in the suffering of a cat, than one that extracts similar delight from the sufferings of human beings. The latter we may fear more, but the moral pronouncement is the same in each case.

INCENTIVES AND CONSEQUENCES

Next it will be noted that on this account the consequences of one's deeds are of little relevance to pronouncing upon the moral significance of those deeds themselves. Here, again, this view is in perfect agreement with Kant, and in complete opposition to Mill. It is not, Kant said, what we happen to produce by our actions that counts, but why we perform those actions to begin with. But Kant, obsessed with rational nature, decided that the only acceptable moral incentive would have to be a rational one: namely, the rational apprehension of one's duty, according to the formula of the categorical imperative. My account, on the other hand, provides no such rational formula at all. Indeed, the impulse of compassion so far transcends reason that it can as easily as not contradict it. It is sometimes the very irrationality of compassion, the residual capacity to respond with tenderness and love when all one's reason counsels otherwise, that confers upon a compassionate act its sweetness, beauty, and nobility. In exactly the same way does the irrationality of malice, the *pointless* but deliberate infliction of suffering, produce its acute and revolting ugliness.

Still, Kant was surely right in directing perception straight to the incentive of action rather than to its results, and Mill quite wrong in wanting to consider only the latter. Thus, it is a great evil that people should suffer and die. Considering these effects by themselves, the evil is the same no matter what produces it. But it is not a *moral* evil. Whether someone dies from being struck by lightning, by an automobile, or by a bullet, the effect is exactly the same in each case; and, considering only the effect, its evil is the same. This, however, is no moral judgment at all. To note that a given man dies from a lightning bolt, and that this is an evil, is to make no moral judgment on the lightning, the man, or his death. It is only to make a pronouncement of good and evil, of the kind considered far back in this discussion. It is, in other words, to describe a fact and add to the description an indication of the reaction to that fact of some conative or purposeful being. This becomes all the more evident when we consider that we *all* suffer and die, simply because we are sentient and mortal beings. No one escapes this fate. Yet, no morality at all turns on it; it is simply a fact, against which we may recoil, but not one that gives rise to any moral praise or blame. Nor is the picture automatically altered when such evils are found to result from human actions. A thousand people die on American highways every week as a result of their own actions, those of others, or both, and although no one doubts that this is a great evil, it is only rarely that the question of moral evil even arises. It is a problem of good and evil not significantly different from the evil of cancer. It is an evil to cope with, to minimize, but not one that normally prompts moral condemnation. Even when we bring the matter down to particular actions that are deliberate and willed, the situation is not significantly changed. That an insect should be killed (by an entomologist, for example), or a cat (by a medical researcher), or even a man (by an enemy soldier) are in varying degrees evil, but it is not the moral sentiment that expresses itself here. What is expressed is a certain reverence for life, and also a fear and horror at its loss, as in wars; but the moral condemnation of a particular deed is far in the background, if not entirely absent. Indeed, if we recall my six stories, it is clear that most of the consequences of the actions described are quite insignificant. All are things that happen normally, all the time; and, yet, the moral judgment is identical, except for degree, in the first three examples and identical again in the rest. In one set of cases an insect dies, a cat dies, and an old man and an infant die, all things that happen pretty regularly. Now one might want, with good reason, to insist that the death of two human beings is hardly trivial, but the thing to note is that even if it were known that these two would have died soon of starvation, had they not been discovered, this would not in the least reduce the moral repugnance of their murders. The moral revulsion arises not from their deaths, but how they died and, in particular, from what was in the hearts of their murderers. And in the second set of stories we find that some pigeons live, to rejoin the millions of them already on earth, a man receives less of a beating than appeared imminent, and another, who had just narrowly escaped death in battle, does not die after all. These are hardly consequences that change the direction of human destiny.

From the standpoint of the good of the world as a whole, they are almost devoid of significance. Yet, we stand in a certain awe of them all, as soon as we see what lies behind them: it is a compassionate heart that manages to overcome fear, hatred, and the sense of duty itself. However little it has won the praise of moralists and theologians, however little it may deck itself out with the ornamentation of intellect and reason, however strange and mysterious it may seem to the mind, it is still the fugitive and unpredictable thing that alone quickens moral esteem and stamps its possessor as one who, although fallible and ignorant and capable of much evil, is nevertheless a person of deep goodness and virtue.

COMPASSION AND JUSTICE

It should be clear by now that the capacity for compassion provides not only the basis for moral approbation, but creates also the possibility of true justice. We are able now to fill in the lacuna left in my previous discussion of this. A philosophical system that, like that of Hobbes, recognizes only self-interest or egoism as a possible human incentive will not only fail to account for any uniquely human virtue or vice, but it will also, if consistent, fail to account for the possibility of justice. If we assume all people to act only from self-interest then we can, as we have seen, envisage how a peaceful society might be formed by such men. There are purely prudential incentives for refraining from injury to others and, beyond this, for cooperating. People can form themselves into a society in which the double principle of justice—not to hinder, but to help—can to some extent govern their conduct without any of them relinquishing their own ultimate interests or goals. This, however, is only a beginning, for the conception of the common good can take no deep root in such a society. The moment people begin to honor this idea a conflict is produced between it and their egoism. And it will by no means do to say that, after all, so long as you are aiming at the common good, or the good of the society of which you are a member, then you are to that extent promoting your own good, simply by virtue of your being a *part* of that society. This may serve as a slogan, but it does not express a philosophical truth. Service to the common good inevitably requires you to subordinate your interests, at times, to the interests of others, and *not* with any expectation or hope that this will even in the long run promote your own good.

If there is in a society a clear and natural distinction between two groups—between those who are black, for instance, and those who are white—and if one of those groups greatly exceeds the other in numbers and power, then there can, from self-interest alone, be no reason why the larger group should be solicitous of the needs of the other. Indeed, so long as we take account only of the incentive of self-interest, there is no reason at all why the larger group should not absolutely enslave the other, reducing its individuals to the status of mere things, to be used and disposed of as one pleases. For so long as the distinction is a natural and not a conventional one, as the distinction between black and white is, then there is no reason for any member of the larger group to fear that any man or law will abolish it, and that he might thus find himself in the very position that he has consigned to his slave. There may be, to be sure, *other* considerations of pure self-interest that might lead the larger group to reexamine such an institution—considerations of economics and the like—but we are on dangerous ground if we appeal entirely to these. There will always be the considerable likelihood that, when all the interests of the larger group are fully considered, the rational verdict will fall clearly on the side retaining such an institution as slavery. We shall get the same result if deprivations of lesser magnitude than slavery are considered. It is not at all clear that the larger group will somehow fail to serve its own interests by denying the smaller group the political right to vote, for example. And in general, it appears a truism that no reason can be given why I, even though my store of wealth may be great, should forfeit a single dime to another who is destitute, or why I should prefer a course of action that would add one dime to his empty purse, rather than one that would add two to my own account. If there is in fact no risk to myself in trivially augmenting my wealth at great deprivation to another—and very often there is no such risk—then an appeal to my self-interest will plainly carry no conviction at all, save the conviction that I should be selfish. It seems fairly clear, beyond this, that no *other* purely rational appeal will serve any better. One will search in vain for any *reason* why I should have more concern for a starving million than for a bit of jam to add to my bread.

The search for an incentive is not, however, so hopeless. For there remains the appeal to the heart, the hope that another's needs can somehow be *felt* as my own, against the very clear knowledge that they are not. This is essential, for without it, the common good ceases to have any life.

The *common* good, by the very meaning of the expression, requires the maximum possible fulfillment of the interests of all, sacrificing the real and entirely legitimate interests of some to the more pressing and important interests of others. It can be increased in no other way than this giving and taking, for the totality of felt needs and purposes that we actually have do not automatically form a symphony, wherein nothing clashes with anything else. Why, then, should any rational person respect this common good? Why, indeed, if it means departing from his self-centered role and offers not the thinnest hope of fulfilling any of his own interests, but offers much threat of the opposite? I believe no real answer to this question exists.

Kant's answer—that it is his duty as a rational being—is perhaps the bravest that has ever been tried, but it carries little conviction. If, on the other hand, we ask why people *do* in fact often behave in this way, and thereby do bring about some realization of the common good, then an answer is possible, and it has no great ring of the absurd. People do this because to some extent they care about others: they have the capacity to feel sympathy for the woe of another that can even override their concern for themselves; they can sometimes respond with compassion. The kind of justice that supplants the Kingdom of Darkness, and then rises above simple trading of good for good and brings into existence a common good, would be impossible without this, and of course without it there would be not the slightest chance for anything remotely resembling a Kingdom of God.

– 16 –

LOVE AND FRIENDSHIP

I T IS FAIRLY common to find love treated as a
virtue, particularly by moralists who are influ-
enced by religion. It was considered by St. Paul to
be the highest virtue, surpassing both faith and
hope. Whatever may have been the fortunes of other
Christian teachings, this one at least has persisted.
Even despisers of religion are apt to stay their criticism of this teaching, however severely they may
wish to deal with the rest.

It was not generally conceived to be a virtue by
the ancients, prior to the rise and spread of Christianity. Most ancient moralists did, to be sure, devote
considerable attention to friendship, but this was
thought of more as a blessing than as a virtue and it
was never, I believe, represented as one of the car-
dinal virtues. They thought of love or friendship as
among the great goods of life, belonging to the same
category as health, learning, honor, and the like, and

284

their thinking was directed to analyzing its different forms and discovering the means to its attainment. They rarely thought of it as a unique incentive to noble and virtuous conduct generally, or as anything one should try to extend to all humankind. So remote was their conception of love from those that prevail today that one can easily read Aristotle's *Ethics* without even realizing that he has devoted more pages to this topic than to any other in the book.

I have already dealt with compassion, which is one form of love, and tried to show that it is a uniquely moral incentive. There seems to be something incomplete in this, however, for compassion is pity, and pity can hardly be the only morally significant aspect of love. That is to say, compassion can be evoked only by pain or suffering, or by the thought or anticipation of them. It is impossible to feel compassion toward one who is faring well, one who rejoices in good fortune or is bathed in pleasures and riches. If moral goodness could shine forth only in the presence of suffering, it would be limited indeed and be essentially negative. One would, therefore, expect there to be a more positive impulse of love, a type of loving kindness not virtually wrenched from one by a pathetic spectacle, but one that can add its warmth to a scene already filled with sweetness and really needing nothing more. I believe love does indeed have this more positive side, and we shall see what it is.

VARIETIES OF LOVE AND FRIENDSHIP

In approaching this it is first essential to distinguish some of the various things that are often referred to as love but that have little or nothing in common other than a name. The considerable differences between them can perhaps be marked at the outset by giving them their classical names, as follows: (1) *Philia*, or mutual friendship; (2) *Eros, amor*, or the love of the sexes; (3) *Agapé, caritas*, or what might quite properly be called Christian love; and (4) *commiseratio, misericordia*, or what I have hitherto referred to as sympathy and compassion.

It is probably unnecessary to say more concerning the last of these, as it would be repetitive. I have already tried to elucidate what compassion is, how it is related to egoism, malice, and self-hatred, and what its significance is to morality. What will be said here is intended to complement earlier discussions.

Nor am I going to discuss the concept of *agapé*, insofar as this is thought to be a uniquely religious idea. For in the first place I find that, as it figures in theological discussion, it is very obscure and is bound up with other theological notions that have little meaning. or interest philosophically. When, therefore, the time arrives to consider this third form of love, I shall avoid the religious expression *agapé*, and speak instead simply of love and its various expressions, such as the love of humankind, love of the world, and so on. If some were to feel that what I am then describing is simply *agapé* or *caritas* all over again, then I would not object; and if others were to claim that my conception of love, as there described, is very remote from what is really meant by *agapé*, then again I would not object. It will be my purpose to describe something that I think is within the ken of all, and it simply does not matter whether it does or does not correspond with any idea of religion.

It will be desirable first, however, to consider briefly the first two forms of love, *philia* and *eros*, to see how little they have in common with each other or with anything else, and to see what is their moral significance, if any.

PHILIA, OR FRIENDSHIP

Love, as it expresses itself in what I shall now refer to simply as friendship, is the mutual affection that sometimes arises between people well known to each other who share certain interests and pursuits. It hardly extends beyond people, although it can. Someone might, for example, with some literal truth, describe a dog as a friend, insofar as the two might really share certain interests and pursuits, such as hunting, and sometimes cooperate in these. A genuine affection of this kind can arise between people and animals, although it is surely not common. No one could describe his relationship to a squirrel or a robin as friendship, without metaphor. To use the term in such a context would only be to express a kind of goodwill toward them, which is of course estimable, but it is not friendship.

Friendship requires for its existence two or more persons having common interests and pursuits and cooperating in their fulfillment; it also requires, of course, frequent association for a considerable time. This latter can perhaps be achieved to a limited extent without actual physical presence, but some personal interaction is quite plainly needed. It is for these reasons—the possession of common interests, cooperation, and frequent association—that no one could truly declare the entire world, or even any considerable part of it, to be his friend. One who is a "friend to man" is simply one who expresses good-will to all. He cannot in any literal sense be a *friend* to all, without emptying the idea of its meaning.

FRIENDSHIP IN ARISTOTELIAN ETHICS

Aristotle's analysis of the various forms of love and friendship[1] and the values of each is probably the best to be found among the ancients, prior to the Gospels. This is not saying much, however, for the Greeks had a limited conception of love. Aristotle distinguished three different kinds of love: friendships based on pleasure, those based on utility or mutual advantage, and those based on character. He rated their significance in that order. The simplest friendships, those of pleasure, rest entirely on mutual enjoyment, and Aristotle quite correctly perceived that these are characteristic of children. Thus, when people seek each other out and form what all would recognize as friendship, and its sole foundation is the pleasure each finds in the other's company, as in the case of playmates, the friendship so formed is one of pleasure. It is, no doubt, an element in all friendship, but it can be the sole element. It is capable, quite by itself, of uniting people in friendship; but usually not, as Aristotle noted, in any lasting way. Resting entirely on the mutual pleasure that each derives from the company of the other and their common pleasurable pursuits, such friendship has nothing whatever to sustain it when the pleasure of the association has ceased. Friend-

---

1. *Nichomachean Ethics*, Books 8 and 9.

ship at this level is of course very common, not only among children, who are capable of no other kind, but among adults. It is easily established and just as easily dissolved. Thus, two men, meeting for the first time and each discovering in the other a passionate devotion to fishing, have between them a very real basis for friendship. They can truly claim to be friends from the moment of that discovery. Nothing more is really required. But, in case that is the only thing uniting them, the friendship must certainly dissolve as soon as the fishing is over, or it can be kept alive only in anticipation of more.

Aristotle was doubtless right, then, in regarding this type of love as both the simplest and least valuable, although he was equally right in regarding it as a good. It is a genuine form of friendship, even though it is neither deep, strong, nor lasting. Somewhat more durable, although not otherwise different in kind, are those friendships based on utility. These arise between people having common purposes other than the pursuit of pleasure, such as partners in business or government, professional colleagues, and the like might enjoy. In such cases, each friend finds the other advantageous to himself in his pursuits, and thus there is formed a bond between them. A successful business partnership sometimes forms the basis of friendship of this kind. One might feel inclined to say that this is no genuine friendship at all, because it expresses no real love except the love of oneself and is plainly motivated by the anticipation of advantage to oneself; but in reply to this it should be insisted that friendship would be rare indeed, and life correspondingly harsh and dismal, if you were expected to love your friends more than yourself and to abandon the concern for yourself that is natural to all. Far from being opposed to real friendship, an honest and unabashed love of oneself is a condition of loving anyone at all, as we shall see more clearly later on.

Aristotle's third kind of friendship is the more interesting, and he quite appropriately called it the love of the good, by which he meant the love of good persons for each other. It is important to remember, however, that by a good person Aristotle did not mean primarily a morally upright one. He meant a superior person, one who excels in intelligence, sensitivity, and nobility of character. Friendships of this kind are based, not primarily on mutual pleasure or mutual advantage, but on the human excellences that each friend perceives in the other; that is to say, on the character of those united in friendship, using character in its laudatory sense. Putting it more plainly, one loves a friend of this kind for his or her own sake, for what he or she is. Aristotle inferred that inferior people cannot form this kind of friendship, because the requisites of character are lacking. They can be friends, in the sense that they derive pleasure and perhaps advantages from their association. They can even, on these bases, be firm, long-lasting, and loyal friends, and such friendship is by no means to be despised. They cannot, however, have between them the kind of friendship that rests on excellence and nobility of character, if such qualities do not exist in them. For the same reason, someone of this character cannot be a friend, in this sense, of inferior persons, even though other things might unite them in a friendship that is perfectly genuine. Friendships of the good are within reach only of the good. Because, however, they are based on human excellence, that is, on character, and because this is not subject to change in those who possess it, this third form of friendship is the most lasting and can be destroyed only by death.

That is a superficial account of Aristotle's thought, but serves to lead us philosophically into the subject. Two things are now worth noting. The first is that Aristotle, like other moralists of his culture, never thought of love as anything but self-regarding. He simply assumes that people love themselves first, and that friendships are for the enhancement of one's own life. The thought of self-sacrificial love is accordingly quite foreign to him. A true friend, he notes, will gladly give generously to a friend, but even this will be motivated by self-love. Aristotle observes that although the friend thus receives the benefit of the gift, the giver is enhancing his own pride and sense of worth, which is the greater of the two goods. The giver, therefore, is the one who comes off best after all. Love, in other words, is considered by Aristotle to be a blessing, rather than a virtue in the modern sense. He never speaks of actions prompted by love as duties, and there is no suggestion that one in any sense owes them to anyone. On the contrary, he explicitly denies that persons far removed from each other in intellect or culture can be friends at all, in his third and highest sense. Aristotle is so far from questioning that friendship, even in its highest expression, rests on the natural love one has for oneself that he describes a friend as an *alter ego*—literally, as another self.

The second thing to note is that Aristotle never confuses love with the sexual passion, or *eros*, and in this his thinking contrasts very sharply with contemporary ideas. Generally, when we think of love we think first of the love of the sexes; we are apt to suppose that this is simply a special and perhaps typical expression of love, differing from other forms of love and friendship only in its special basis. This, I think, would have moved Aristotle and his contemporaries to laughter. Sexual activity is an obvious source of pleasure and is also, manifestly, the means of perpetuating the species, but few of the ancients thought of it as having any essential connection with love and friendship.

EROS, OR THE LOVE OF THE SEXES

In this I think the ancients were basically right, and to see this we need to examine the sexual passion, as objectively as possible, to see what is its explanation and what connection it has, if any, with love and friendship and with good and evil.

The general conception most persons seem quite unthinkingly to have formed is something like this: Sexual union is a great good, an allurement that presents itself to the mind and the imagination; and, because it is thus viewed, one who is thus seized with this vision directs his will to the attainment of it. But this is to put the whole thing backward. The sexual embrace is not first seen as a great good and delight, and for that reason pursued; it is the reverse of this. That is, it is because it is keenly, and blindly, desired, that it is deemed a great good. The impulse and passion are what first make themselves felt and, in the younger portion of humankind, sometimes quite irresistibly felt. Then, in response to this impulse, which lacks any intellectual direction whatever, that which is imagined as fulfilling it is deemed a great good. People want to think otherwise, because they like to think they have reasons and even conscious reasons for pursuing the things they pursue. And what could the reason be, in the present case, other than the great goodness and delight of the thing sought? But this is to overlook what is in general true of all willing: the things we deem good are so considered because they are sought. They are not sought because they are first deemed good. Indeed, as we have seen, the good and evil of things generally is simply a consequence, and not a cause, of their promising fulfillment or threatening frustration of one's aims and purposes.

This becomes obvious, I think, if we consider the urge to sexual union as it finds expression in other creatures, and then note how unessential are the differences between these and ourselves. Certain fishes, such as the salmon and herring, for example, leave the salty oceans in vast numbers at a certain time of the year, seeking out the fresh waters where they spawn. This is nothing they would do ordinarily, for the environmental change, to which their bodily functions are so delicately attuned, is very great and abrupt. Evidently they are driven by a powerful force. This becomes more evident when we observe how they persevere against every obstacle, constantly exposing themselves to every danger, to sudden destruction among the rocks and in shallow waters, leaping against the powerful currents and high waterfalls, often persisting in this time after time, until one would suppose their energy and even their lives would long since have been spent in the effort. Finally, some of them do make it. Now then, after all this struggle, struggle against which no obstacle or danger can ever avail, and from which no force or danger can divert them, with what great good are they then rewarded? What allurement awaited them in the spawning beds, solicited from them such feats and exertions, and made it all so worthwhile? What actually happens is nothing more than this: the female fishes go about laying eggs, and the males follow behind to fertilize them, the two having no more concern for or contact with each other than is described here.

This is, of course, pretty much how the sexual urge expresses itself throughout nature, as anyone having any acquaintance with animals knows. It would be strange indeed if, coming to humans, we were to find this picture suddenly *reversed*. What we do find is an impulse that is absolutely blind, at least from the point of view of that creature in whom it arises. From another point of view, it is of course not blind, for the function it actually serves is the perpetuation of the species. That this is no conscious or deliberate aim of other animals is perfectly obvious, for it would be laughable to suppose that one of these—one of the fishes just described, for example—framed in its mind the objective of producing others like itself and then embarked on the means it thought might lead to the goal. Nor is it just that such creatures lack the necessary wit to have purposes and plan the means to their attainment. It is more absurd than that. For if we could somehow imagine them endowed with the necessary intelligence, then we could not imagine them applying it in that fashion. What their intelligence or reason would tell them, if they had any, is that it is not worth it. Few animals show any interest in or concern for their young, once they have produced them, and in those that do, it persists only until the young are able to shift for themselves. Clearly, it was no hope of begetting these that lured them on. It was, instead, a blind urge that goaded them on, then produced this result. One might say that nature's great plan is thereby fulfilled, which would be rather poetic; but beneath the poetry there is, of course, a truth that could be expressed scientifically.

If one looks at eros in this way and considers that its human expression is not fundamentally different from its expression throughout nature, then many apparent mysteries begin to dissolve. They dissolve when one considers the blindness of eros, its incredible power, and its unfailing result, this latter being the perpetuation of the race—which is not, however, the end that is consciously sought even in the case of human beings, who can foresee it. We get inklings of its great power when we see what must give way before it. Prudence and good sense collapse almost at once, the moment an outlet for this demonic urge presents itself, even if but for a moment; it is no wonder, then, that heroic efforts are made, continuously and on every side, to cage and confine it. These take the form of conventions and attitudes of shame and modesty that are instilled in one from the tenderest age, and are woven so tightly that they often enable men and women to dwell in close proximity, day after day, without breaking them. All such efforts notwithstanding, however, we continuously see great careers brought to ruin, even thrones abandoned, and sometimes the interests of nations endangered by the insufficiency of such efforts, in the face of what they seek to restrain. This urge usurps a large part of the thinking of youth and infects all its emotions, day and night. No allusion to it fails to quicken immediate interest and, more often than not, to shove from the stage for the time being whatever other interests one has. No crime is so heinous that it has not been committed in response to this impulse, and no deed seems too heroic to attempt in response to the same. Thus does it become the central ingredient of most song, poetry, and story—and, oddly enough, of much humor. For most humor appears to result simply from this: someone, seemingly aware and knowing what he is up to, is nevertheless guided in his actions by things over which he has no control, and in such a way that he is carried to some absurd end that he could not really ever have intended. It is the surprise of this outcome, a surprise produced by the tension between planning and fate, that so often produces the inner tension that is expressed in laughter. Thus, the clown, apparently knowing what he is about, suddenly has something blow up in his face, precisely as a result of what he was so deliberately doing—and onlookers are bent over in laughter. The inebriate, similarly, plans his own motions, but is constantly foiled by a force he cannot control, presenting a ridiculous spectacle of thought versus force that culminates in a victory of force at the actor's expense. This is at the heart of much that presents itself to the mind as ridiculous, and it finds its purest and clearest expression in the sexual passion. For here we have, par excellence, the spectacle of an agent apparently planning and executing his own actions—deliberately, and often at great pains and expense of time, fortune, and effort—seemingly knowing what he is doing and why, yet all the time being entirely goaded from behind by a force that he never created and can now in no way abate or ignore. Like the clown, his labor carries him to a result that his mind or reason could never have chosen, and he is landed precisely in what all can at least dimly see as absurd. If you try to divest the thing of its passional associations—so as to be blinded as little as possible—and bring clearly before your mind an actual image of the culmination and goal of the erotic drive, you can see that nothing could possibly be more totally absurd, nothing less likely as a candidate for a sane being's aspiration. It is without doubt our perception of this, of the unsurpassable ridiculousness in the image of sexual union, that prompts people everywhere to conceal it as nothing else on earth is concealed, and almost to pretend that it does not exist. It is not mere shame begotten by custom, for no mere custom could be so universally and tenaciously held—and in any case it is everywhere declared not to be shameful when certain conditions are met. It is, therefore, its inherent absurdity to the mind, together with its ineluctable appeal to the will, that has invested it with this feeling of embarrassment and shame that without fail leads lovers to places of darkness and concealment. What they do must never be seen, for it is so immensely absurd.

This is of course a large subject, and an intriguing one, about which much more could be said; but perhaps the brief and general description before us will suffice to answer the questions that now arise. Namely, is eros, or the sexual passion, an expression of love? What has it to do with love? And what is its moral significance?

Clearly, it is no form of love at all, beyond the fact that it happens to be called by that name, and it has almost nothing to do with love, in any sense in which this is of special moral significance. Eros, or the attraction of the sexes, is found in virtually everything that lives and appears to differ in people only in certain accidental details. We are, for example, aware of this drive, can formulate and act on deliberate plans with respect to it, can to some degree at least understand it, and can foresee its consequences; but none of these things changes its essential nature. It is in us as irrational, blind, and unchosen as in any insect; it is something that is simply thrust on us by nature, we then to act out our response to it. The fact that we know what we are doing and are aware of what is going on does not change this in the least, for no more did anyone ever choose *not* to be impelled by its urging, than did any ever choose to be so impelled. One could not aptly describe a pair of copulating grasshoppers, or mice, or dogs, as making *love*; they are simply copulating. The expression is no less inept when applied to people—except that here we feel some euphemism is needed, and this one serves.

Love, as a sentiment, expresses itself naturally in sympathetic kindness, even sometimes in a kind of identification of oneself with the thought, feelings, and aspirations of another. It is compatible with sexual passion, but it by no means rests on it nor, contrary to what so many would like to believe, does it find its highest expression there. This is made obvious by a number of things; for example, by the natural love of parents for their children, and by the fact that sentiments of genuine love and friendship can exist and sometimes persist through a lifetime among persons of either sex, wherein the erotic element is sometimes entirely absent. And on the other side, it is notorious that the sexual passion can be kindled by one for whom one cares nothing at all, and equally, that one may have a friend who is truly beloved who nevertheless stirs this passion not in the least. Looking at it from still another point of view, it is obvious to anyone having a knowledge of human affairs that genuine love, as St. Paul put it, "never fails"; that is to say, it is inseparable from loving kindness in action, and absolutely ennobles everything that it touches. The erotic passion, on the other hand, left to itself seldom succeeds, for it is a notoriously fertile source of folly, of madness, sometimes of human degradation, and very often of cruelty and unspeakable crime.

None of this is of course intended to deny that the two can dwell together; it is only meant to deny that they are one and the same, and even spring from a common source—all of which would probably be obvious if people did not insist on adorning in their own case whatever behavior they share with other animals. Certainly the adoration of lovers is increased by erotic fulfillment, and the latter is itself ennobled by loving sympathy, but an excursus on that theme belongs in manuals for lovers rather than in a philosophical treatise.[2]

ABSOLUTE LOVE

By this, I mean, not a love of which human beings are the special objects, but rather, the love of which they are alone capable. I shall try to convey some idea of what it is, and what it is not, to relate it to the moral life, and to enunciate an aspiration that this human capacity yields.

---

2. For a similar treatment of erotic love, see Schopenhauer, "On the Metaphysics of Sexual Love," in *The World As Will and Representation*, vol. 2, trans. E. F. J. Payne (New York: Dover Publications, 1966).

Human beings have a capacity to rejoice in the sheer existence of things, first of all in their own existence, then in the existence of things around them, both human and nonhuman, animate and inanimate. It is a rejoicing that goes far beyond aesthetic pleasure, encompassing things that are perfectly banal and without any aesthetic significance, and far beyond the mere utility of things. Insofar as we are conative beings, with diverse desires and aims, both great and trivial, then we can, in the manner already described at length, divide things in the world into good and evil. But this in itself gives rise to no love of things, as I am now using the term. To love a thing is not merely to use it, except in a degraded sense of the term, and anyone can recognize an ineptness in speaking, as is so often done, of loving money, food, reputation, and such things as are merely useful in the fulfillment of aims. Behind this recognition is the perception of a rejoicing over things, not merely as they can be turned to advantage, but simply and solely in their existence.

The first such existence that fills the heart with love is one's own, and it cannot possibly be anything else. I have used the expression *the heart* to indicate that this love of being is entirely nondiscursive, nonintellectual, and nonrational, and although obviously no mindless being could possess it, it is at the same time nothing for which any reason or justification could be given. It is one's own being that is, thus, first loved; for if it is not, then nothing is ever loved at all. Self-love, by which is meant something far more than narrow self-interest, is an absolute precondition of loving anything, and one who is devoid of it is as deprived—indeed, as inhuman—as a vegetable or a machine. And such rejoicing must, if it is to exist at all, begin with one's own existence, because it is that which you first feel and in terms of which the existence of other things first becomes meaningful. Behind any view of the world there must be a viewer, but you differ in this: you are yourself the lens through which all the rest is seen. Thus, one who is filled with warmth in the sheer joy of his own being finds warmth in the world, whereas one who is bereft of this is automatically chilled, forsaken, and quite alone in the world.

This joy of being, which could with equal felicity be called love for the world, is nothing rare or esoteric, nothing that any learning or religion is needed to impart. It exists all around. We find it in children, who practically come into the world with it, and in them it is easily, almost casually, destroyed, often by the most innocent neglect. It usually survives as one grows older, although in very different degrees. In some it has been utterly suffocated, usually in their tender years and as often as not through sheer accident, whereas in others no suffering can diminish it and no fortune add to it. These latter go through to the day of their death bathed in the warmth of love that arose first in their own hearts, was at first absorbed in their own existence, and then for the rest of their years poured in on them as echoes are sent back to one from the hills of a valley. Such persons fill others with awe, not because their lives are dramatic or even filled with achievement, but because we see in them intimations of what is divinely good. It is the crowning virtue of St. Francis, and of the numberless unknowns who have been exactly like him. At times it seems to shine with such brightness that people are willing to declare and believe, quite solemnly, that its possessors are gods, as in the case of Jesus or Gotama Buddha. This is however misleading if it suggests that such love is mysterious or even rare, for nothing could in fact be more distinctively human.

However narrow and superficial may have been the conception of love and friendship discoursed on by the ancient moralists, there is one particular in which they were undoubtedly right, and that was in viewing love as a blessing rather than thinking of it, as moralists since have tended to do, as a duty. The child is born with the capacity for it, but that capacity is either nourished or destroyed by forces over which it has no control; it is entirely at the mercy of others. Nothing which is so clearly a gift or deprivation of fortune can be represented as a duty. To say otherwise is as absurd as to declare it one's duty to be born in the first place. It is not up to the child to be tenderly loved, but up to others; and failing this, the child is damaged as severely and irreparably as if deprived of a limb. A line that is sometimes interjected by a clergyman into the ritual of marriage is therefore most fitting and reflects profound wisdom in every detail. He says, ". . . and may the love you will lavish on your children be returned to you a thousandfold." Here they are not exhorted to love children; it is simply taken for granted that they will. And such love is without grotesque exaggeration represented as a palpable substance, to be "lavished" on them; it is not merely a feeble inner prompting of appropriate actions, nor a mere precept to be borne in the mind and heeded from time to time as the occasion demands. And, finally, it is quite unabashedly recognized that it needs to come back, and the more the better—"a thousandfold." Such a wish is incomparably better than dozens of vows.

Physicians and nurses in children's hospitals well know the consequences to children who lack love, even at the very beginning of life, before the children can have any thoughts of it or know what is going on. Psychologists know, too, that such deprivation can seldom be redeemed. An infant so deprived is as surely starved as if denied food, and the consequences are hardly less horrible. In many ways they are more so, for it is the very spirit that is crippled, and it is seldom that it can ever be reached and healed again. A child thus damaged is divested of the most precious quality anyone can possess, never to be restored. Such a child cannot rejoice in her own being, can never love herself, is thus rendered incapable of loving anything else, and hence of ever becoming loved. It is a vicious and almost unbreakable circle that dooms its victim to be frozen out of the world forever.

The disease is well recognized in a children's ward, and its symptoms are quite clear and uniform. The infant, although it is fed, does not grow much. Its nourishment is simply not assimilated, even though nothing is organically wrong. All development is profoundly retarded, and a blank, passive, unhappy look takes the place of what one expects to find in an infant. It is not apt to cry, but not apt to laugh either. The head droops, there appears to be little awareness of anything, even of its own hands or of moving objects around it, and it languishes into a state of inner nothingness. The child looks sick, and remains in that passive, rather vegetative state, although there seems to be "nothing wrong." The disease was at one time called marasmus, and it greatly puzzled medical science. It is now perfectly well known that its cause is simply deprivation of love. Interns and nurses are now directed to do what they can in supplying some semblance of the love such a child would normally receive from its mother, by holding it while it is fed and actions of this sort. Even such makeshift efforts as these produce visible improvement.[3]

In the face of such considerations as this we should not think of love as an ornament to human life, as something that brightens it and makes life more agreeable. We need to recognize that it is the very nourishment of a life that is human, from one's very first breath to his last. It is not something with which we should be exhorted to embellish our lives; it is something without which we cannot even be humans. It requires more than the possession of arms and legs and the human form to be human, for corpses and statues have these; and it requires more than a body that is quickened and warm, for an animal has this. Aristotle thought that reason was what lifted us above the rest of nature, and this has become pretty much a part of our intellectual tradition; but it does not really seem possible that one can measure human goodness by this quality. Concerning someone who is rational, perhaps preeminently so, one can only say that this person is, indeed, rational; but of one filled with love, of the kind I have been trying to describe—not love that is a mere sentiment of kindness, nor of the kind that rises no higher than a decent sense of justice—one can say that such a person is good and noble, and unfailingly so.

---

3. See Ashley Montagu, *On Being Human* (New York: Hawthorn Books, 1966), chap. 5.

– 17 –

LOVE AND ASPIRATION

I HAVE ALREADY said that absolute love must begin with oneself and cannot possibly begin anywhere else. There is nothing novel or odd in this claim, and you need only to reflect on what your own existence is to you, as compared with everything else, to see that this has to be so. One would never be tempted to think otherwise, except for certain debased moral ideals whose authors, in their zeal for loving all of humankind, have tended to treat such love as mere altruism and service to others and thus to disregard the fact that one is himself a man. Spinoza has perhaps declared more forceably than anyone the necessity of first loving oneself as a condition of loving anything at all; but even when the rule of Christianity says you must love your neighbors it immediately adds, *"as yourself."*

POSSESSIVE LOVE

Such self-love, it should be clear by now, is not what one would ordinarily think of as selfishness; indeed, it is the other way around. A selfish person, in the ordinary sense, is precisely one who to whatever degree he is selfish does *not* love himself. Selfishness in this sense is self-serving behavior, and the selfish person is accordingly one who, *not* loving his or her own existence and being to that extent discontent, seeks to accumulate all sorts of things precisely in order to make up what seems a deficiency. It is largely from this that the boundless love of possessions arises. It represents a vain and futile attempt to compensate for what seems lacking in one's own being, and thus bring oneself up to a level comparable to the goodness one finds, and sometimes bitterly rues, in others. I refer to it as vain and futile because, being so motivated, it can obviously never succeed. It is not surprising, therefore, that such self-hatred, whether great or small, is a fertile source of envy, spite, and hatred. Self-love, on the other hand, which is an agreeable total satisfaction with one's own being, has no need of self-serving, and can never be a source of hatred toward anything. It is, on the contrary, the first step toward love for the sheer existence of all sorts of things.

But it is only the first step. Love can stop at that point, at love of yourself, and in that case everything else you love only for your own sake, not theirs. This is the essence of possessive love, and it is not uncommon in husbands and wives whose love for each other, and even for their children, has not gone beyond that. I mention these two relationships, conjugal and parental, because they constitute something of a test case, usually presenting the clearest and closest opportunity one can ever have for stepping beyond oneself. Some persons do, nonetheless, think of their spouses and children first of all as ornaments to themselves, the wife drawing her inner satisfaction from the achievements of the man in whose eyes she has found favor, the husband relishing the physical beauty and talents of his wife, and both prizing the achievements of their children as though they were somehow their own. Such possessive love easily extends to other things, of course, particularly to things of beauty with which you can surround yourself and call your own; and while such love of possession can, as already suggested, express a certain degree of self-hatred, it can also be the expression of self-love that has failed to get beyond itself. As self-love it is not to be despised or berated; indeed, all love for other things must begin there. It nevertheless falls far short of the ideal of human nature that now begins to emerge.

LOVE AS A DUTY

Kant saw perfectly the incompatibility of love and duty. To the extent that you are prompted by love to render assistance to others, or to do anything else, then to that extent, Kant noted, you are *not* being prompted to do it by the incentive of duty. Your motivation clearly lies in your own feelings and inclinations; you are merely doing what you want to do; and although this might indeed be precisely what duty would bid you to do if you did not love, it is nevertheless not a dutiful act. Kant, accordingly, dismissed such actions as being without genuine

moral worth and referred to feelings of love as
pathological. A similar claim had been made by the
Stoics of antiquity, who endeavored to rid their lives
of all passions and hearken only to reason and the
sense of duty. Thus Epictetus advised that, in case
you should come upon a friend sitting in the gutter
who is groaning and wailing from the misfortunes
that have befallen him, you should try to comfort
him in whatever ways duty suggests, even to the
extent of groaning with him, if necessary. However,
Epictetus immediately added, "Be careful that you
do not groan inwardly too." Feelings of love and
compassion, just because they are passions and,
hence, not within our power or control, are thus
claimed to be unsuitable incentives to action. Only
the sense of duty provides this.

This seems a strange and grotesquely perverse
turn for the thinking of a moralist, and it is aston-
ishing how many have been impressed by it, and
even inspired.[1] The insight is certainly correct, that
love and duty do not mix as incentives to action,
and that love, as a feeling, cannot be commanded. It
is, as I have noted, a passion and not an action, and
therefore it cannot be evoked or banished at will.
But from none of this does it follow that the passion
of love is without moral significance, *unless* you
simply presuppose a morality of duty. Another
inference is perfectly possible, and it is this: Love is
a passion that cannot be commanded, and hence
cannot be represented as a duty, but because it is,

---

1. Thus Gilbert Murray, commenting on the Stoic devotion to
duty and indifference to consequences, said that "this view is so sub-
lime and so stirring that at times it almost deadens one's power of
criticism." *Stoic, Christian and Humanist* (London: Allen & Unwin,
Ltd., 1940), p. 109.

nevertheless, a virtue and the noblest incentive to action, then, to that extent, the concept of duty has no place in the moral life. Kant, with perfect consistency, could have developed his insight in that direction. The insight that love, as a feeling, is incompatible with the incentive of duty, is plainly correct. In the light of it one can expunge feelings of love from theoretical ethics, or one can expunge the incentive of duty. Kant took the former course, and I take the latter.

And why, anyway, should it seem so obvious to so many that the concept of duty is inseparable from ethical thought? It plays no significant role in some of the most inspiring moral philosophy that history provides. Duty, in any abstract and uniquely moral sense, hardly entered the thinking of the Greeks; one can read Plato and Aristotle without finding it, and without missing it. Good and evil were what concerned them, and it was in terms of good and evil, rather than in terms of dutiful conduct, that they interpreted virtue and vice. Spinoza's philosophy provides another example—a system that is fatalistic throughout, in which the idea of performance of duty hardly makes an appearance, but the idea of finding the supreme good is everything. And this is, surely, a proper aim of moral philosophy—*not* to discover one's duty, so that one may *perform* it, but rather to find the greatest good, so that one may hope to *attain* it.

Having a duty, as I pointed out earlier, involves the idea of *owing* something, and is in fact one and the same notion. It implies having some kind of *debt*. To whom, then, do we owe any actions? Well, obviously we owe them to whomever we have contracted to perform them. Later this idea was extended to include the idea of owing them to the state, inasmuch as they are prescribed by the laws. The idea was then extended still further, to include owing certain actions to God because they are demanded in the Scriptures. But what, now, if we lift this concept of duty even from the theological context, in which it still preserves a meaning, and speak of actions that are owed—that is, actions that it is our duty to perform—but not owed *to* any person or thing? This is the extension that Kant has tried to give the idea, and at that point the idea becomes completely empty. It maintains its powerful grip, though, mostly because of the conditioning that religion has had on our culture. The idea of goodness has suffered no such preemption of meaning, and it is still very worthy of being the central and noblest concern of philosophy.

LOVE AS A BLESSING

It has been altogether too common to represent love as a social virtue and recommend it as an incentive to action because of its fruits and the agreeableness it adds to social life. We need another emphasis, and that I try to effect by representing love as a blessing. By this I mean that it is a good to be attained, but not a thing to be used. Calling it a blessing is inept, as it suggests themes of devotional literature rather than philosophy; but I do not know what else to call it. Perhaps it should simply be called the greatest good.

I have indicated the possibility of the passion of love beginning with oneself and then extending beyond, first, no doubt, to other persons, but not ending with them or including all humankind, which seems quite impossible. Such things are loved, not for what they can do, but for exactly the same reason you love yourself; namely, because they are there. It extends to things both trivial and great and need not even make much of a distinction between these, because the existence of things is not something that admits of degrees. Thus you can love, in the sense I am suggesting, not only another person, but a sunset, a flock of migrating geese, and even the pebbles and insects at your feet. It is, then, not primarily an incentive to actions, but a passional state, something that is to be possessed rather than used. It need not call upon one to *do* anything whatever, for it is instead the aspiration to *be* a certain kind of person, to exemplify an ideal of human nature that is found to be good, not primarily for what it does, but for what it is. To look at it otherwise—to think of its worth, for example, solely in terms of what it produces in conduct—is to take a utilitarian, almost commercial view of the matter and to risk missing its goodness entirely.

What, then, is so good about it? Now to ask that question is, it seems to me, to miss the point. It is like asking what is so good about a sunset, when after all it yields so little light. The goodness of something cannot be shown, it can only be found.

Earlier I tried to show that good and evil are relative to needs, purposes, and desires, that the goodness of a thing consists of its being sought, and evil, of its being shunned. It is nevertheless possible, although it seems at first to contradict this, to pursue what is not good, and shun what is not evil; for it is perfectly possible to find that something that has been pursued and won is not after all satisfying, or that something that has been avoided but nevertheless thrust upon one is, after all, satisfying of the purposes and desires he in fact has. The truth of this is what is at the heart of Socrates' claim, so misleadingly expressed, that one cannot voluntarily and knowingly pursue what is evil. The goodness of the ideal I have portrayed therefore consists simply in this and cannot be anything else: It entirely fulfills the need that human beings naturally have, and this remains true even for those who may not know it. But this is a truth that can only be said. To be shown, there must be eyes that can see it.

MORAL RULES AND ASPIRATIONS

Moral philosophy, at least since the rise of Christianity, has for the most part been concerned with imperatives, commands, rules, or principles, all of which are essentially the same. The reason for this is obvious; namely, that it has been considered the task of moral philosophy, largely under the influence of religion as it was conditioned by Roman law, to specify what *actions* we should perform. The normal way to express this is by a rule.

Imperatives and commands are one and the same; namely, expressions of what some person or persons must do in compliance with the will of another. "Remember the Sabbath day and keep it holy," for example, is a command, representing in Scripture the will of God. Such commands may be positive, as this is, or negative, as in the case of prohibitions. In either case, however, it is actions that are enjoined or prohibited.

Rules are simply commands or expressions of the will of another that are continuously binding. Thus, the command "Come forward," addressed to a particular man or group, is no rule, although it is a command; whereas "Thou shall not steal" is a command that is a rule. Like other commands, therefore, rules enjoin and prohibit actions.

Moral rules and principles, as they are elaborated by moral philosophy, are entirely general, inasmuch as they are supposed to apply to all rational beings. They differ from other commands, rules, and laws in one very significant respect: they are not represented as expressing the will of any author or commander. They are instead supposed to be expressions of the will of the person who is commanded, provided that person is rational. Thus, if you understand why you should, for example, try to promote the greatest happiness of the greatest number, which is a moral rule, then you presumably will, in obedience to your reason, impose that rule on yourself. No other commander is needed.

I have already raised doubts concerning the intelligibility of a command that issues from no commander and is thus assumed to express no will except the will of the person to whom it is meant to apply. I have also maintained that no moral rules are really binding, because they all admit of exceptions that are made on some basis other than rules themselves. Any moral rule of the form "always act such that . . ." is entirely canceled by acceptance of a single dictum having the same content but asserting "In *this* case do not act such that . . . ," and I have argued that, in the case of every such moral rule, there is such a dictum. There is, then, no need to reintroduce any of those doubts concerning the legitimacy and value of moral rules.

What does need to be emphasized, however, is

that moral rules or imperatives, like any others, are rules of *action*. Like laws, commands of Scripture, or any other imperatives and rules, they have to do with what we are supposed to do and to refrain from doing. And this obviously presupposes that the things we are, by such rules, supposed to do or refrain from are things we *can* do or refrain from; or in other words, that they are actions.

From this it can be seen that the foregoing reflections on the beatitude of love and the incentive of compassion can give rise to no moral rules whatsoever. Love and compassion are passions, not actions, are therefore subject to no rule or command, and can in no way be represented in terms of duties or moral obligations. This is in any case obvious just from consideration of any moral rule that might appear to have such a content. If, for example, you are commanded to love your neighbor, then the love that is commanded cannot be any passion or feeling; it can only be a command to act toward your neighbor as one acts who does love his neighbor. Love, as a feeling, cannot be commanded, even by God, simply because it is not up to anyone at any given moment how he feels about a neighbor or anything else. Regardless of how you may feel, however, you can be commanded to treat your neighbor in certain ways, or in other words, to act in the manner enjoined.

Hence, one could never represent it as a moral rule that one should act from compassion, and the claim I have made, that compassion is a uniquely moral incentive, gives rise to no moral rule whatever. To act from compassion, your action must really be prompted by compassion. But this is a feeling or state of mind, not subject even to your own will, and so not subject to any other. It can, therefore, be subject to no command. You can, indeed, command one to act as a compassionate person would act, and you could even try to make of this a moral rule, because such a command or rule reaches only to the act and not to its incentive. But such actions are no longer acts of compassion and are, in fact, acts of hypocrisy. A compassionate act, as so conceived, is only an act that is intended to resemble a real act of compassion and does not in any way require the presence of the one thing that would make it genuine.

Sometimes, partly perhaps in response to the felt need for rules and commands, and for exhorting people to desirable actions, words that once referred solely to passions come instead to apply only to actions. The word *charity* is an instance of this, for this word is derived from *caritas*, which is the Latin for *agapé*, or religious love. A genuine act of charity is therefore not, as it is now generally thought to be, merely an act of giving; it is in its original sense an act that springs from love and is prompted by nothing else. And, clearly, there can be no such thing as giving *to* charity; one can only give *from* charity, in its true sense. Because, however, this too is a passion and not something that can be commanded, society has generally settled for the imitation, which is just the external act, and something that can be enjoined. This has become so complete that even the word has nearly lost its original sense.

LOVE AS ASPIRATION

Taking such things as this into account, many moralists, such as Kant and even Mill, have tended to treat the passions as of secondary importance to moral philosophy. We can be instructed about what to do, or what our actions must be in order to be dutiful, but no one can presume to dictate how we should feel. But here, I suggest, moral philosophy has simply taken the wrong turn. Instead of aiming at the elaboration of moral rules, which has been notoriously unsuccessful from the start, moral philosophy should aim at the presentation of moral aspirations, which do extend to the passions and to the inner person. Moral rules—as contrasted with positive laws and other conventions that need have no moral content and can be justified on purely practical grounds—are already sufficiently dubious, even if there were agreement concerning which ones should be honored. When taken in dead earnest they can become a source of untold mischief, even enabling men to spread suffering around them and providing what appears as an excuse for so doing—or even better than an excuse, something that one can really believe is a moral justification. Thus has malice, for example, expressed itself in genocide, accompanied by moral justification, or in attacks upon women, described as witches, the attacks thus being given biblical justification. The clearest recent examples of malice with pretended moral justification are the attacks upon clinics and upon physicians willing to abort pregnancies, under the guise of some kind of divine necessity. Hate organizations, dedicated to the extermination of whole groups, wave the banners of religion.

But quite apart from all this, we are surely capable of something better than going about from one day to the next busying ourselves doing all sorts of things in accordance with moral principles and rules and congratulating ourselves that we have, just by virtue of this, attained morally significant lives. One of Socrates' claims was surely true: It is the inner person that matters, for what one is, is infinitely more important than what he from time to time does. No mere rule of morality, however strenuous and noble, is going to reverse the relative worth of these two things.

The passion of love, as I have described it, has two sides, a negative and a positive one. Negatively, it expresses itself in compassion for suffering. Positively, it is the absolute love for the existence of persons and things, of oneself and others. This yields no rule of morality, but what of an ultimate or final moral aspiration? Clearly it points to this, and I express it in the most banal and unpretentious way I can, in order that its transparently simple meaning cannot be lost, and to foil any temptation to make war on it with dialectical reason. The ultimate moral aspiration is simply this: *To be a warm-hearted and loving human being.* I call this an *ultimate* aspiration because no question of *why* can be asked concerning it, without misunderstanding it. It is not deemed good on account of any beneficial deeds that it prompts, or because of its usefulness, nor is it fulfilled by anything that one merely does. It invites you to *be* rather than commanding you to *do*, and yet it cannot fail to ennoble whatever you do. There is in this simple aspiration no rationalization, no requirement to measure the consequences of your deeds against some goodness outside of yourself, no reasoning upon your incentives to see if they are consistent, no rule or principle whatever. It commands nothing, and so requires no commander either within or without. It simply invites, and replaces moral sanction, which is negative, with solicitation, which is not. Its solicitation is to be a kind of person that the nature of absolute love shows to be supremely good.

But is not such an aspiration just a moral principle all over again, something one is expected somehow to fulfill? Not at all, for it is very likely that no one really can, and very certain that no one can do so at will. In this it resembles, but by no means pretends to be the same, as an aspiration enunciated by Jesus—namely, the aspiration to be *perfect*, like God. Clearly this is not a command, much less a moral rule, because it in no way says what to do, but only what to be, and what it exhorts one to be is something impossible.

– 18 –

THE MEANING OF LIFE

THE QUESTION WHETHER life has any meaning is difficult to interpret, and the more you concentrate your critical faculty on it the more it seems to elude you, or to evaporate as any intelligible question. You want to turn it aside, as a source of embarrassment, as something that, if it cannot be abolished, should at least be decently covered. And yet I think any reflective person recognizes that the question it raises is important, and that it ought to have a significant answer.

If the idea of meaningfulness is difficult to grasp in this context, so that we are unsure what sort of thing would amount to answering the question, the idea of meaninglessness is perhaps less so. If, then, we can bring before our minds a clear image of meaningless existence, then perhaps we can take a step toward coping with our original question by seeing to what extent our lives, as we actually find them, resemble that image, and draw such lessons as we are able to from the comparison.

MEANINGLESS EXISTENCE

A perfect image of meaninglessness, of the kind we are seeking, is found in the ancient myth of Sisyphus. Sisyphus, it will be remembered, betrayed divine secrets to mortals, and for this he was condemned by the gods to roll a stone to the top of a hill, the stone then immediately to roll back down, again to be pushed to the top by Sisyphus, to roll down once more, and so on again and again, *forever*. Now in this we have the picture of meaningless, pointless toil, of a meaningless existence that is absolutely *never* redeemed. It is not even redeemed by a death that, if it were to accomplish nothing more, would at least bring this idiotic cycle to a close. If we were invited to imagine Sisyphus struggling for a while and accomplishing nothing, perhaps eventually falling from exhaustion, so that we might suppose him then eventually turning to something having some sort of promise, then the meaninglessness of that chapter of his life would not be so stark. It would be a dark and dreadful dream, from which he eventually awakens to sunlight and reality. But he does not awaken, for there is nothing for him to awaken to. His repetitive toil is his life and reality, and it goes on forever, and it is without any meaning whatever. Nothing ever comes of what he is doing, except simply, more of the same. Not by one step, nor by a thousand, nor by ten thousand does he even expiate by the smallest token the sin against the gods that led him into this fate. Nothing comes of it, nothing at all.

This ancient myth has always enchanted people, for countless meanings can be read into it. Some of the ancients apparently thought it symbolized the perpetual rising and setting of the sun, and others the repetitious crashing of the waves upon the shore. Probably the commonest interpretation is that it symbolizes our eternal struggle and unquenchable spirit, our determination always to try once more in the face of overwhelming discouragement. This interpretation is further supported by that version of the myth according to which Sisyphus was commanded to roll the stone *over* the hill, so that it would finally roll down the other side, but was never quite able to make it.

I am not concerned with rendering or defending any interpretation of this myth, however. I have cited it only for the one element it does unmistakably contain, namely, that of a repetitious, cyclic activity that never comes to anything. We could contrive other images of this that would serve just as well, and no myth-makers are needed to supply the materials of it. Thus, we can imagine two persons transporting a stone—or even a precious gem, it does not matter— back and forth, relay style. One carries it to a near or distant point where it is received by the other; it is returned to its starting point, there to be recovered by the first, and the process is repeated over and over. Except in this relay nothing counts as winning, and nothing brings the contest to any close, each step only leads to a repetition of itself. Or we can imagine two groups of prisoners, one of them engaged in digging a prodigious hole in the ground that is no sooner finished than it is filled in again by the other group, the latter then digging a new hole that is at once filled in by the first group, and so on and on endlessly.

Now what stands out in all such pictures as oppressive and dejecting is not that the beings who enact these roles suffer any torture or pain, for it need not be assumed that they do. Nor is it that their labors are great, for they are no greater than the labors commonly undertaken by most people most of the time. According to the original myth, the stone is so large that Sisyphus never quite gets it to the top and must groan under every step, so that his enormous labor is all for nought. But this is not what appalls. It is not that his great struggle comes to nothing, but that his existence itself is without meaning. Even if we suppose, for example, that the stone is but a pebble that can be carried effortlessly, or that the holes dug by the prisoners are but small ones, not the slightest meaning is introduced into their lives. The stone that Sisyphus moves to the top of the hill, whether we think of it as large or small, still rolls back every time, and the process is repeated forever. Nothing comes of it, and the work is simply pointless. That is the element of the myth that I wish to capture.

Again, it is not the fact that the labors of Sisyphus continue forever that deprives them of meaning. It is, rather, the implication of this: that they come to nothing. The image would not be changed by our supposing him to push a different stone up every time, each to roll down again. But if we supposed that these stones, instead of rolling back to their places as if they had never been moved, were assembled at the top of the hill and there incorporated, say, in a beautiful and enduring temple, then the aspect of meaninglessness would disappear. His labors would then have a point, something would come of them all, and although one could perhaps still say it was not worth it, one could not say that the life of Sisyphus was devoid of meaning altogether. Meaningfulness would at least have made an appearance, and we could see what it was.

That point will need remembering. But in the meantime, let us note another way in which the image of meaninglessness can be altered by making only a very slight change. Let us suppose that the gods, while condemning Sisyphus to the fate just described, at the same time, as an afterthought, waxed perversely merciful by implanting in him a strange and irrational impulse; namely, a compulsive impulse to roll stones. We may if we like, to make this more graphic, suppose they accomplish this by implanting in him some substance that has this effect on his character and drives. I call this perverse, because from our point of view there is clearly no reason why anyone should have a persistent and insatiable desire to do something so pointless as that. Nevertheless, suppose that is Sisyphus' condition. He has but one obsession, which is to roll stones, and it is an obsession that is only for the moment appeased by his rolling them—he no sooner gets a stone rolled to the top of the hill than he is restless to roll up another.

Now it can be seen why this little afterthought of the gods, which I called perverse, was also in fact merciful. For they have by this device managed to give Sisyphus precisely what he wants—by making him want precisely what they inflict on him. However it may appear to us, Sisyphus' fate now does not appear to him as a condemnation, but the very reverse. His one desire in life is to roll stones, and he is absolutely guaranteed its endless fulfillment. Where otherwise he might profoundly have wished surcease, and even welcomed the quiet of death to release him from endless boredom and meaningless-ness, his life is now filled with mission and meaning, and he seems to himself to have been given an entry to heaven. Nor need he even fear death, for the gods have promised him an endless opportunity to indulge his single purpose, without concern or frustration. He will be able to roll stones *forever*.

What we need to mark most carefully at this point is that the picture with which we began has not really been changed in the least by adding this supposition. Exactly the same things happen as before. The only change is in Sisyphus' view of them. The picture before was the image of meaning-less activity and existence. It was created precisely to be an image of that. It has not lost that mean-inglessness, it has now gained not the least shred of meaningfulness. The stones still roll back as before, each phase of Sisyphus' life still exactly resembles all the others, the task is never completed, nothing comes of it, no temple ever begins to rise, and all this cycle of the same pointless thing over and over goes on forever in this picture as in the other. The *only* thing that has happened is this: Sisyphus has been reconciled to it, and indeed more, he has been led to embrace it. Not, however, by reason or per-suasion, but by nothing more rational than the potency of a new substance in his veins.

THE MEANINGLESSNESS OF LIFE

I believe the foregoing provides a fairly clear con-tent to the idea of meaninglessness and, through it, some hint of what meaningfulness, in this sense, might be. Meaninglessness is essentially endless pointlessness, and meaningfulness is therefore the opposite. Activity, and even long, drawn out and repetitive activity, has a meaning if it has some significant culmination, some more or less lasting end that can be considered to have been the direction and purpose of the activity. But the descriptions so far also provide something else; namely, the suggestion of how an existence that is objectively meaningless, in this sense, can nevertheless acquire a meaning for him whose existence it is.

Now let us ask: Which of these pictures does life in fact resemble? And let us not begin with our own lives, for here both our prejudices and wishes are great, but with the life in general that we share with the rest of creation. We shall find, I think, that it all has a certain pattern, and that this pattern is by now easily recognized.

We can begin anywhere, only saving human existence for our last consideration. We can, for example, begin with any animal. It does not matter where we begin, because the result is going to be exactly the same.

Thus, for example, there are caves in New Zealand, deep and dark, whose floors are quiet pools and whose walls and ceilings are covered with soft light. As you gaze in wonder in the stillness of these caves it seems that the Creator has reproduced there in microcosm the heavens themselves, until you scarcely remember the enclosing presence of the walls. As you look more closely, however, the scene is explained. Each dot of light identifies an ugly worm, whose luminous tail is meant to attract insects from the surrounding darkness. As from time to time one of these insects draws near it becomes entangled in a sticky thread lowered by the worm, and is eaten. This goes on month after month, the blind worm lying there in the barren stillness waiting to entrap an occasional bit of nourishment that will only sustain it to another bit of nourishment until. . . . Until what? What great thing awaits all this long and repetitious effort and makes it worthwhile? Really nothing. The larva just transforms itself finally to a tiny winged adult that lacks even mouth parts to feed and lives only a day or two. These adults, as soon as they have mated and laid eggs, are themselves caught in the threads and are devoured by the cannibalist worms, often without having ventured into the day, the only point to their existence having now been fulfilled. This has been going on for millions of years, and to no end other than that the same meaningless cycle may continue for another millions of years.

All living things present essentially the same spectacle. The larva of a certain cicada burrows in the darkness of the earth for seventeen years, through season after season, to emerge finally into the daylight for a brief flight, lay its eggs, and die— this all to repeat itself during the next seventeen years, and so on to eternity. We have already noted, in another connection, the struggles of fish, made only that others may do the same after them and that this cycle, having no other point than itself, may never cease. Some birds span an entire side of the globe each year and then return, only to insure that others may follow the same incredibly long path again and again. One is led to wonder what the point of it all is, with what great triumph this ceaseless effort, repeating itself through millions of years, might finally culminate, and why it should go on and on for so long, accomplishing nothing, getting nowhere. But then you realize that there is no point to it at all, that it really culminates in nothing, that each of these cycles, so filled with toil, is to be followed only by more of the same. The point of any living thing's life is, evidently, nothing but life itself.

This life of the world thus presents itself to our eyes as a vast machine, feeding on itself, running on and on forever to nothing. And we are part of that life. To be sure, we are not just the same, but the differences are not so great as we like to think; many are merely invented, and none really cancels the kind of meaninglessness that we found in Sisyphus and that we find all around, wherever anything lives. We are conscious of our activity. Our goals, whether in any significant sense we choose them or not, are things of which we are at least partly aware and can therefore in some sense appraise. More significantly, perhaps, we have a history, as other animals do not, such that each generation does not precisely resemble all those before. Still, if we can in imagination disengage our wills from our lives and disregard the deep interest we all have in our own existence, we shall find that they do not so little resemble the existence of Sisyphus. We toil after goals, most of them—indeed every single one of them—of transitory significance and, having gained one of them, we immediately set forth for the next, as if that one had never been, with this next one being essentially more of the same. Look at a busy street any day, and observe the throng going hither and thither. To what? Some office or shop, where the same things will be done today as were done yesterday, and are done now so they may be repeated tomorrow. And if we think that, unlike Sisyphus, these labors do have a point, that they culminate in something lasting and, independently of our own deep interests in them, very worthwhile, then we simply have not considered the thing closely enough. Most such effort is directed only to the establishment and perpetuation of home and family; that is, to the begetting of others who will follow in our steps to do more of the same. Everyone's life thus resembles one of Sisyphus's climbs to the summit of his hill, and each day of it one of his steps; the difference is that whereas Sisyphus himself returns to push the stone up again, we leave this to our children. We at one point imagined that the labors of Sisyphus finally culminated in the creation of a temple, but for this to make any difference it had to be a temple that would at least endure, adding beauty to the world for the remainder of time. Our achievements, even though they are often beautiful, are mostly bubbles; and those that do last, like the sand-swept pyramids, soon become mere curiosities while around them the rest of humankind continues its perpetual toting of rocks, only to see them roll down. Nations are built upon the bones of their founders and pioneers, but only to decay and crumble before long, their rubble then becoming the foundation for others directed to exactly the same fate. The picture of Sisyphus is the picture of existence of the individual man, great or unknown, of nations, of the human race, and of the very life of the world.

On a country road one sometimes comes upon the ruined hulks of a house and once extensive buildings, all in collapse and spread over with weeds. A curious eye can in imagination reconstruct from what is left a once warm and thriving life, filled with purpose. There was the hearth, where a family once talked, sang, and made plans; there were the rooms, where people loved, and babes were born to a rejoicing mother; there are the musty remains of a sofa, infested with bugs, once bought at a dear price to enhance an ever-growing comfort, beauty, and warmth. Every small piece of junk fills the mind with what once, not long ago, was utterly real, with children's voices, plans made, and enterprises embarked upon. That is how these stones of Sisyphus were rolled up, and that is how they became incorporated into a beautiful temple, and that temple is what now lies before you. Meanwhile other buildings, institutions, nations, and civilizations spring up all around, only to share the same fate before long. And if the question "What for?" is now asked, the answer is clear: so that just this may go on forever.

The two pictures—of Sisyphus and of our own lives, if we look at them from a distance—are in outline the same and convey to the mind the same image. It is not surprising, then, that we invent ways of denying it, our religions proclaiming a heaven that does not crumble, their hymnals and prayer books declaring a significance to life of which our eyes provide no hint whatever.[1] Even our philosophies portray some permanent and lasting good at which all may aim, from the changeless forms invented by Plato to the beatific vision of St.

---

1. A popular Christian hymn, sung often at funerals and typical of many hymns, expresses this thought:

>　Swift to its close ebbs out life's little day;
>　Earth's joys grow dim, its glories pass away;
>　Change and decay in all around I see:
>　O thou who changest not, abide with me.

Thomas and the ideals of permanence contrived by the moderns. When these fail to convince, then earthly ideals such as universal justice and brotherhood are conjured up to take their places and give meaning to our seemingly endless pilgrimage, some final state that will be ushered in when the last obstacle is removed and the last stone pushed to the hilltop. No one believes, of course, that any such state will be final, or even wants it to be in case it means that human existence would then cease to be a struggle; but in the meantime such ideas serve a very real need.

THE MEANING OF LIFE

We noted that Sisyphus' existence would have meaning if there were some point to his labors, if his efforts ever culminated in something that was not just an occasion for fresh labors of the same kind. But that is precisely the meaning it lacks. And human existence resembles his in that respect. We do achieve things—we scale our towers and raise our stones to the hilltops—but every such accomplishment fades, providing only an occasion for renewed labors of the same kind.

But here we need to note something else that has been mentioned, but its significance not explored, and that is the state of mind and feeling with which such labors are undertaken. We noted that if Sisyphus had a keen and unappeasable desire to be doing just what he found himself doing, then, although his life would in no way be changed, it would nevertheless have a meaning for him. It would be an irrational one, no doubt, because the desire itself would be only the product of the substance in his veins, and not any that reason could discover, but a meaning nevertheless.

And would it not, in fact, be a meaning incomparably better than the other? For let us examine again the first kind of meaning it could have. Let us suppose that, without having any interest in rolling stones, as such, and finding this, in fact, a galling toil, Sisyphus did nevertheless have a deep interest in raising a temple, one that would be beautiful and lasting. And let us suppose he succeeded in this, that after ages of dreadful toil, all directed at this final result, he did at last complete his temple, such that now he could say his work was done, and he could rest and forever enjoy the result. Now what? What picture now presents itself to our minds? It is precisely the picture of infinite boredom! Of Sisyphus doing nothing ever again, but contemplating what he has already wrought and can no longer add anything to, and contemplating it for an eternity! Now in this picture we have a meaning for Sisyphus' existence, a point for his prodigious labor, because we have put it there; yet, at the same time, that which is really worthwhile seems to have slipped away entirely. Where before we were presented with the nightmare of eternal and pointless activity, we are now confronted with the hell of its eternal absence.

Our second picture, then, wherein we imagined Sisyphus to have had inflicted on him the irrational desire to be doing just what he found himself doing, should not have been dismissed so abruptly. The meaning that picture lacked was no meaning that he or anyone could crave, and the strange meaning it had was perhaps just what we were seeking.

At this point, then, we can reintroduce what has

been until now, it is hoped, resolutely pushed aside in an effort to view our lives and human existence with objectivity; namely, our own wills, our deep interest in what we find ourselves doing. If we do this we find that our lives do indeed still resemble that of Sisyphus, but that the meaningfulness they thus lack is precisely the meaningfulness of infinite boredom. At the same time, the strange meaningfulness they possess is that of the inner compulsion to be doing just what we were put here to do, and to go on doing it forever. This is the nearest we may hope to get to heaven, but the redeeming side of that fact is that we do thereby avoid a genuine hell.

If the builders of a great and flourishing ancient civilization could somehow return now to see archaeologists unearthing the trivial remnants of what they had once accomplished with such effort— see the fragments of pots and vases, a few broken statues, and such tokens of another age and great- ness—they could indeed ask themselves what the point of it all was, if this is all it finally came to. Yet, it did not seem so to them then, for it was just the building, and not what was finally built, that gave their life meaning. Similarly, if the builders of the ruined home and farm that I described a short while ago could be brought back to see what is left, they would have the same feelings. What we construct in our imaginations as we look over these decayed and rusting pieces would reconstruct itself in their very memories, and certainly with unspeakable sadness. The piece of a sled at our feet would revive in them a warm Christmas. And what rich memories would there be in the broken crib? And the weed-covered remains of a fence would reproduce the scene of a great herd of livestock, so laboriously built up over so many years. What was it all worth, if this is the final result? Yet, again, it did not seem so to them through those many years of struggle and toil, and they did not imagine they were building a Gibraltar. The things to which they bent their backs day after day, realizing one by one their ephemeral plans, were precisely the things in which their wills were deeply involved, precisely the things in which their interests lay, and there was no need then to ask questions. There is no more need of them now—the day was sufficient to itself, and so was the life.

This is surely the way to look at all of life—at one's own life, and each day and moment it contains; of the life of a nation; of the species; of the life of the world; and of everything that breathes. Even the glow worms I described, whose cycles of existence over the millions of years seem so pointless when looked at by us, will seem entirely different to us if we can somehow try to view their existence from within. Their endless activity, which gets nowhere, is just what it is their will to pursue. This is its whole justification and meaning. Nor would it be any salvation to the birds who span the globe every year, back and forth, to have a home made for them in a cage with plenty of food and protection, so that they would not have to migrate anymore. It would be their condemnation, for it is the doing that counts for them, and not what they hope to win by it. Flying these prodigious distances, never ending, is what it is in their veins to do, exactly as it was in Sisyphus's veins to roll stones, without end, after the gods had waxed merciful and implanted this in him.

You no sooner drew your first breath than you responded to the will that was in you to live. You no more ask whether it will be worthwhile, or whether

anything of significance will come of it, than the
worms and the birds. The point of living is simply to
be living, in the manner that it is your nature to be
living. You go through life building your castles,
each of these beginning to fade into time as the next
is begun; yet it would be no salvation to rest from all
this. It would be a condemnation, and one that
would in no way be redeemed were you able to gaze
upon the things you have done, even if these were
beautiful and absolutely permanent, as they never
are. What counts is that you should be able to begin
a new task, a new castle, a new bubble. It counts
only because it is there to be done and you have the
will to do it. The same will be the life of your children, and of theirs; and if the philosopher is apt to
see in this a pattern similar to the unending cycles
of the existence of Sisyphus, and to despair, then it
is indeed because the meaning and point he is
seeking is not there—but mercifully so. The meaning
of life is from within us, it is not bestowed from
without, and it far exceeds in both its beauty and
permanence any heaven of which men have ever
dreamed or yearned for.

INDEX

335